L. CAMPBELL · PARALIPOMENA SOPHOCLEA

LEWIS CAMPBELL

Paralipomena Sophoclea

Supplementary Notes on the Text and Interpretation of Sophocles

1969

GEORG OLMS VERLAG
HILDESHEIM

Die Originalvorlage befindet sich im Besitz der Niedersächsischen Staats- und Universitätsbibliothek Göttingen.

Signatur: 8⁰ Auct. gr. II, 7148

Reprografischer Nachdruck der Ausgabe London 1907
Printed in Germany
Herstellung: Druckerei Lokay, 6101 Reinheim/Odw.
Best.-Nr. 5102 319

PARALIPOMENA SOPHOCLEA

PARALIPOMENA SOPHOCLEA

SUPPLEMENTARY NOTES ON THE TEXT
AND INTERPRETATION OF SOPHOCLES

BY

LEWIS CAMPBELL, M.A

HON. D.LITT., OXON.; HON. LL.D., GLASGOW; EMERITUS PROFESSOR OF GREEK
IN THE UNIVERSITY OF ST. ANDREWS, SCOTLAND; HONORARY FELLOW
OF BALLIOL COLLEGE AND FORMERLY FELLOW AND TUTOR
OF QUEEN'S COLLEGE IN THE UNIVERSITY OF OXFORD

RIVINGTONS

34 *KING STREET, COVENT GARDEN*

LONDON

1907

PREFACE

THESE notes were ready for publication a year ago, but were withheld in consequence of the illness and death of Sir Richard Jebb. This fact must excuse the absence of reference to recent criticisms, those, for example, of the veteran scholar, Mr. F. W. Blaydes.

Tragic fragments are quoted according to the second edition of Nauck's *Tragicorum Graecorum Fragmenta* (1889).

LEWIS CAMPBELL.

ALASSIO, *December* 1906.

CONTENTS

	PAGE
INTRODUCTION,	ix
ANTIGONE,	1
AJAX,	48
OEDIPUS TYRANNUS,	83
ELECTRA,	125
TRACHINIAE,	156
PHILOCTETES,	195
OEDIPUS COLONEUS,	232

INTRODUCTION

I DESIRE to place on record, for what it is worth, my matured opinion on disputed points in the text and interpretation of Sophocles. These are fewer now than formerly, for English scholars, since the late Sir Richard Jebb, in his edition of the seven plays, by his rare faculty of exposition, by the fineness of his analysis, and an abundant copiousness of illustration, has placed the meaning of innumerable passages in the clearest light. It is a subject of sincere self-congratulation to me that a considerable portion of Sir Richard's commentary coincides with, and so corroborates, the views put forward in my edition (1871-1881), but I find on reconsidering both that, while I stand corrected in several places, there are others in which I adhere to my former view, and some also where I am now disposed to differ from both judgments.

The following notes make hardly any mention of the very numerous places in which Professor Jebb's views accord with mine. I am equally silent, where, as often happens, Sir Richard decides in favour of an interpretation which, in my more tentative method, I had put forward as the first of two or more alternatives. The points herein to be discussed are (1) those in which I now agree with Sir Richard Jebb against my former opinion : (2) those in which I adhere to the view expressed in my edition: and (3) the comparatively few places where, on further consideration, I have come to conclusions differing more or less both from his commentary and from my own. For the sake of brevity, in quoting from Sir Richard Jebb, I simply use the proper name, and in speaking of my own edition I refer to that of 1879 (vol. I.) and 1881 (vol. II.). I have also found it convenient to quote occasionally from the smaller edition—prepared by Dr. Evelyn Abbott and myself, as *CA*.

The famous saying of Cobet '*Commenta delet dies*' may be applied, with at least equal truth, to the majority of conjectural emendations. At Florence in 1882, when desirous of verifying my collation, I had the honour of sharing the use of the Laurentian MS. with M. Pappageorg, who was preparing his notes upon the Scholia, and I was struck by his remark that the text of Sophocles appeared to him exceptionally sound, but that a few great errors had probably crept into it from a very early time. This view has been recently confirmed by the discovery amongst the Oxyrhynchus Papyri (I. xxii.) of a few lines of the *Oedipus Tyrannus* (375-385 and 429-441) in which there are two remarkable variants, and one manifest error (l. 376) which is found in all our MSS. The Papyrus is of the 5th century A.D., and the corruption is, therefore, not to be attributed to Byzantine scholarship.

In such cases, even a conservative critic must allow that boldness is not always to be censured as temerity. 'Good reasons must of force give way to better', and palaeographical arguments must sometimes yield to the requirements of the context. That is after all the final test. The '*ductus literarum*' is an excellent guide. But the sources of error are varied and complex, and obvious causes may sometimes mislead. '*Opinio copiæ*' is apt to be '*causa inopiæ.*' General learning is of less account than an intimate acquaintance with the spirit of an author. One who possesses that may sometimes guess rightly, even if he fail to show how the mistake which he corrects originated.

It may suffice to adduce one instance of an emendation that was palaeographically faultless, but certainly not justifiable. In Aeschylus, *Ag.* 1172, ἐγὼ δὲ θερμόνους τάχ' ἐν πέδῳ βαλῶ, early scholars did not perceive that the intransitive verb is excused by tmesis of ἐμβαλῶ; and Canter conjectured θερμὸν οὖς. This was printed by Hermann in his text, and gravely defended by Professor Kennedy on the ground that 'as a frantic prophetess she may use wild language.' But who does not now see the absurdity? The Cassandra of Aeschylus is not a Tilburina.

The printed text of Sophocles was fortunate in its beginning. The Aldine *Editio princeps* appears to have been based on the Venetian MS. 467, of the 14th century (V.[3]), containing all the seven dramas written in a very legible hand. The Codex in its present condition bears evidence of the printer's industry, having been taken to pieces and afterwards *mis-bound*. Some readings were derived from other MSS. and some possibly from the conjectures of scholars, but the general agreement of the Aldine with V.[3] is such as to confirm the supposition here advanced. Unfortunately the edition of Turnebus, which quickly followed, made use of the Parisian MS. T., also of the 14th century, but representing the Triclinian recension. This gained considerable vogue in the succeeding century, until the error was redressed by Philip Brunck's discovery of the superior age and authority of Paris A. (2712), a 13th century MS. in remarkably close agreement with V.[3]. Meanwhile conjecture had not been idle. Sixteenth century scholars such as Auratus, H. Stephanus, and Canter had introduced corrections which still remain, and in the 18th century a group of scholars, of whom Porson was chief, had applied new canons of textual criticism in a manner which does not always convince.

Peter Elmsley was the first to appreciate the supreme value for Sophocles of the Laurentian MS., which the Juntine editors (1547) appear to have used without estimating it aright. (They retained ἐν καιροῖς, *O.T.* 1031.) Elmsley's collation made at Florence in 1825 was published after his death by Dean Gaisford, and his transcription of the Scholia is still, I presume, where I saw it formerly, in the Bodleian Library at Oxford.

It may be said of Godfrey Hermann that while English grammarians were insisting on logical precision, he initiated a higher, psychological method which was capable of more fruitful results. Of the editors of Sophocles belonging to the early 19th Century the interpreters whose work has lasted best are Hermann, Lobeck, and August Boeckh. But it was still a period of experiment and of uncertainty, and the collection of notes published by Erfurdt in 1824 must prove to anyone who examines them how much which had then been attempted is now obsolete.

As I am not re-editing Sophocles, I have not dwelt in the following notes on metrical questions, except when they bear directly on interpretation, nor on matters of orthography—although I accept θνῄσκειν, σῴζειν, and some other forms which are beyond dispute. My attention will be chiefly confined to difficulties of interpretation.

Two causes of difficulty in Sophoclean diction are concentration and emphasis. Many anomalies of language, or 'idiotisms,' may be traced to one or both of these motives. In particular cases the question remains whether the anomaly assumed in interpretation transcends the limit of what is natural or even possible.

1. *Condensed expression.* The determination to express in a single clause what in ordinary prose would be expanded into a sentence gives rise to the 'figures' named by grammarians 'prolepsis,' 'zeugma,' etc, In comparisons, the image and the thing compared are thought of together, and the result is something intermediate between simile and metaphor. A familiar instance is *O.T.* 922,3 ἐκπεπληγμένον | κεῖνον βλέποντες

ὡς κυβερνήτην νεώς. To the same category belong the use of cases without prepositions, of optatives without ἄν, of εἰ with the subjunctive, of a compound adjective equivalent to a clause (*El.* 857, etc.).

2. *Emphasis.* The desire to fix attention on what is prominent in thought, gives rise to various departures from the obvious or normal mode of expression—such as 'enallage,' 'hyperbaton,' etc. An epithet is transferred from the agent to the act or the emotion, etc. Where the *Subject* is important the active voice is preferred, although the passive would have been used in prose, and, *vice versa*, where the action is chiefly in question, a passive—sometimes impersonal— verb is chosen. Words that usually begin a sentence are postponed, in order to bring to the front that on which the stress is laid. And Sophocles, like other poets, sometimes excites attention by inverting the natural or logical order or relation of ideas (*El.* 782). See on this subject Schmidt's *Shakespeare Lexicon* pp. 1423, 4, (Grammatical observations, Section 14). An extraordinary situation is sometimes marked by a verbal contradiction (oxymoron). Whether in such passages as *Aj.* 195, 640; *Phil.* 1149; *O.C.* 1219; the application of the above observations has been stretched too far, is a point still admitting of debate.

Once more, a point not sufficiently considered, especially in emendation, is *parcimony* of emphasis. Much both of the strength and beauty of Sophoclean style depends on this. See, *e.g.*, the conjectural emendations of *Trach.* 554, λυτήριον λύπημα.

The uses of negation and of antithesis are also affected by the force of emphasis. The familiar idiom in which the negation is strengthened by reduplication calls for no remark.[1] But the rare instances in which a complex sentence introduced with a prohibitory μή has an independent negation in a subordinate place may be accounted for by the strength of the primary negation pervading the whole (*O.C.* 277,8).

3. The poets of the 5th Century enjoyed a degree of liberty in the choice and employment of words and phrases which was denied to the writers of Attic prose. Meanings could be suggested, through etymological and other associations, beyond the ordinary connotation of the vocables used. In particular, words culled from Epic and lyric poetry could be thus forged anew: see, for example, τηλύγετον in Eur. *Iph. T.* 828. And, as a consequence of this freedom, the same combination may have a different significance when recurring in a different context (*e.g.*, οὐδ' ἀνίεσαν in *O.T.* 1277, *O.C.* 1608). Thus ἄκρας νυκτός may mean, according to the context, 'at dead of night,' or, 'on the verge of night.' Verbs commonly intransitive may have an active or causative sense: *e.g.*, βαίνειν πόδα in Eur. *El.* 94, 1173.

---

[1] In *Tragic Drama* I quoted a sentence from Prof. Huxley's *Hume*:—'No event is too extraordinary to be impossible.' The following examples are still more recent. Lord Kelvin in his obituary notice of Prof. Tait (Transactions of R. S. E.) observed 'I cannot say that our meetings were never unruffled.' And in the *Times* article on the Anglo-Japanese Alliance (March 22, 1905) these words occur:—'Few things are too valuable not to be sacrificed on the altar of money-getting.'

ANTIGONE

Obs. 1. As I have elsewhere remarked, the apparent anomaly by which the burial of Polynices precedes the attempt to rescue Antigone, is explained by the character of Creon. The change in him is produced not by any compunction on account of Antigone, nor by any apprehension of the real danger to Hæmon, but simply by the superstitious fear which Tiresias has awakened, that the anger of the Gods is directed against himself and the state. His first impulse, therefore, is to reverse his previous action in violating the sacred rites of burial.

2. The resemblance between ll. 454-460 and [Lys.] c. Andoc., § 10 f. is remarkable. The words of the orator are these:—καίτοι Περικλέα ποτέ φασι παραινέσαι ὑμῖν περὶ τῶν ἀσεβούντων, μὴ μόνον χρῆσθαι τοῖς γεγραμμένοις νόμοις περὶ αὐτῶν, ἀλλὰ καὶ τοῖς ἀγράφοις, καθ' οὓς Εὐμολπίδαι ἐξηγοῦνται, οὓς οὐδείς πω κύριος ἐγένετο καθελεῖν οὐδὲ ἐτόλμησεν ἀντειπεῖν, οὐδὲ αὐτὸν τὸν θέντα ἴσασιν· ἡγεῖσθαι γὰρ ἂν αὐτοὺς οὕτως οὐ μόνον τοῖς ἀνθρώποις ἀλλὰ καὶ τοῖς θεοῖς διδόναι δίκην.

3. Against Goethe's æsthetic judgment condemning ll. 904-912 may be set the poetic instinct of Mr. Swinburne, who in his *Atalanta* has effectively employed the same idea. Althæa, when about to slay her son to avenge her brothers, ends a long speech with the reflection—

> 'For all things else and all men may renew;
> Yea, son for son the gods may give and take;
> But never a brother or sister any more.'

1. I still think that κοινόν is intended to *suggest* 'having common interests,' assuming a bond of union that is broken in the sequel.

2, 3. ἆρ' οἶσθ' ὅτι Ζεὺς τῶν ἀπ' Οἰδίπου κακῶν
ὁποῖον οὐχὶ νῷν ἔτι ζώσαιν τελεῖ;

Of the many explanations I still prefer that of Boeckh, which is not condemned by Professor Jebb,—viz., reading ὅτι, the conjunction,—that 'ὁποῖον is substituted for the direct ποῖον.' Only I take τελεῖ as future, and νῷν as dative. '*Art* thou aware that Zeus will fulfil on us, while we yet live, what not? (*i.e.* all without exception) of the ills derived from Oedipus?' 'The familiarity of the combination οἶδ' ὅτι,' as Jebb remarks, makes this easier, and also (I may add), renders οἶσθ' ὅ τι less probable. (For the twofold interrogation, however, cp. Eur. *Heracl.* 661.

ἀτὰρ τί χώρᾳ τῇδε προσβαλὼν πόδα
ποῦ νῦν ἄπεστι;)

4-6. οὐδὲν γὰρ οὔτ' ἀλγεινὸν οὔτ' ἄτης *γέμον
οὔτ' αἰσχρὸν οὔτ' ἄτιμόν ἐσθ', ὁποῖον οὐ
τῶν σῶν τε κἀμῶν οὐκ ὄπωπ' ἐγὼ κακῶν.

The reading of the MSS. in l. 4, ἄτης ἄτερ, although proved to be as early as the first century B.C., is almost certainly corrupt. The most plausible of the many attempted explanations, that the words are a parenthesis,—'leaving aside the ruin of our fortunes'—is excluded by the nature of the speech, which would be injured by any break in its impetuous flow.

Porson's suggestion of a gloss is inadmissible, because we do not know how soon the habit of interlinear annotation began. But *dittographia* is a not improbable cause. When the second ἄτης had been read as ἄτερ, the line appeared complete, and the final syllables, whatever they were, were

ANTIGONE 3

dropped. See infr. 1. 1301, where the repetition of ἥδε has caused the extrusion of two syllables.

ἥδ' ὀξυθήκτῳ (ἥδε) βωμία περὶ ξ(ίφει).

In such cases it is not necessary to suppose the lost syllables to resemble the repeated word. Thus a wide field is opened for conjecture. The emendation above adopted is Hermann's. It is recommended (1) by the strength of the expression; (2) by the resemblance to the latter part of ἀλγεινόν, which may have assisted the corruption, and (3) because involving an alliteration which is not unpleasing.

10.   πρὸς τοὺς φίλους στείχοντα τῶν ἐχθρῶν κακά.

I still prefer the interpretation of the scholiasts: τὰ ἀπὸ τῶν ἐχθρῶν κακά. The antithesis is not without point, but expresses the bitter feeling of Antigone: cp. infr. 942, οἵα πρὸς οἵων ἀνδρῶν πάσχω.

20.   ἔπος is what Ant. is about to tell.

23, 24.   σὺν δίκῃ
               *προθεὶς δικαίᾳ καὶ νόμῳ.

The correction is mine. The Scholiast accepted the traditional reading χρησθείς as = χρησάμενος. This cannot be defended. J. W. Donaldson proposed σὺν δίκῃ, προσθεὶς δίκαια, καὶ νόμῳ. προθεὶς δικαίᾳ requires hardly any more alteration, and avoids the harshness of the parenthesis between δίκῃ and νόμῳ.

29, 30.   οἰωνοῖς γλυκὺν
               θησαυρὸν εἰσορῶσι πρὸς χάριν βορᾶς.

'To the birds, as they eye him, a welcome store of feeding to their pleasure.'

Jebb says, 'Take πρὸς χαρὶν βορᾶς with γλυκὺν θησαυρόν, not with εἰσορῶσι'. I quite agree. But in that case the genitive goes better with θησαυρόν than the prepositional phrase, while the adverbial πρὸς χάριν may be attached to the verbal notion in βορᾶς. The parallel use in Phil. 1156, ἀντίφονον κορέσαι στόμα πρὸς χάριν, is then exactly in point. ('*ad vescendum ut volupe est*,' Herm.). For general sense, cp. Eur. *Suppl.* 282, χάρματα θηρῶν.

31, 32.   τοιαῦτά φασι τὸν ἀγαθὸν Κρέοντά σοι
κἀμοί, λέγω γὰρ κἀμέ, κηρύξαντ' ἔχειν.

λέγω γὰρ κἀμέ, 'For I count myself also'—amongst those forbidden. I still take σοι as enclitic, and as ethical dative, supposing the following words to be an afterthought, suggested by Antigone's rising indignation. Jebb thinks that 'such a transition is hardly possible.' But, on the other hand, to read σοὶ κἀμοί continuously, implying that 'Creon's edict touches the sisters first,' makes the transition in λέγω γὰρ κἀμέ somewhat too abrupt. Cp. Eur. *Alc.* 630, οὔτ' ἐν φίλοισι σὴν παρουσίαν λέγω. Aesch. *Pr. V.* 973. Her. iii. 95, τὸ δ' ἔτι τούτων ἔλασσον ἀπιεὶς οὐ λέγω.

39, 40.   τί δ', ὦ ταλαῖφρον, εἰ τάδ' ἐν τούτοις, ἐγὼ
λύουσ' ἂν ἢ 'φάπτουσα προσθείμην πλέον;

ταλαῖφρον—perhaps implies not only pity, as *infr.* 866, but some disparagement of her sister's judgment. Cp. 68.

ἢ 'φάπτουσα. Against Porson's εἴθ' ἅπτουσα may be urged that the 'knot' is already tied. Schol. ἀντὶ τοῦ λύουσα τὸν νόμον ἢ ἐπιβεβαιοῦσα αὐτόν. (So in L distinctly: not ἢ βεβαιοῦσα.)

42.   ποῦ γνώμης ποτ' εἶ;

I am now inclined to read ποῖ γνώμης ποτ' εἶ; 'whither will your thoughts carry you?' comparing *El.* 922, ὅποι γνώμης φέρει, Eur. *Iph. Aul.* 480, εἶμι δ' οὗπερ εἶ σὺ νῦν.

46. οὐ γὰρ δὴ προδοῦσ' ἁλώσομαι.
Cp. Eur. *Androm.* 191, ὅμως δ' ἐμαυτὴν οὐ προδοῦσ' ἁλώσομαι.

50. ὡς νῷν ἀπεχθὴς δυσκλεής τ' ἀπώλετο.
ἀπεχθής—διὰ τὸν γενόμενον λοιμόν. Schol.

57. I am inclined to place the comma after ἀμπλακημάτων. Cp. 170.

58. νῦν αὖ μόνα δὴ νώ λελειμμένα σκόπει
ὅσῳ κάκιστ' ὀλούμεθ'.

νῦν αὖ seems more forcible than νῦν δ'αὖ. It belongs to the energy of tragic diction to give such a word as αὖ the effect of a conjunction.

71. ἀλλ' ἴσθ' ὁποία σοι δοκεῖ, κεῖνον δ' ἐγὼ θάψω.
Cp. Aesch. *S. c. T.* 1053.
ἀλλ' αὐτόβουλος ἴσθ', ἀπεννέπω δ' ἐγώ.

74. Cp. *fr.* 518.

83. μὴ 'μοῦ is better than μή μου.

86, 87. πολλὸν ἐχθίων ἔσει
σιγῶσ', ἐὰν μὴ πᾶσι κηρύξῃς τάδε.
Cp. Eur. *fr.* 163.
ἀνδρὸς φίλου δὲ χρυσὸς ἀμαθίας μέτα
ἄχρηστος, εἰ μὴ κἀρετὴν ἔχων τύχοι.

99. ἄνους μὲν ἔρχει, τοῖς φίλοις δ' ὀρθῶς φίλη.

I still prefer to give the active sense to φίλη. Schol. εὐνοϊκῶς δὲ τῷ θανόντι (πράττεις). Ismene's heart approves what her judgment condemns. This prepares for her conduct afterwards, 536 ff. Cp. Eur. *Iph. T.* 610, τοῖς φίλοις τ' ὀρθῶς φίλος. *Or.* 424, ἀληθὴς δ' ἐς φίλους ἔφυν φίλος.

121. στεφάνωμα πύργων.

Cp. Eur. *Hec.* 910, ἀπὸ δὲ στέφανον κέκαρσαι πύργων; Pind. *Ol.* viii. 32, Ἰλίῳ μέλλοντες ἐπὶ στέφανον τεῦξαι. Hes. *Theog.* G. F. F., εὐστεφάνῃ ἐνὶ Θήβῃ.

126. ἀντιπάλῳ δυσχείρωμα δράκοντι.

The difficulty of this verse has hardly been removed. Jebb reads ἀντιπάλῳ—δράκοντος (which is supported by the Venetian MS. 468), and renders, 'a thing too hard for him to conquer, as he wrestled with his dragon foe.' But the phrase ἀντιπάλῳ δράκοντι is so appropriate to the serpent successfully struggling against the eagle's attack, as in *Il.* 12, 203 ff.

καὶ οὔ πω λήθετο χάρμης·
κόψε γὰρ αὐτὸν ἔχοντα κατὰ στῆθος παρὰ δειρὴν
ἰδνωθεὶς ὀπίσω,

that it is preferable to join δράκοντι as dative of the agent with ἐτάθη. Retaining the reading of LA. etc., I believe the solution to be supplied by the observation of Solger in the Appendix to his German translation (Berlin 1824) p. 217, that 'the noun in μα sometimes signifies not the object or result of the action, but the action itself. So ἄμυγμα in *Aj.* 634, στέργημα in *Trach.* 1138, ὕβρισμα in Eur. *H. F.* 181, *Bacch.* 779, στεφάνωμα, *ib.* 355, πλήρωμα *Troad.* 822, ἀγεμόνευμα, *Phœn.* 1492, ζήτημα, *Bacch.* 1139, φυσήματα, *Iph. A.* 1114. δυσχείρωμα is then 'an act of hard achievement,' an accusative in apposition to the sentence. For ἀντιπάλῳ=

'successfully resisting,' 'equal in might,' cp. Pind. *Isthm.* v. (iv.) 59-61, αἰνέω δὲ καὶ Πυθέαν ἐν γυιοδάμαις | Φυλακίδᾳ πλαγᾶν δρόμον εὐθυπορῆσαι | χερσὶ δεξιὸν νόῳ ἀντίπαλον. Eur. *Phœn.* 797, ἀσπιδοφέρμονα θίασον ... ἀντίπαλον. Jebb says, 'In itself, δυσχείρωμα might mean 'a thing achieved with difficulty'; but here the irony is clearly pointed against the routed Argives : the poet does not mean that the Thebans won with difficulty.' But why should not this be seriously intended? The note of triumph is presently saddened in the lines, πλὴν τοῖν στυγεροῖν κ.τ.λ., and the difficulty of achievement may prepare the way for the direct intervention of Zeus.

The form δυσχείρωμα is certainly, as Jebb says, very unusual and bold. The lexicons have δυσοιωνισμός, δυσέργημα, but these do not appear in classical Greek. For a similar construction, cp. Eur. *Phœn.* 655, Βάκχιον χόρευμα παρθένοισι Θηβαίαις, 1492, ἀγεμόνευμα νεκροῖσι πολύστονον.

130.   χρυσοῦ καναχῆς *ὑπεροπλίαις.

Vauvilliers' conjecture is now generally accepted. I have rendered it in my translation.

132.   νίκην ὁρμῶντ' ἀλαλάξαι.

The subject of the participle is not τινά, but is supplied as the sentence proceeds in πυρφόρος ὃς τότε κ.τ.λ. Capaneus, although not named, is present to the mind.

138.   εἶχε δ' ἄλλᾳ μὲν ἄλλ|ᾳ· τὰ δ' ἐπ' ἄλλοις ...

Hermann's reading involves the slightest change, and the mode of expression well indicates the various fortunes of the fight. The *third* alternative is characteristic: cp. *El.* 1291, ἀντλεῖ, τὰ δ' ἐκχεῖ, τὰ δὲ διασπείρει μάτην. The transition from cretics to choriambi involves no break in the rhythm, so that μέν taking the place of a long syllable in the other reading is hardly justified.

8   PARALIPOMENA SOPHOCLEA

148. μεγαλώνυμος. Cp. Eur. *Iph. T.* 905, τὸ κλεινὸν ὄνομα τῆς σωτηρίας.

151.   θέσθε λησμοσύναν.

The reading is doubtful between θέσθε and θέσθαι, which as Jebb observes may be infinitive for imperative.

153.   ὁ Θήβας δ' ἐλελίχθων.

Jebb explains ὁ τὴν Θήβης χθόνα ἐλελίζων. But the note of the Scholiast has more solemnity:—ὁ Θήβας Βακχεῖος, ὁ Θηβαγένης Διόνυσος,—ὁ ἐλελίχθων, ἄρχοι τῆς χορείας.

159.   μῆτιν ἐρέσσων

Rather 'advances' than 'meditates.' *Aj.* 251, 2, ἐρέσσουσιν ἀπειλάς . . . ἡμῶν.

176.   πρὶν ἄν
ἀρχαῖς τε καὶ νόμοισιν ἐντριβὴς φάνῃ.

Although these words might simply mean 'until he hath been versed in rule,' etc., I still think that the metaphor from coin that is proved by wearing is at least suggested by the poet : 'till he have been proved' in office and administration.

189, 190.   ἥδ' ἐστὶν ἡ σῴζουσα, καὶ ταύτης ἔπι
πλέοντες ὀρθῆς τοὺς φίλους ποιούμεθα.

Cp. Eur. *fr.* 798.
πατρὶς καλῶς πράσσουσα τὸν τυχόντ' ἀεὶ
μείζω τίθησι, δυστυχοῦσα δ' ἀσθενῆ.

211, 212.   σοὶ ταῦτ' ἀρέσκει, παῖ Μενοικέως Κρέον,
τὸν τῇδε δύσνουν καὶ τὸν εὐμενῆ πόλει.

If Κρέον has displaced a dissyllable, is not ποιεῖν better than παθεῖν? The accusatives as with εὖ, κακῶς ποιεῖν.

218.   τί δῆτ' ἂν ἄλλῳ τοῦτ' ἐπεντέλλοις ἔτι;

I do not admit that ἄλλῳ is a 'bad reading.' τί... τοῦτο quite intelligibly asks for an explanation of ὡς ἂν σκοποί νυν ἦτε κ.τ.λ., and ἄλλῳ, 'to another than the guards already set,' refers modestly to the chorus themselves. But ἄλλο is an early variant, and not impossible.

219.   τὸ μὴ 'πιχωρεῖν τοῖς ἀπιστοῦσιν τάδε.

ἐπιχωρεῖν is rather 'to allow' than 'to join with.' There is quite sufficient authority for such a use.

229.   τλήμων, μενεῖς αὖ.

'Will you on the other hand not go?' Jebb calls this impossible, and (reading μένεις) renders 'are you tarrying again?' which is vivid certainly, but hardly represents the inward dialogue which this crude dialectician is reporting. For αὖ cp. *O. T.* 233, εἰ δ' αὖ σιωπήσεσθε.

231.   τοιαῦθ' ἑλίσσων ἤνυτον *σπουδῇ βραδύς.

ἑλίσσων; cp. Eur. *fr.* 674, λόγους ἑλίσσων, and the imagery in Plat. *Phil.* 15 e.

I cannot think that Seyffert's *σπουδῇ βραδύς is a 'bad' conjecture. The following line implies that the preceding words contained an oxymoron in accordance with the vulgar wit of the φύλαξ. This seems to have been felt by the author of the variant σχολῇ ταχύς, 'with leisurely haste' (καί τοι ταχὺς ὤν, βραδέως ἤνυτον τὴν ὁδόν Schol.), which harmonises ill, however, with the opening words:

ἄναξ, ἐρῶ μὲν οὐχ ὅπως τάχους ὕπο
δύσπνους ἱκάνω, κοῦφον ἐξάρας πόδα.

'My very eagerness retarded me,' is much more suitable. And the MS. reading σχολῇ βραδύς, however it may be defended, is flat and tautological. Because the γνώμη, σπεῦδε

PARALIPOMENA SOPHOCLEA

βραδέως, frequent in later prose, is seriously applied, it does not follow that the watchman may not give the same verbal paradox a different turn.

234. The emphatic position of σοὶ at the beginning of the line rather militates against Jebb's punctuation here.

241. εὖ γε στοχάζει.

The grammarian Pollux (5, 36) says that στοχάς and στοχασμός were hunting terms for a method of setting nets for game. Schneidewin's suggestion, to give στοχάζεσθαι the same meaning here, was approved by Prof. E. L. Lushington. The sense is certainly not weakened by the assumption that a single image is contemplated in both parts of the line.

259, 260. λόγοι δ' ἐν ἀλλήλοισιν ἐρρόθουν κακοί,
φύλαξ ἐλέγχων φύλακα.

Cp. Thuc. viii. 93, § 2, πρὸς αὐτοὺς ἀνὴρ ἀνδρὶ διελέγοντο. Eur. *Hel.* 1549, 50, ἡμῖν δ' ἦν μὲν ἥδ' ὑποψία | λόγος τ' ἐν ἀλλήλοισι.

262, 263. εἷς γάρ τις ἦν ἕκαστος οὐξειργασμένος,
κοὐδεὶς ἐναργής, ἀλλ' ἔφευγε μὴ εἰδέναι.

While Jebb's rendering, 'pleaded in defence that he knew nothing of it' (sc. ἕκαστός τις, the positive evolved from the negative οὐδείς) is, of course, admissible, I do not think that my explanation, 'he (οὐξειργασμένος) escaped our knowledge,' is condemned by the continuous tense, which accords with ἐρρόθουν, ἐγίγνετο, above. All down to 268, τέλος δ' κ.τ.λ., describes a protracted state of uncertainty. The imperfect need not be 'conative.' The latter explanation gives a more exact antithesis to ἐναργής.

275. For καθαιρεῖ cp. *Her.* vi. 38, κατέλαβε, [*Lys.*] 13, 37, τὴν δὲ καθαιροῦσαν (ψῆφον) ἐπὶ τὴν ὑστέραν (τράπεζαν τίθεσθαι).

280. παῦσαι, πρὶν ὀργῆς *καί με μεστῶσαι λέγων.

καί με is probably right, though the MS. reading κἀμέ might mean 'even me' ('however slow to wrath').

286, 287. ναοὺς πυρώσων ἦλθε κἀναθήματα,
καὶ γῆν ἐκείνων καὶ νόμους διασκεδῶν;

It seems doubtful whether γῆν is to be joined with πυρώσων or διασκεδῶν. Either involves a *zeugma*, and the phrasing is more natural if the comma is placed after ἀναθήματα.

288, 289. ἀλλὰ ταῦτα καὶ πάλαι πόλεως
ἄνδρες μόλις φέροντες ἐρρόθουν ἐμοί.

I explained ταῦτα as adverbial, and so Schneidewin, and apparently the Scholiast. I still think this more expressive, although the absolute use of such a phrase as μόλις φέρειν is elsewhere supported by a participle or prepositional phrase. For the adverbial ταῦτα cp. Eur. *Androm.* 212, ταῦτά τοί σ' ἔχθει πόσις; *Iph. T.* 932, ταῦτ' ἄρ' ἐπ' ἀκταῖς κἀνθάδ' ἠγγέλης μανείς; Ar. *Nub.* 320.

291, 292. οὐδ' ὑπὸ ζυγῷ
λόφον δικαίως εἶχον.

δικαίως, 'rightly,' but perhaps with an association from the familiar notion of horses bearing the yoke evenly or fairly, as Donaldson thought. See the use of δίκαιος in Xen. *Cyr.* ii. 2, 26, οὔτε γὰρ ἅρμα δήπου ταχὺ γένοιτ' ἂν βραδέων ἵππων ἐνόντων οὔτε δίκαιον ἀδίκων συνεζευγμένων.

303. χρόνῳ ποτ' ἐξέπραξαν ὡς δοῦναι δίκην.

χρόνῳ ποτέ: not 'at some time or other,' but 'now at last.' Cp. *Phil.* 816, 1041.

309.
πρὶν ἂν
ζῶντες κρεμαστοὶ τήνδε δηλώσηθ' ὕβριν.

Of the two explanations of δηλώσητε: (1) 'show the nature of your crime,' by suffering for it (Erfurdt), and (2) 'reveal the author of the crime' (Hermann, Jebb). I prefer the former, as more vehement. Cp. *infr.* 325, 6, *O. T.* 624, ὅταν προδείξῃς οἷόν ἐστι τὸ φθονεῖν.

311. Cp. Eur. *Tro.* 1041, ἵν' εἰδῇς μὴ καταισχύνειν ἐμέ.

317. Cp. *Her.* viii. 39.

325, 326.
εἰ δὲ ταῦτα μὴ
φανεῖτέ μοι τοὺς δρῶντας, ἐξερεῖθ' ὅτι
τὰ δειλὰ κέρδη πημονὰς ἐργάζεται.

Cp. Eur. *Heracl.* 863-6.

τῇ δὲ νῦν τύχῃ
βροτοῖς ἅπασι λαμπρὰ κηρύσσει μαθεῖν
τὸν εὐτυχεῖν δοκοῦντα μὴ ζηλοῦν πρὶν ἂν
θανόντ' ἴδῃ τις.

332. Cp. Eur. *fr.* 27.

337. For ὑπὸ, cp. *Bacchyl.* xii. 125. ὑπὸ κύμασιν.

351.
λασιαύχενά θ'
ἵππον *ὑφέλκεται ἀμφίλοφον ζυγόν.

MS. reading $\overset{\epsilon}{_{a}}\xi$εται.

Jebb rightly says that a present tense is required, and admits that the words of the Scholiast may be merely a paraphrase of ἀμφίλοφον. Against ζυγῶν it may be urged that the continuation of the dactylic run suggested by the

ANTIGONE

corresponding line of the strophe (340) is otherwise more probable than the logaoedic close. The conjecture ὑφέλκεται supposes the loss of two letters ὑφ (ΥΠΗ with ΙΠΠ preceding)—see also Schol. ὑπὸ κοινοῦ τὸ ὑπὸ ζυγὸν ἕξεται, implying an earlier reading ὑφέξεται (in which the future form may be due to assimilation with ἐπαξεται *inf.*)—the substitution of Α for Λ and of ΚC for Κ. The verb, taken in the primary sense, 'he drags beneath the yoke upon their necks,' is not unsuitable to the harnessing or subjugation of the wild horse and mountain bull.

356, 357.   πάγων *διαίθρεια καὶ
            δύσομβρα φεύγειν βέλη.

In favour of διαίθρεια—the darts of the frost descend *through* the clear sky.

367.   *τοτὲ μὲν κακόν, ἄλλοτ' ἐπ' ἐσθλὸν ἕρπει.

Jebb is probably right in reading τοτὲ μέν.

368.   νόμους †παρείρων χθονός.

Of the conjectures, περαίνων, 'fulfilling,' agrees best with the *ductus litterarum*, and with the Schol. ὁ πληρῶν τοὺς νόμους καὶ τὴν δικαιοσύνην : (gloss in L.[2] πληρῶν, τηρῶν).

370.   ὑψίπολις.   For the compound, cp. Eur. *Tro.* 602, ἐρημόπολις.

375.   ὃς τάδ' ἔρδοι.

L gives ἔρδει, but the form of the second ε is unusual, and suggests that the scribe began to write an ο and finished off the letter as an ε.

Cp. Aesch. *fr.* 303, μὴ παρασπιστὴς ἐμοί, | μηδ' ἐγγὺς εἴη.

14 PARALIPOMENA SOPHOCLEA

381, 382. οὐ δή που σέ γ' ἀπιστοῦσαν
τοῖς βασιλείοις *ἀπάγουσι νόμοις.

Because ἀπάγειν has a specific technical meaning as an Attic law term, it does not follow that it may not be used generally for 'to arrest and bring before the magistrate,' as in Her. and Eur. (see L. and S.). See Jebb's note on 160, *supr*. σύγκλητον. ἀπάγουσι is more *graphic* than ἄγουσι.

392. Cp. Eur. *fr.* 550, ἐκ τῶν ἀέλπτων ἡ χαρὰ μείζων βροτοῖς.

395. καθῃρέθη is probable.

414. εἴ τις τοῖσδ' ἀφειδήσοι πόνου.

Hermann's explanation of ἀφειδήσοι is not to be lightly rejected. It is quite possible that the word may have passed from 'to be lavish' or 'reckless' to the more general sense of 'to be careless,' and so, 'to neglect.' Against Bonitz' conjecture ἀκηδήσοι, it may be urged that κήδεσθαι implies feeling for a *person*, or at least some personal feeling. In the apparent exception, Ar. *Nub.* 106, the *vis comica* depends on the παρὰ προσδοκίαν. 'If you have any *affection* for your father's *dinner-table*.' The verb ἀφειδεῖν is used absolutely in Eur. *Iph. T.* 1354.

424, 425. ὡς ὅταν κενῆς
εὐνῆς νεοσσῶν ὀρφανὸν βλέψῃ λέχος.

Cp. Eur. *Med.* 435.
τᾶς ἀνάνδρου
κοίτας ὀλέσασα λέκτρον.

431. χοαῖσι τρισπόνδοισι τὸν νέκυν στέφει

Cp. *El.* 440.
τάσδε δυσμενεῖς χοὰς
οὐκ ἄν ποθ', ὅν γ' ἔκτεινε, τῷδ' ἐπέστεφε.

and Eur. *Hec.* 128.
τὸν Ἀχίλλειον τύμβον στεφανοῦν
αἵματι χλωρῷ.

ANTIGONE

436. ἀλλ' ἡδέως ἔμοιγε κἀλγεινῶς ἅμα.
See my note *in loco*. Jebb reads ἅμ' ἡδέως κ.τ.λ. Whether he is right or wrong in this, his parallels from Plato, *Gorg.* 496 *b.*, *Tim.* 38 *b.*, are not in point. He might fairly have quoted *Gorg.* 497 A., ἅμα διψῶν . . . πέπαυται καὶ ἅμα ἡδόμενος. For the facile confusion of μ and λλ, cp. *O. C.* 1266.

439, 440. ἀλλὰ πάντα ταῦθ' ἥσσω λαβεῖν
ἐμοὶ πέφυκε τῆς ἐμῆς σωτηρίας.

The suggestion that λαβεῖν here nearly=ὑπολαβεῖν (Schol. οὐδὲν γὰρ προκρίνω τῆς ἐμῆς σωτηρίας), may be defended, not only by Thuc. 2, 42, § 5, τὴν δὲ τῶν ἐναντίων τιμωρίαν ποθεινοτέραν αὐτῶν λαβόντες, but also by Eur. *fr.* 781, l. 57.

φιλεῖ τὰ τοιάδε
ληφθέντα φαύλως ἐς μέγαν χειμῶν' ἄγειν.

Cp. also Eur. *H. F.* 223, κακίστην λαμβάνων ἐς παῖδ' ἐμόν (τὴν Ἑλλάδα); *Suppl.* 194, δι' οἴκτου . . . λαβεῖν, *Iph. T.* 637, τὸ μέντοι δυσμενὲς μή μοι λάβῃς, also *Oed. Col.* 1678, as commonly interpreted, see Jebb's note.

(It should be observed, however, that I gave this as an alternative view. I had quoted *El.* 1015-16, for the other, which I gave first.)

443. καὶ φημὶ δρᾶσαι κοὐκ ἀπαρνοῦμαι τὸ μή.

μή echoes Creon's words. If Antigone had spoken at length, she would have said, οὐκ ἀπαρνοῦμαι μὴ οὐ δεδρακέναι. In *O. T.* 1388 (quoted by Jebb), μή is preferred, because the case is hypothetical (οὐκ ἂν ἐσχόμην).

447. ᾔδης τὰ κηρυχθέντα μὴ πράσσειν τάδε.

I am not convinced that ᾔδης τὰ is wrong. That Creon should prefix the article to *his* edict is significant. The reply of Antigone is also more exactly in point—ἐμφανῆ ἦν, sc. τὰ κηρυχθέντα.

16 PARALIPOMENA SOPHOCLEA

452. οἵ τούσδ' ἐν ἀνθρώποισιν ὥρισαν νόμους.

I still prefer οἱ τούσδ' of the MSS. to τοιούσδ' (Valcknär, approved by Jebb). The Scholiast and Donaldson seem to me to have apprehended the dramatic force of the passage. Creon had emphasised τούσδε νόμους, '*my* laws.' Antigone echoes him with still more indignant emphasis, τούσδε νόμους, 'the laws which *I* obey.' This is not a 'tame statement of fact,' but a solemn asseveration. And solemnity, not 'pathetic force,' is what is wanted here. So far from being 'awkward,' the stress on τούσδε has thus a dramatic import.

454, 455. ἄγραπτα κἀσφαλῆ θεῶν νόμιμα.

[Lysias] *c. Andocidem*, p. 104, l. 8, who quoted from Pericles a prosaic version of this account of the unwritten laws, implies that it belonged to the teaching of the Eumolpidae: νόμοις ... τοῖς ἀγράφοις, καθ' οὓς Εὐμολπίδαι ἐξηγοῦνται. The correspondence is remarkable. See above, p. 1, *Obs.* 2.

468. 'This series of three clauses, in which the second is opposed to the first, and the third reiterates the sense of the first is peculiarly Sophoclean.'—(Jebb.)

471, 472. δηλοῖ τὸ γέννημ' ὠμὸν ἐξ ὠμοῦ πατρὸς τῆς παιδός.

Jebb explains τὸ γέννημα τῆς παιδός as = ἡ γεννηθεῖσα παῖς. But that the noun ln -μα may signify, not the thing produced, but the process, or even the manner of production, appears, not only from *Prom.* 850 (where no change is probable), and Plat. *Soph.* 266 *d.* (where I agree with Ast), but from Plat. *Polit.* 272 *e.*, where σπέρματα are not 'things sown,' but 'acts of sowing.' See my note in loco, and cp. *supra.* 126 and note. I believe the meaning in Soph. *O. T.* 1246 to be the same. And so here τὸ γέννημα τῆς παιδός is 'the breeding of

ANTIGONE 17

the maid': 'Her strain is fierce, derived from a fierce sire.'
Cp. Eur. *fr.* 166.

τὸ μωρὸν αὐτῷ τοῦ πατρὸς νόσημ' ἔνι.

476.   θραυσθέντα καὶ ῥαγέντα πλεῖστ' ἂν εἰσίδοις.

θραύειν is to break in small pieces. Eur. *Hipp.* 1239, θραύων τε σάρκας. I think that here, as sometimes elsewhere, the strongest word comes first.

477-79. σμικρῷ χαλινῷ δ'οἶδα τοὺς θυμουμένους
         ἵππους καταρτυθέντας· οὐ γὰρ ἐκπέλει
         φρονεῖν μέγ' ὅστις δουλός ἐστι τῶν πέλας.

Cp. *Fr.* 785, πολλῶν χαλινῶν ἔργον οἰάκων θ' ἅμα.
and Eur. *fr.* 49.

δούλου φρονοῦντος μᾶλλον ἢ φρονεῖν χρεὼν
οὐκ ἔστιν ἄχθος μεῖζον, οὐδὲ δώμασι
κτῆσις κακίων οὐδ' ἀνωφελεστέρα.

490. For τοῦδε . . . τάφου, cp. Eur. *Alc.* 620.

510.   σὺ δ' οὐκ ἐπαιδεῖ, τῶνδε χωρὶς εἰ φρονεῖς;

Cp. *supr.* 375, ἴσον φρονῶν, and note.

514.   πῶς δῆτ' ἐκείνῳ δυσσεβῆ τιμᾷς χάριν;

ἐκείνῳ, 'in relation to him': dative of interest, rather than (as Jebb) 'in his judgment.' Cp. *Trach.* 140, τέκνοισι . . . ἄβουλον.

520.   ἀλλ' οὐχ ὁ χρηστὸς τῷ κακῷ λαχεῖν ἴσος.

ἴσους, the conjecture of Nauck and Semitelos, is not convincing. Not the desire of the dead man, but his rights as a citizen, should be prominent in Creon's mind. I therefore hold to the construction which Jebb thinks impossible. The expression is condensed, and an instance of the 'personal' construction, in place of οὐκ ἴσον ἐστὶν αὐτὸν ἴσον λαχεῖν.

521.   τίς οἶδεν εἰ κάτω 'στὶν εὐαγῆ τάδε;

γρ. κάτωθεν is written above by S. (or an ancient hand). The line would not perhaps be approved in a College exercise; but τίς οἶδεν if it would offend an Attic ear?

527.   φιλάδελφα κάτω δάκρυ' εἰβομένη.

The reading of one MS. δάκρυα εἰβομένη helps to explain the slight corruption, Λ having been read for Α, which was afterwards inserted as a v. r.

529. For ῥέθος, cp. Eur. *H. F.* 1205, ῥέθος ἀελίῳ δεῖξον.

531.   σὺ δ', ἢ κατ' οἴκους ὡς ἐχιδν' ὑφειμένη.

The notion of secrecy is not implied in the preposition ὑπὸ, but in the whole word, which might be used of a serpent lurking under a stone. On the other hand, the notion of submission (Jebb) is hardly present except in so far as submissiveness has been a cloke for disobedience.

533.   τρέφων δύ' ἄτα κἀπαναστάσεις θρόνων.

For ἄτα, cp. Eur. *Androm.* 103.

οὐ γάμον, ἀλλά τιν' ἄταν
ἀγάγετ' εὐναίαν ἐς θαλάμους Ἑλέναν.

537. Cp. also Hes. *Theog.* 474.

541. ξύμπλουν. For the image, cp. Eur. *Iph. T.* 600.

542. Eur. *Alc.* 339, λόγῳ γὰρ ἦσαν οὐκ ἔργῳ φίλοι.

547. Cp. Eur. *Iph. A.* 1418, 1419.

548. Eur. *Iph. A.* 1418,

ἡ Τυνδαρὶς παῖς διὰ τὸ σῶμ' ἀρκεῖ μάχας
ἀνδρῶν τιθεῖσα καὶ φόνους.

551. ἀλγοῦσα μὲν δῆτ', εἰ γέλωτ' ἔν σοι γελῶ.

Aj. 79, quoted by Jebb, supports γέλωτ' against the conjecture γελῶ γ'. The sense is obvious if a stress is laid on εἰ =κεἰ, 'I do so with pain, though I do laugh at thee.' Ismene has not spoken of laughter. The same meaning belongs to Dindorf's conjecture, δή, κεἰ.

556. ἀλλ' οὐκ ἐπ' ἀρρήτοις γε τοῖς ἐμοῖς λόγοις.

Besides Eur. *Ion.* 228, see *fr.* adespot. 224.

οὐκ εὖ λέγειν χρὴ μὴ 'πὶ τοῖς ἔργοις καλοῖς.

561. Read τὼ παῖδε φημὶ with Jebb.

563, 564. οὐδ' ὃς ἂν βλάστῃ μένει
νοῦς τοῖς κακῶς πράσσουσιν, ἀλλ' ἐξίσταται.

Cp. Eur. *Androm.* 365.

καί σου τὸ σῶφρον ἐξετόξευσεν φρενός.

Eur. *fr.* 267, νῦν δ' οἶνος ἐξέστησέ μ'; Melanthius, *fr.* 1 (p. 760 *N.*). [θυμός] τὰ δεινὰ πράσσει τὰς φρένας μετοικίσας —on which Plutarch observes—οὔκ· ἀλλ' ἐξοικίσας τελείως. Perhaps Eur. (*Ant.*) *fr.* 165, οὐ γὰρ οἱ κακῶς πεπραγότες | σὺν ταῖς τύχαισι τοὺς λόγους ἀπώλεσαν, intended a contradiction of this saying.

20 PARALIPOMENA SOPHOCLEA

575.   Ἅιδης ὁ παύσων τούσδε τοὺς γάμους ἔφυ.

Jebb reads ἐμοί with L. But is not Creon shifting the responsibility from himself to Hades? Cp. Eur. *fr.* 465, (Ἅιδης) κρινεῖ ταῦτ᾽.

577.   καὶ σοί γε κἀμοί.

σοί, not 'for thee,' as Jebb, but as in δοκεῖ μοι. 'You hold it as determined, do you? So do I. It is my resolve.' So the words may be paraphrased. In Creon's case the δόγμα is a determination of the will. He takes advantage of the double meaning of δοκεῖν.

583.   οἷς γὰρ ἂν σεισθῇ θεόθεν δόμος, ἄτας
οὐδὲν ἐλλείπει.

θεόθεν : cp. *fr.* adespot. 303.

θεόθεν δὲ πνέοντ᾽ οὖρον ἀνάγκη
τλῆναι καμάτοις ἀνοδύρτοις.

585.   γενεᾶς ἐπὶ πλῆθος ἕρπον.

For πλῆθος = 'the full number,' cp. Eur. *Phoen.* 715, σμικρὸν τό πλῆθος τῆσδε γῆς, οἳ δ᾽ ἄφθονοι.

587, 588.   οἶδμα δυσπνόοις ὅταν
Θρήσσαισιν ἔρεβος ὕφαλον ἐπιδράμῃ πνοαῖς.

Cp. *fr.* adespot. 377.

φεύγει μέγα λαῖφος ὑποστολίσας
ἐρεβώδεος ἐκ θαλάσσης.

590 *f.* I see no reason for altering the reading here.

597.   οὐδ' ἔχει λύσιν.

The subject of ἔχει is not τα πήματα exactly, but a general notion drawn from it, such as τὰ κακά (Hermann), or τὸ πρᾶγμα. Cp. *O. C.* 545, ἔχει δέ μοι ... πρὸς δίκας τι, and note. Jebb suggests ἡ γενεά in the larger sense. But this is rather remote, and a neuter subject is better.

600.   νῦν γὰρ ἐσχάτας ὑπὲρ
ῥίζας *ὃ τέτατο φάος ἐν Οἰδίπου δόμοις.

Jebb's reasons in favour of *ὃ τέτατο are, I think, convincing. In the scholion on the margin of L the words are λείπει ἄρθρον τὸ ὅ· τὸ δὲ λεγόμενον ἐστὶ τοιοῦτο. νῦν γὰρ ὅπερ ἐπέτατο (*sic*) φησί (? an error for φῶς) καὶ σωτηρία ἐν τοῖς οἴκοις τοῦ Οἰδίποδος.

601-603. κατ' αὖ νιν φοινία θεῶν τῶν
νερτέρων ἀμᾷ κόνις
λόγου τ'ἄνοια καὶ φρενῶν Ἐρινύς.

My objection to the conjectural κοπίς is not merely the vulgarity (which may or may not be true), but the *distinctness* of the image. The language of Sophocles in treating of the supernatural has a vagueness which adds to its solemnity. In dealing with the world beneath, especially, he nowhere indulges in those graphic and picturesque touches which we find in Euripides. He does not arm Death or Hades with a material sword. His Pluto is not 'black-haired,' nor is Charon seen at the oar in his dark skiff, or with his hand on the boat-pole and the rudder (*Alc.* 253-263). Only in *O. C.* 1568 ff. the superstitious elders hint at the legendary form of Cerberus. Also, as Professor Jebb in his second edition well remarks, νερτέρων κοπὶς is not in harmony with the following words, λόγου τ'ἄνοια κ.τ.λ.

The whole passage is one of those in which suggestiveness prevails over clearness. The phraseology is condensed, and every word is deeply tinged with association. Cp. *Trach.* 573 and note; *ib.* 831-840.

I agree with Jebb and Hermann that the object of καταμᾷ is not ῥίζαν but φάος. Now, to 'reap' or to 'cut down' a spreading light, does not seem to me an harmonious metaphor. But the brightness on the root may be 'swept under' by dust heaped over it; and that I take to be the image suggested. I have never thought that ἀμᾶν could primarily mean to 'cover.' When I spoke of two vocables, to 'gather' and to 'cut' were the meanings in my mind. If the latter is derived from the former, then I think that in καταμᾶν the primitive meaning has prevailed (as it certainly has in καταμᾶσθαι (see L. and S.) and in διαμᾶσθαι (Plut. *de Iside*, 379 A, διαμώμενοι τὴν κόνιν). And for similar use of the simple verb, see L. and S., s. v. ἀμάω, ii. The linguistic process which I meant to suggest is as follows:

(1) καταμᾶν κόνιν τινός, 'to gather or heap dust over something.'

(2) καταμᾶν τι κόνει, 'to heap over with dust.'

(3) ἡ κόνις καταμᾷ τι, 'the dust overspreads it'—and so 'covers it from sight.'

I grant that this is bold: but is it impossible? It is what the scholiast meant who explained the word by καλύπτει.

603.   λόγου τ'ἄνοια καὶ φρενῶν 'Ερινύς.

With Hermann and Ellendt I take λόγου rather as 'discourse' than 'speech.' At all events it recalls her talk with Ismene as well as her answer to Creon. For φρενῶν, cp. Eur. *Med.* 1265, φρενῶν βαρὺς χόλος.

606.   ὕπνος . . . ὁ παντογήρως.

The reasons against παντογήρως are strong. On the other side, I can only repeat the comparison with *O. T.* 870, 817, οὐδὲ ... λάθα κατακοιμάσει ... οὐδὲ γηράσκει, as showing a possible association of old age with slumber. Sleep and death are brothers, and the threshold of old age is near to death.

607. *οὔτε θεῶν ἀκάμαντες
μῆνες.

I now read οὔτε θεῶν ἀκάμαντες with εἰδότι δ'οὐδὲν *ἐφέρπει in the antistrophe (618). ἀκάμας is more suited to lyric verse than ἄκματος. Cp. Eur. *fr.* 594.

ἀκάμας τε χρόνος περί γ'ἀενάῳ
ῥεύματι πλήρης φοιτᾷ τίκτων
αὐτὸς ἑαυτόν.

609. ἀγήρῳ δὲ χρόνῳ δυνάστας.
Cp. Eur. *fr.* 910.
ἀθανάτου καθορῶν φύσεως
κόσμον ἀγήρω.

ἀγήρως is a MS. emendation, and would only be admissible if χρόνῳ were causal dative.

613, 614. οὐδὲν *ἕρπων
θνατῶν βιότῳ πάμπολις ἐκτὸς ἄτας.

It is difficult not to agree with Dindorf and Linwood that that there is here some corruption too deep for remedy. I do not know in what sense πάμπολύ γ' was first conjectured, but I cannot think that οὐδὲν πάμπολυ='nothing vast' is a natural expression. The scholiasts certainly read πάμπολις, and also apparently ἕρπων. Hermann gives the general drift of the passage thus: '*Dicit autem legem eam, quam modo indicaverat, invictum esse Jovis imperium. " In aeternum," inquit, " haec lex valebit, nulla in re mortalium vitam permulta* (πάμπολυ?) *sine malo expetens": i.e. valet quidem semper haec lex, sed nulla in re perdiu sine malo. Quod cur ita fiat statim in sequente stropha explicat.*'

πάμπολις, as explained by the scholiasts, is quite intelligible, 'a law prevailing in all cities,' unlike human laws, which differ between city and city. The difficulty lies in the order of the words: cp. δυσχείρωμα, *supr.* 126. Taking the words as they stand, however, I would still try to explain them thus: 'The sovereignty of Zeus, an all-embracing law, in its eternal course fails not to bring calamity to men, whom Hope deceives.' The tone of the Chorus here is pessimistic; cp. *O.C.* 1211 ff. For ἕρπων, cp. Eur. *Hipp.* 557, ἁ Κύπρις οἷον ἕρπει.

615, 616. ἁ γὰρ δὴ πολύπλαγκτος ἐλπὶς
πολλοῖς μὲν ὄνασις ἀνδρῶν.

πολύπλαγκτος—'far-wandering.' Hope, like calamity, has a wide range. Aesch. *Prom.* 278, 279.

ταὐτά τοι πλανωμένη
πρὸς ἄλλοτ' ἄλλον πημονὴ προσιζάνει.

It is better not to anticipate ἀπάτη.

618. εἰδότι δ' οὐδὲν *ἐφέρπει.

The change, though affecting strophe and antistrophe, is slight in both, and the scholiast here explains, τῷ ἀνθρώπῳ οὐδὲν εἰδότι ἐπέρχεται. Cp. Eur. *Alc.* 269, σκοτία δ' ἐπ' ὄσσοισι νὺξ ἐφέρπει.

620-624. σοφίᾳ γὰρ ἔκ του
κλεινὸν ἔπος πέφανται,
τὸ κακὸν δοκεῖν ποτ' ἐσθλὸν
τῷδ' ἔμμεν ὅτῳ φρένας
θεὸς ἄγει πρὸς ἄταν.

Cp. also *fr.* adespot. 296.

ὅταν γὰρ ὀργὴ δαιμόνων βλάπτῃ τινά,
τοῦτ' αὐτὸ πρῶτον, ἐξαφαιρεῖται φρενῶν
τὸν νοῦν τὸν ἐσθλόν· εἰς δὲ τὴν χείρω τρέπει
γνώμην, ἵν' εἰδῇ μηδὲν ὧν ἁμαρτάνει.

ANTIGONE

625. πράσσει δ' †ὀλιγοστὸν χρόνον ἐκτὸς ἄτας.

It is, of course, easy to read ὀλίγιστον. An early corrector of L. seems to have been puzzled and corrected ὀλιγοστὸν to ὀλίγως τὸν (sc. χρόνον).

635, 636. σύ μοι γνώμας ἔχων
χρηστὰς ἀπορθοῖς, αἷς ἔγωγ' ἐφέψομαι.

Jebb is probably right in making γνώμας the object of ἀπορθοῖς. Haemon is anxious to soothe his father; but he is also anxious to lead him gently to a different point of view, and he prepares for this by the form of his submission. His opening words contain a suggestion, τοῖς συνετοῖσι, that Creon is not infallible. As Schneidewin observes, the participles may represent a sentence with either εἰ or ἐπεί. Creon does not take the hint.

637. ἐμοὶ γὰρ οὐδεὶς ἀξίως ἔσται γάμος.

There is no sufficient reason for reading ἀξιώσεταί (fut. pass.).

646, 647. τί τόνδ' ἂν εἴποις ἄλλο πλὴν αὐτῷ πόνους
φῦσαι, πολὺν δὲ τοῖσιν ἐχθροῖσιν γέλων;

Cp. Eur. *fr.* 84.

ἢ τί πλέον εἶναι παῖδας ἀνθρώποις, πάτερ,
εἰ μὴ 'πὶ τοῖς δεινοῖσιν ὠφελήσομεν;

650. For παραγκάλισμα, cp. Eur. *Hel.* 242, Διὸς ὑπαγκάλισμα σεμνόν. And for a similar use of the noun in μα, Her. vii. 156, δῆμον εἶναι συνοίκημα ἀχαριτώτατον.

654. μέθες
τὴν παῖδ' ἐν Ἅιδου τήνδε νυμφεύειν τινί.

I still take νυμφεύειν of the husband. 'Leave her for some one down there to marry.'

666, 667. ἀλλ' ὃν πόλις στήσειε, τοῦδε χρὴ κλύειν
καὶ σμικρὰ καὶ δίκαια καὶ τἀναντία.

See also *fr*. 226.

ἀλλ' εἰς θεοὺς ὁρῶντα, κἂν ἔξω δίκης
χωρεῖν κελεύῃ, κεῖσ' ὁδοιπορεῖν χρεών.

671. δίκαιον κἀγαθὸν παραστάτην.

Cp. *fr*. adespot, 14 (of the Dioscuri).

σωτῆρες—κἀγαθοὶ παραστάται.

673. αὕτη πόλεις τ' ὄλλυσιν, ἥδ' ἀναστάτους
οἴκους τίθησιν.

ἥδ', not ἦδ', is certainly right. πόλεις τ' is, of course, irregular; but I am not convinced that it is wrong. As the sentence proceeds, one rhetorical form is substituted for another.

674. ἥδε σὺν μάχῃ δορὸς
τροπὰς καταρρήγνυσι·

Why συμμάχου δορός? Does not the remark apply to every army?

676. σῴζει τὰ πολλὰ σώμαθ' ἡ πειθαρχία.

τὰ πολλὰ σώματα: not 'the greater part,' but 'the many persons' who form one host. The single principle of obedience is the cause of safety to all.

680. κοὐκ ἂν γυναικῶν ἥσσονες καλοίμεθ' ἄν.

Not 'and then,' but simply 'and.' 'I had rather be overthrown by a man; and certainly I am not going to have it said that I was beaten by a woman.'

ANTIGONE

687. γένοιτο μεντἂν χἀτέρῳ καλῶς ἔχον.

Haemon is so far roused by his father's vehemence as to throw out this further hint, which is certainly not well calculated to mollify Creon. But he is bent on reasoning with his father, as he does below, 705 ff. The line is commonly taken to mean 'and yet another man, too, might have some useful thought.' I do not see that this is more propitiatory or less irritating than the meaning which I prefer, and which seems also to have occurred to Linwood: 'In another, who is not thy son, such criticism might not be unbecoming'; *i.e.* εἰ καὶ ἕτερος οὕτως εἴποι, γένοιτ᾽ ἂν αὐτῷ καλῶς ἔχον. In this way, a subject for ἔχον is more easily supplied (sc. τὸ οὕτω λέγειν), and in contrasting persons, καί is sometimes used illogically, *e.g.* in *Aj.* 1103, 1104.

οὐδ᾽ ἔσθ᾽ ὅπου σοὶ τόνδε κοσμῆσαι πλέον
ἀρχῆς ἔκειτο θεσμὸς ἢ καὶ τῷδε σέ.

(they could not each command the other). Compare the well-known idiomatic use of ἄλλος. It is not necessary to this view (with Linwood) to assume an *hyperbaton*. Cp. also *Oed. Col.* 488, αὐτὸς κεἴ τις ἄλλος; *El.* 1145, 1146, οὔτε γάρ ποτε | μητρὸς οὐ γ᾽ ἦσθα μᾶλλον ἢ κἀμοῦ φίλος; *Bacchyl.* vii. 46, παῖς ἐὼν ἀνήρ τε—where see Jebb's note.

709. οὗτοι διαπτυχθέντες ὤφθησαν κενοί.

Cp. Eur. *Hipp.* 985, τὸ μέντοι πρᾶγμ᾽, ἔχον καλοὺς λόγους | εἴ τις διαπτύξειεν, οὐ καλὸν τόδε.

715. ναὸς ὅστις ἐγκρατῆ πόδα
τείνας ὑπείκει μηδέν.

It is necessary to take ἐγκρατῆ as 'proleptic'? Is it not the sheet (πούς) in any case that determines the course of the vessel? For ἐγκρατῆ, cp. *fr.* adespot, 380.

ναῦς ὥς τις ἐκ μὲν γῆς ἀνήρτηται βρόχοις,
πνεῖ δ᾽ οὖρος, ἡμῖν δ᾽ οὐ κρατεῖ τὰ πείσματα.

28   PARALIPOMENA SOPHOCLEA

And for the general sense, *ib.* 413.

μικρὸν δὲ ποδὸς χαλάσαι μεγάλῃ
κύματος ἀλκῇ.

718.   ἀλλ' εἶκε· θυμῷ καὶ μετάστασιν δίδου.

I now agree with Hermann and Gaisford in thinking this the true reading. Hermann rightly says of the asyndeton: 'quae est per asyndeton instantius precantis oratio.' Jebb seems to have overlooked H.'s explanation of καί, *i.e.* 'ut iratus fuisti, ita fac etiam ut cesset ira.' 'Allow your angry spirit to remove.' Cp. *Phil.* 807, καὶ θάρσος ἴσχ', and for μετάστασιν, Eur. *Alc.* 1122.

λύπης δ' εὐτυχῶν μεθίστασο.

See also Eur. *Bacch.* 647, ὀργῇ δ' ὑπόθες ἥσυχον πόδα.

723.   Cp. *fr.* adespot. 535.

χρὴ δ'ἢ λέγειν τι χρηστὸν ἢ λέγουσιν εὖ
μὴ δυσμεναίνειν τῷ φθόνῳ νικώμενον.

729.   οὐ τὸν χρόνον χρὴ μᾶλλον ἢ τἄργα σκοπεῖν.

I still think that Haemon means by τἄργα, not his own merits, but the facts of the case. Creon, however, may have understood him in the former way, and Jebb's explanation of ἔργον in 730 is then justified. Cp. *fr.* adespot. 374.

ὦ τλῆμον ἀρετή, λόγος ἄρ' ἦσθ', ἐγὼ δὲ σὲ
ὡς ἔργον ἤσκουν.

737.   πόλις γὰρ οὐκ ἔσθ' ἥτις ἀνδρός ἐσθ' ἑνός.

Cp. Eur. *fr.* 172.

οὔτ' εἰκὸς ἄρχειν, οὔτ' ἐχρῆν ἄνευ νόμου
τύραννον εἶναι· μωρία δὲ καὶ θέλειν,
ὃς τῶν ὁμοίων βούλεται κρατεῖν μόνος.

747. Jebb treats αἰσχρῶν as neuter; and certainly αἰσχρὸς, in a moral sense, is rarely used of persons. But cp. *Phil.* 906, αἰσχρὸς φανοῦμαι.

751. ἥδ' οὖν θανεῖται καὶ θανοῦσ' ὀλεῖ τινά.

Jebb says 'ὀλεῖ τινά, *i.e.* ἐμέ: Creon understands him to mean σέ.' I think that he means σέ, not as a threat, but as a warning. Creon's authority in the State will be ruined by his arbitrary and cruel act. Haemon certainly has no thought of threatening his father's life. Creon wrongly imagines that he is going to put himself at the head of a revolt (768).

767. νοῦς δ'ἐστὶ τηλικοῦτος ἀλγήσας βαρύς.

βαρύς. This word implies not only resentment, but suggests the 'something dangerous' in the angry man. Cp. Eur. *Med.* 38, βαρεῖα γὰρ φρήν, and *Phil.* 1045.

βαρύς τε καὶ βαρεῖαν ὁ ξένος φάτιν
τήνδ' εἶπ', Ὀδυσσεῦ.

The words of the chorus harp upon Creon's fear of rebellion.

768. δράτω, φρονείτω μεῖζον ἢ κατ' ἄνδρ' ἰών.

ἄνδρα is not exactly = ἄνθρωπον here, but is suggestive of active energy.

775. φορβῆς τοσοῦτον ὡς ἄγος μόνον προθείς.

Cp. Eur. *fr.* 379.

ἤν τις οἴκων πλουσίων φάτνην ἔχῃ.

785. Cp. Eur. *Hipp.* 447, 448; 1272, 1273, ποτᾶται 'πὶ γαῖαν εὐάχητόν θ' ἁλμυρὸν ἐπὶ πόντον.

786-796.

786.   καὶ σ' οὔτ' ἀθανάτων †φύξιμος οὐδείς.

796.   νύμφας τῶν μεγάλων †πάρεδρος ἐν ἀρχαῖς.

I propose καὶ σ' οὔτ' ἀθανάτων *πέφευγεν οὐδεὶς ... νύμφας, τῶν μεγάλων πάρεδρος *ἀρχαῖς. φύξιμος occurs once in *Od.* 5, 359, where the neuter is used impersonally, and not as here. Otherwise the word seems to belong to later prose. May not the text here be affected by a marginal gloss, φύξιμός ἐστιν, explaining πέφευγεν (the gnomic perfect) as = δυνατός ἐστι φυγεῖν? If that is so, the deletion of ἐν in 796 is a very simple change. 'Yoke-fellow with the authority of great Ordinances.' The law of filial obedience is tempered by the influence of beauty. An assessor may either confirm a judgment or modify it.

The loves in Eur. *Medea*, 843, are co-workers with wisdom: justice in O.C. 1382, sits in council with the ancient laws of Zeus. The assessor in the present instance over-rules the finding of the judge. Cp. *Moschion, fr.* 6, l. 16.

ἦν δ'ὁ μὲν νόμος
ταπεινός, ἡ βία δὲ σύνθρονος δίκῃ.

790.   οὔθ' ἀμερίων ἐπ' ἀνθρώπων, ὁ δ'ἔχων μέμηνεν.

The change from ἐπ' ἀνθρώπων to σέ γ' ἀνθρώπων is simple and plausible. But ἐπί with the genitive denoting extent may be compared to the use with the accusative in Homer, *Il.* 24, 202, ἔκλε' ἐπ' ἀνθρώπους, *ib.* 10, 213.

800.   ἄμαχος γὰρ ἐμπαίζει θεὸς Ἀφροδίτα.

ἐμπαίζει. Either (with Jebb) sc. τοῖς βλεφάροις = 'is at play therein'; or rather sc. τῷ ἡσσωμένῳ τοῦ ἔρωτος, = 'mocks at her victim.' Cp. Hor. *Od.* iii. 28, 49.

Fortuna saevo laeta negotio et
Ludum insolentem ludere pertinax.

ANTIGONE

806-808. ὁρᾶτ' ἔμ', ὦ γᾶς πατρίας πολῖται
τὰν νεάταν ὁδὸν
στείχουσαν, νέατον δὲ φέγγος
λεύσσουσαν ἀελίου
κοὔποτ' αὖθις.

Jebb says, 'νέατον, in contrast with αὖθις, is best taken as adv.' It is a nice point, but I think it should be determined rather by what precedes than by what follows, which can easily be construed κατὰ σύνεσιν. Cp. *Trach*. 835, ἀέλιον ἕτερον ἢ τανῶν. See, however, Eur. *Hec*. 411, *Tro*. 201.

820. οὔτε ξιφέων ἐπίχειρα λαχοῦσ'.

In spite of parallels, I think the genitive ξιφέων here is descriptive.

821, 822. ἀλλ, αὐτόνομος, ζῶσα μόνη δὴ
Θνητῶν Ἀίδην καταβήσει.

αὐτόνομος. This is taken to mean 'of your own free will,' 'mistress of thine own fate.' So Jebb, with Hermann. But the scholiast's explanation may yet be justified: ἰδίῳ καὶ καινῷ νόμῳ περὶ τὸ τέλος χρησαμένη. Antigone's case is an exception to all rules. If that is the meaning, she may well say 'Miserable comforters are ye all.'

823. ξέναν. Cp. Pind. *Nem*. iv. 23, where Thebes is ξένιον ἄστυ to Aegina.

828-840. πετραία βλάστα δάμασεν· καί νιν *ὄμβροι τακομέναν
. . . οὐκ *οἰχομέναν ὑβρίζεις.

I accept Jebb's defence of the conjectures ὄμβροι and οἰχομέναν.

32 PARALIPOMENA SOPHOCLEA

836-838. καίτοι φθιμένη μέγα *κἀκοῦσαι
τοῖς ἰσοθέοις ἔγκληρα λαχεῖν
ζῶσαν καὶ ἔπειτα θανοῦσαν.

There is likewise much force in Jebb's argument about these lines. But I do not see why ἔγκληρα λαχεῖν may not mean 'having a share amongst.' Words in poetry are not tied down to the precision of their legal application.

849.   πρὸς *ἔρυμα τυμβόχωστον ἔρχομαι.

The ¨ over ἔρῠ̈μα does not mark ἔργμα as corrupt, but indicates that what looks like a γ is really a deeply indented ῠ̈. The same thing may be seen two lines higher up over the ῠ̈ of ξυμμάρτῠ̈ρας, which, in linking it to the ρ, the scribe has made too shallow. On the other hand, in the Scholion, ἕρμα περίφραγμα, ἕρμα seeems to be miswritten for ἔργμα.

850.   *βροτοῖς οὔτε *τις ἐν νεκροῖσιν.

I still think that this correction of the text, proposed by me in the small edition of 1886 (C.A.) may compete with that of Seyffert adopted by Jebb, βροτοῖς οὔτε νεκροῖς κυροῦσα.

862-865. ἰὼ ματρῷαι λέκτρων ἆται
κοιμήματά τ'αὐτογέννητ'
ἐμῷ πατρὶ δυσμόρῳ ματρός.

'Alas for my mother's horrid fate in marriage,—alas, for what befel my hapless father,—incestuous intercourse with her from whom he sprang.'

I read δυσμόρῳ and understand Antigone to refer to both her parents. πατρί, dative of interest after the compound adj.

866.   οἵων ἐγώ ποθ' ἁ ταλαίφρων ἔφυν.

οἵων is not merely exclamatory, but relative : and the vague ποτε looks back to the hour of her birth, 'I sprang, what time I sprang.'

ANTIGONE   33

879. Cp. *fr*. adespot, 28.

ὦ κλεινὸν ὄμμα, νῦν πανύστατόν σ' ἰδὼν
λείπω φάος τοδ'.

887, 888.   ἄφετε μόνην ἔρημον, εἴτε χρὴ θανεῖν
εἴτ' ἐν τοιαύτῃ ζῶσα *τυμβεύσει στέγῃ.

Certainly, if 888 is sound, the change from χρὴ to χρῇ is justified. But there is something to be said for τυμβεύσει, though of weak MS. authority. The notion of Antigone choosing between life and death when insepulchred, is too *bizarre* even for Creon's caprice. For χρή, cp. Eur. *Med.* 355, εἰ μένειν δεῖ, μίμν' ἐφ' ἡμέραν μίαν.

899.   φίλη δὲ σοί, κασίγνητον κάρα.

I agree that κασίγνητον κάρα in this line is addressed to Eteocles.

904-920.   καίτοι σ'ἐγὼ 'τίμησα τοῖς φρονοῦσιν εὖ.
οὐ γάρ ποτ' οὔτ' ἂν εἰ τέκνων μήτηρ ἔφυν
οὔτ' εἰ πόσις μοι κατθανὼν ἐτήκετο,
βίᾳ πολιτῶν τόνδ' ἂν ᾐρόμην πόνον.
τίνος νόμου δὴ ταῦτα πρὸς χάριν λέγω;
πόσις μὲν ἄν μοι κατθανόντος ἄλλος ἦν,
καὶ παῖς ἀπ' ἄλλου φωτός, εἰ τοῦδ' ἤμπλακον,
μητρὸς δ' ἐν Ἅιδου καὶ πατρὸς κεκευθότοιν,
οὐκ ἔστ' ἀδελφὸς ὅστις ἂν βλάστοι ποτέ.
τοιῷδε μέντοι σ' ἐκπροτιμήσασ' ἐγώ
νόμῳ, Κρέοντι ταῦτ' ἔδοξ' ἁμαρτάνειν
καὶ δεινὰ τολμᾶν, ὦ κασίγνητον κάρα.
καὶ νῦν ἄγει με διὰ χερῶν οὕτω λαβὼν
ἄλεκτρον, ἀνυμέναιον, οὔτε του γάμου
μέρος λαχοῦσαν οὔτε παιδείου τροφῆς,
ἀλλ' ὧδ' ἔρημος πρὸς φίλων ἡ δύσμορος
ζῶσ' εἰς θανόντων ἔρχομαι κατασκαφάς.

It may seem an act of unpardonable temerity to defend this passage from the hosts of critics who, since Goethe's *obiter dictum* on the subject have pronounced against it. But I must venture. The fallacy which seems to me to lie at the root of the objection is that of demanding absolute logical consistency from a tragic heroine in the immediate prospect of death. That Antigone's faith does waver for a moment appears from 922, which no one suspects, τί χρή με τὴν δύστηνον ἐς θεοὺς ἔτι | βλέπειν; In this moment of utter desertion she marvels at her own act, and in a state of mind approaching to delirium, tries to account for it. The reasoning put into her mouth by the poet is peculiar to the age, but the fact which it expresses has a universal import. The ground of her proceeding in defiance of all men was something deeper, not only than Creon's edict, but than the unwritten immemorial tradition to which she had appealed. It lay in her unique affection for Polynices. Under the shadow of death she is conscious of a motive more constraining than reason, 'the primal sympathy, which, having been, must ever be.' But the shadow lifts, and she recovers the resolute unbending mood which breathes through 925-928.

Such an alternation of pathos with stern resolve does not seem to me to detract either from the *Antigone* as a work of art, or from the character of the heroine.

In line 904, I would not punctuate after φρονοῦσιν. 'Those who consider wisely will agree that I *did* honour thee.'

What Jebb thinks the inexcusable clumsiness of 910, appears to me to arise from condensation. She means, 'if, after the loss of a husband, her only child were lost to her.' And her imagination about such things is that of an inexperienced girl.

In 916, I do not think that διὰ χερῶν is 'in his hands,' but 'between the hands of ministers'; see L. and S. διαλαμβάνω, ii. 1; Her. i. 114, ἐκέλευε αὐτὸν τοὺς ἄλλους παῖδας διαλαβεῖν.

For a further defence of the passage, see above, p. 1, *Obs.* 3.

ANTIGONE

927. εἰ δ' οἵδ' ἁμαρτάνουσι, μὴ πλείω κακὰ πάθοιεν.

For μὴ πλείω, cp. Eur. *Heracl.* 576.

δίδασκέ μοι
τοιούσδε τούσδε παῖδας, ἐς τὸ πᾶν σοφούς,
ὥσπερ σύ, μηδὲν μᾶλλον· ἀρκέσουσι γάρ.

940. λεύσσετε, Θήβης οἱ κοιρανίδαι.

I still think, as I did in 1879, that οἱ κοιρανίδαι is addressed chiefly to the θεοὶ προγενεῖς, and that πρὸς οἵων ἀνδρῶν expresses contempt for the upstart Creon. Cp. [*Lys.*] xiii. 64, δεῖ γὰρ ὑμᾶς εἰδέναι ὅτι δοῦλος καὶ ἐκ δούλων ἐστίν, ἵν' εἰδῆτε οἷος ὢν ὑμᾶς λυμαίνεται.

959, 960. οὕτω τὰς μανίας δεινὸν ἀποστάζει
ἀνθηρόν τε μένος.

Previous interpreters, including the Scholiast, Hermann and Schneidewin, have understood these words to mean, 'So fell and so acute is the rage that flows' (lit. 'exudes') 'from madness.' Linwood says, 'ἀποστάζει *dicit, metaphorâ a viro stillante sumta*.' Jebb renders, 'There the fierce exuberance of his madness slowly passed away.' This innovation will hardly stand: οὕτω naturally connects with δεινόν, which is predicative with ἀποστάζει. ἄνθος is a natural metaphor for the *acme* or acute stage of a disease. And κεῖνος ἐπέγνω μανίαις κ.τ.λ. confirms the *general* statement (Hermann) by the example in question.

966. παρὰ δὲ Κυανεᾶν *πελάγει διδύμας ἁλός.

Jebb's conjecture πελάγει for πελάγεων is decidly preferable to Wieseler's σπιλάδων. I have no hesitation in accepting it.

36 PARALIPOMENA SOPHOCLEA

For διδύμας ἁλός, cp. Aesch. *fr*. 191.

δίδυμον χθονὸς Εὐρώπης
μέγαν ἠδ' Ἀσίας τέρμονα Φᾶσιν.

Also Eur. *Iph. T.* 392, κυάνεαι σύνοδοι θαλάσσας; *ib*. 421-422, τὰς ξυνδρομάδας πέτρας ... Φινεΐδας αὐτόνους ἀκτάς.

970. Σαλμυδησός, ἵν' ἀγχίπτολις Ἄρης.

I prefer to read ἀγχίπτολις Ἄρης with ἀρχαιογενήτων in the antistrophe. See below.

977-980. κατὰ δὲ τακόμενοι μέλεοι μελέαν πάθαν
κλαῖον ματρός, ἔχοντες ἀνύμφευτον γονάν.

Jebb thinks the comma at ματρός makes the sentence harsh and obscure. But, if it is intended to indicate that 'they mourn for their mother's fate also,' such an indirect way of expressing this is even more obscure.

981. ἃ δὲ σπέρμα μὲν ἀρχαιογόνων.

I would read ἀρχαιογενήτων. Cp. ἀγένητος (Plat. *Phaedr.* 245 *d*).

987. ἀλλὰ κἀπ' ἐκείνᾳ
Μοῖραι μακραίωνες ἔσχον, ὦ παῖ.

ἐπέσχον is well explained by Schneidewin, '*irruerunt, mit der Nebenbezeichnung des καθελεῖν*).' The aorist tense has this effect. Cp. Eur. *Hec.* 692, οὐδέ ποτ' ἀστένακτος, ἀδάκρυτος ἁμέρα μ' ἐπισχήσει, Pind. *fr*. 50 (*Bergk*.) ἀλόχῳ ποτὲ θωραχθεὶς ἔπεχ' ἀλλοτρίᾳ | Ὠαρίων.

989, 990. τοῖς τυφλοῖσι γὰρ
αὕτη κέλευθος ἐκ προηγητοῦ πέλει.

Cp. Eur. *fr*. 816.

εἴ τιν' εἰσίδοιμ' ἀνὰ πτόλιν
τυφλὸν προηγητῆρος ἐξηρτημένον.

ANTIGONE 37

994. τοιγὰρ δι' ὀρθῆς τήνδε ναυκληρεῖς πόλιν.

If ἐναυκλήρεις is read, with Jebb, the echo to the previous line is more exact. But the present has some point in contrast to the impending peril.

1012, 1013. τοιαῦτα παιδὸς τοῦδ' ἐμάνθανον πάρα
φθίνοντ' ἀσήμων ὀργίων μαντεύματα.

I take τοιαῦτα adjectively with μαντεύματα.

1017, 1018. πλήρεις ὑπ' οἰωνῶν τε καὶ κυνῶν βορᾶς
τοῦ δυσμόρου πεπτῶτος Οἰδίπου γόνου.

The construction which Jebb thinks less natural seems to me to give a better *phrasing*. 'Are tainted by the feeding of birds and dogs upon the unhappily fallen son of Œdipus.'

1029, 1030. ἀλλ' εἶκε τῷ θανόντι, μηδ' ὀλωλότα
κέντει. τίς ἀλκὴ τὸν θανόντ' ἐπικτανεῖν;

Cp. Eur. *fr.* 176.

τίς γὰρ πετραῖον σκόπελον οὐτάζων δορὶ
ὀδύναισι δώσει; τίς δ' ἀτιμάζων νέκυς,
εἰ μηδὲν αἰσθάνοιντο τῶν παθημάτων;

1035, 1036. ἄπρακτος ὑμῖν εἰμι, τῶν δ' ὑπαὶ γένους
ἐξημπόλημαι κἀμπεφόρτισμαι πάλαι.

Jebb has L.'s authority for retaining δ'. I seem to have neglected this in my collation. He is also probably right in retaining κἀμπεφόρτισμαι, 'I am bought and taken on board.'

1044. θεοὺς μιαίνειν οὔτις ἀνθρώπων σθένει.

In rejoinder to Jebb's note, I will only say that a general acknowledgment of Divine sovereignty is elsewhere combined with contempt for divination. See especially Jocasta's attitude in *O. T.* 709 ff. For the sentiment, cp. Eur. *H. F.* 232, οὐ μιαίνεις θνητὸς ὢν τὰ τῶν θεῶν.

1051. ὅσφπερ, οἶμαι, μὴ φρονεῖν πλείστη βλάβη.

I do not see that μὴ φρονεῖν is aimed at Teiresias. It is simply the acceptance of a truism.

1062. οὕτω γὰρ ἤδη καὶ δοκῶ τὸ σὸν μέρος;

I take the words interrogatively, but still understand τὸ σὸν μέρος, as *quantum ad te attinet*. 'Do I seem to be speaking for gain in regard to you?' This does not mean 'for your advantage,' but 'so as to win reward from you.' The former would sound oddly after εἰ κέρδος λέγοι in l. 1032. The meaning is well expressed by Dindorf (quoted by Linwood *in loco*): 'Significat his verbis Tiresias ea se dicturum quae nihil lucri ab Creonte ei allatura sint.'

1070-1072. ἔχεις δὲ τῶν κάτωθεν ἐνθάδ' αὖ θεῶν
ἄμοιρον, ἀκτέριστον, ἀνόσιον νέκυν.
ὧν οὔτε σοὶ μέτεστιν.

I still think that the gen. depends on ἄμοιρον, 'without the honour due to the gods below, and that ὧν in 1072 is neuter, 'in which things' (the dues of burial which you withhold).

1078. φανεῖ γάρ, οὐ μακροῦ χρόνου τριβή.

This punctuation, which is Schneidewin's, seems to me far more vivid and expressive than the deletion of the commas, making τριβή the subject of φανεῖ.

1094. μή πώ ποτ' αὐτὸν ψεῦδος ἐς πόλιν λακεῖν.

The correction from λαβεῖν to λακεῖν in L. is made by the Scholiast, who wrote φθέγξασθαι in the margin.

1098. εὐβουλίας δεῖ, παῖ Μενοικέως, λαβεῖν.

I agree in reading λαβεῖν.

ANTIGONE

1102. καὶ ταῦτ' ἐπαινεῖς καὶ δοκεῖς παρεικαθεῖν;

Jebb conjectures δοκεῖ somewhat doubtfully. But is not this tautological? I prefer δοκεῖς παρεικαθεῖν (sc. ταῦτα ἐμέ): 'Do you expect that I will yield it?'

1103, 1104. συντέμνουσι γὰρ
θεῶν ποδώκεις τοὺς κακόφρονας βλάβαι.

As ποδώκεις shows, there is at least an association from the secondary meaning of συντέμνειν (sc. ὁδόν). This seems to be admitted by Jebb in rendering, 'Cut short *their careers*.' Cp. Eur. *Rhes.* 450, συντεμὼν τοὺς σοὺς πόνους. For a secondary use of ποδώκης, cp. *fr.* adespot. 519.

οὐ χρὴ ποδώκη τὸν τρόπον λίαν φέρειν.

1106. ἀνάγκῃ δ' οὐχὶ δυσμαχητέον.

Cp. *fr.* adespot. 312.

θεῷ μάχεσθαι δεινόν ἐστι καὶ τύχῃ.

1112. αὐτός τ' ἔδησα καὶ παρὼν ἐκλύσομαι.

I agree with 'Nauck and others,' including Schneidewin, in taking these words figuratively. 'As I have made the tangle, I will unravel it.' Creon is not moved by compassion for Antigone, nor by anxiety on Haemon's account, but by the fear for the State, which Tiresias's prophecy has awakened. His first thought is to undo his primal error by burying Polynices. For the language, cp. Eur. *Hipp.* 671, κάθαμμα λύειν.

1116. Καδμείας νύμφας ἄγαλμα.

Cp. *fr.* adespot. 126, Αἰτωλίδος ἀγάλματα νύμφας (sc. Deianira's sons), Eur. *Suppl.* 1163, οὐκέτι φίλον | φίλας ἄγαλμ' ὄψομαί σε ματρός, *Iph. T.* 273.

1119. κλυτὰν ὅς ἀμφέπεις Ἰταλίαν.

See the reference to Soph. *Triptol.* in Pliny, *H. N.* 18, 12 (quoted by Nauck, *fr.* 543), et fortunatam Italiam frumento canere candido.'

1122-1124. I would arrange the lines—

ναίων παρ' ὑγρὸν Ἰσμηνοῦ ῥέεθρον,
ἀγρίου τ' ἐπὶ σπορᾷ δράκοντος.

− ! ᴗ ! ᴗ ! − ! ᴗ ᴗ ≘
! ᴗ ! ᴗ ! ᴗ ! ᴗ ! ᴗ.

For the final short syllable, cp. *Phil.* 679. As sometimes happens, even in the earlier period, the dactyl comes in a different part of the logaoedic line in str. and antistr. Thus in the antistr. (1135) we have—

*τῶν ἀμβρότων ἐπέων εὐαζόντων

− ! ᴗ ! ᴗ ᴗ ! − ! − .

1127. ἔνθα Κωρύκιαι στείχουσι Νύμφαι Βακχίδες.

By all means transpose Νύμφαι στείχουσι to στείχουσι Νύμφαι.

1141. ἔχεται πάνδαμος *ἁμὰ πόλις ἐπὶ νόσου.

ἔχεται. Cp. Plato, *Phileb.* 45 *b*, οἱ πυρέττοντες καὶ ἐν τοιούτοις νοσήμασιν ἐχόμενοι.

1150. προφάνηθι Ναξίαις σαῖς ἅμα περιπόλοις.

Jebb reads ὦναξ, σαῖς with Bergk. I prefer Böckh's method.

1155. Κάδμου πάροικοι καὶ δόμων Ἀμφίονος.

It seems more natural to construe Κάδμου with πάροικοι, δόμων being introduced by an afterthought. Amphion was the *builder*.

ANTIGONE

1156, 1157. οὐκ ἔσθ' ὁποῖον στάντ' ἂν ἀνθρώπου βίον
οὔτ' αἰνέσαιμ' ἂν οὔτε μεμψαίμην ποτε.

Cp. *fr.* 102.

τίς δή ποτ' ὄλβον ἢ μέγαν θείη βροτῶν,
ἢ σμικρόν, ἢ τὸν μηδαμοῦ τιμώμενον;
οὐ γάρ ποτ' αὐτῶν οὐδὲν ἐν ταὐτῷ μένει.

I still think the Scholiast's explanation, τινὰ στάσιν ἔχοντα, gives the true sense, 'No life of man, howsoe'er it stand' in apparent fixity). Jebb seems to take στάντα as a secondary predicate following αἰνέσαιμι, and 'giving the ground for the praise or blame.'

1165. τὰς γὰρ ἡδονὰς
ὅταν προδῶσιν ἄνδρες.

Note the inverted expression, and *see* Prefatory Remarks, p. x.

1168. πλουτεῖ τε γὰρ κατ' οἶκον, εἰ βούλει, μέγα.

I retain the present indicative. The hypothetical imperative' in the 2nd person seems doubtful and less expressive here than the hypothetical use of the indicative, for which cp. Eur. *Androm.* 334.

τέθνηκα δὴ σῇ θυγατρὶ καὶ μ' ἀπώλεσε, Plat. *Theaet.* 192 e, Σωκράτης ἐπιγινώσκει Θεόδωρον καὶ Θεαίτητον, ὁρᾷ δὲ μηδέτερον, μηδὲ ἄλλη αἴσθησις αὐτῷ πάρεστι περὶ αὐτῶν· οὐκ ἄν ποτε ἐν ἑαυτῷ δοξάσειεν ὡς ὁ Θεαίτητός ἐστι Θεόδωρος.

In either case εἰ βούλει is idiomatic; though with πλούτει and ζῇ it would require the same subject (σύ) to be continued. But 'Be wealthy, if you will' is less to the point than 'Grant, if you will, that the man is wealthy,' and with the latter meaning ἀνδρί, 1171, is more in harmony.

1195. ὀρθὸν ἀλήθει' ἀεί.

Cp. *fr.* 529.

θάρσει· λέγων τἀληθὲς οὐ σφαλεῖ ποτε.

42 PARALIPOMENA SOPHOCLEA

***fr.* adespot. 30.** οὐκ οἶδα· τἀληθὲς γὰρ ἀσφαλὲς φράσαι.

Eur. *fr.* 1036. πότερα θέλεις σοι μαλθακὰ ψευδῆ λέγω
ἢ σκληρ᾽ ἀληθῆ· φράζε· σὴ γὰρ ἡ κρίσις.

Aesch. *Ag.* 620, 1.

1196. ἐγὼ δὲ σῷ ποδαγὸς ἑσπόμην πόσει.
ποδαγὸς ἑσπόμην : 'Accompanied as guide.'

1204. For the feeling in λιθοστρώτῳ, cp. Eur. *H. F.* 52 ἀστρώτῳ πέδῳ | πλευρᾶσ τιθέντες.

1216. ἁρμὸν χώματος λιθοσπαδῆ.
For ἁρμόν, cp. Eur. *fr.* 781, l. 45.
δι᾽ ἁρμῶν ἐξαμείβεται πύλης
καπνοῦ μέλαιν᾽ ἄησις ἔνδοθεν στέγης, *Med.* 1315.

1219. τάδ᾽ ἐξ ἀθύμου δεσπότου κελεύσμασιν.
Burton's κελευσμάτων, adopted by Jebb, is attractive. But cp. the datives in Eur. *Phœn.* 91, στράτευμ᾽ ἰδεῖν Ἀργεῖον ἱκεσίαισι σαῖς, *Bacch.* 441, 442, οὐχ ἑκὼν | ἄγω σε, Πενθέως δ᾽, ὅς μ᾽ ἔπεμψ᾽, ἐπιστολαῖς.

1224. εὐνῆς ἀποιμώζοντα τῆς κάτω φθοράν.
I do not see the awkwardness of understanding εὐνῆς as = marriage.

1232. πτύσας προσώπῳ κοὐδὲν ἀντειπὼν ξίφους
ἕλκει διπλοῦς κνώδοντας.

I am not convinced by Jebb's note that the Scholiast is wrong concerning πτύσας προσώπῳ. Cp. *fr.* 617, ἀπέπτυσεν λόγους.

ANTIGONE

1238. καὶ φυσιῶν ὀξεῖαν ἐκβάλλει πνοήν.

ὀξεῖαν πνοήν, 'keen breath,' seems to me more natural than ὀξεῖαν ῥοήν, 'the swift stream.' The dying man 'breathes hard, Aesch. *Ag.* 1389,

κἀκφυσιῶν ὀξεῖαν αἵματος σφαγὴν
βάλλει μ' ἐρεμνῇ ψακάδι φοινίας δρόσου.

1241. τέλη λαχὼν δείλαιος εἰν Ἅιδου δόμοις.

I see no objection to reading ἕν γ', with Heath ('ay, in the home of Death'), although I think with Jebb that εἰν may be defended.

1259, 1260. εἰ θέμις εἰπεῖν, οὐκ ἀλλοτρίαν
ἄτην, ἀλλ' αὐτὸς ἁμαρτών.

εἰ θέμις εἰπεῖν : not only because it is a heavy charge, but because reverence forbids rash accusation of the sovereign, *Trach.* 809, εἰ θέμις δ', ἐπεύχομαι.

1265. *ὤμοι ἐμῶν ἄνολβα βουλευμάτων.

ἄνολβα βουλευμάτων. Cp. Eur. *Hec.* 192, ἀμέγαρτα κακῶν.

1266. ἰὼ παῖ, νέος νέῳ ξὺν μόρῳ.

I agree with the Scholiast: νέᾳ ἡλικίᾳ καὶ καινοπρεπεῖ θανάτῳ τετελεύτηκας.

1272-1274. ἐν δ' ἐμῷ κάρᾳ
θεὸς τότ' ἄρα τότε μέγα βάρος μ' ἔχων
ἔπαισεν.

I agree with Jebb's excellent note, except that I take μέγα βάρος to be primarily adverbial, and ἔχων to be added supplementarily : 'Smote me with mighty force which he held.'

44 PARALIPOMENA SOPHOCLEA

1274. ἐν δ' ἔσεισεν ἀγρίαις ὁδοῖς.

The use of ἐπισείω in Eur. *Or.* 255 is closely parallel to ἐνέσεισεν here.

μὴ 'πίσειέ μοι
τὰς αἱματωποὺς καὶ δρακοντώδεις κόρας.

1278-1280. ὦ δέσποθ', ὡς, ἔχων τε καὶ κεκτημένος,
τὰ μὲν πρὸ χειρῶν τάδε φέρων, τὰ δ' ἐν δόμοις
ἔοικας ἥκειν καὶ τάχ' ὄψεσθαι κακά.

I take ὡς to be exclamatory; for the rest I am in agreement with Jebb's elaborate explanation.

Observe that πρὸ χειρῶν does not necessarily imply that Creon is himself carrying the dead body. Cp. Eur. *Rhes.* 274, μάχας πρὸ χειρῶν καὶ δόρη βαστάζομεν.

1282. τί δ' ἔστιν αὖ κάκιον ἢ κακῶν ἔτι.

Without rejecting Canter's emendation I still think that the MS. reading has a possible meaning: 'What is there worse, or what more of ill?'

1288. τί φῄς; τίνα λέγεις νέον μοι λόγον;

Jebb's reading is
τί φῄς, ὦ παῖ, τίνα λέγεις μοι νέον.

But (1), although the form of dochmiac ⏑ ⏑́ ⏑́ – ⏓́ is not incorrect, it is extremely rare and not identical with 1341, with which Jebb compares it.

(2) Although ὦ παῖ might be addressed to the messenger, there is a certain awkwardness in its occurring in the line of the antistrophe which corresponds to 1266, ἰὼ παῖ κ.τ.λ. The eye of the scribe may have wandered back from the antistrophe to the strophe. In *O. T.* 1008, 1030, which Jebb compares, the Corinthian regards Œdipus as his foster-son. Creon is too self-absorbed to appeal for sympathy.

ANTIGONE

(3) Although in Jebb's reading νέον may be construed with μόρον, the phrase τίνα νέον γυναικεῖον μόρον is not in point. Creon asks, not 'What new slaughter of a woman dost thou tell me of?' but 'dost thou tell me also of the slaughter of a wife?' He seeks confirmation, not further information. Cp. Macduff's 'My wife killed too?'

1301. ἥδ' *ὀξυθήκτῳ βωμία περὶ *ξίφει.

I now accept Arndt's emendation with Jebb. The repetition of ἥδε gave the appearance of an hypermetric line. And in cutting off the two last syllables the ξ of ξίφει adhered to περί; while ὀξυθήκτῳ changed to ὀξύθηκτος. See note on l. 4, *supra*.

1303. τοῦ πρὶν θανόντος Μεγαρέως κλεινὸν λέχος.

I admit that λάχος is probable. But see Eur. *Phœn.* 931 *ff.*

1308. τί μ' οὐκ ἀνταίαν
ἔπαισέν τις ἀμφιθήκτῳ ξίφει.

For ἀνταίαν, cp. Eur. *Androm.* 843, ἵν' ἀνταίαν | ἐρείσω πλαγάν.

1321. ἄγετέ μ' ὅτι τάχος, ἄγετέ μ' ἐκποδών.

If the lengthening of the last syllable of τάχος *in arsi* between the dochmiacs may not be allowed, ὅτι τάχιστ' is certainly an easy remedy. But cp. the hiatus in *O. T.* 657, σὺν ἀφανεῖ λόγῳ ἄτιμον βαλεῖν.

1327. βράχιστα γὰρ κράτιστα τἀν ποσὶν κακά.

Cp. *fr.* 172, βράχιστον· βραχύτατον. Σοφοκλῆς Δανάῃ. —(Antiatt.)

1329, 1330. φανήτω μόρων ὁ κάλλιστ' ἐμῶν
ἐμοὶ τερμίαν ἄγων ἀμέραν
ὕπατος·

Jebb reads with Pallis
μόρων ὁ κάλλιστ' *ἔχων
ἐμοί.

I will not dispute his *dictum* that μόρος is not thus used elsewhere. But I would urge (1) that the language is more forcible without the periphrasis, which Sophocles has rarely employed in lyric verse. (An exception is *O. T.* 879, τὸ καλῶς ἔχον πόλει πάλαισμα, where the sense is less emotional than here.)
(2) A somewhat similar use of μοῖρα occurs in Plato, *Polit.* 271 c, ὅσους μὴ θεὸς αὐτῶν εἰς ἄλλην μοῖραν ἐκόμισεν. And δαίμων is sometimes similarly particularised as the special destiny attending a critical moment: *e.g. El.* 1306, τῷ παρόντι δαίμονι: *ib.* 916 *f.*,   τοῖς αὐτοῖσί τοι
οὐχ αὐτὸς αἰεὶ δαιμόνων παραστατεῖ.

1332. ὕπατος: 'Best fate of all' (Jebb). But why may not ὕπατος, like the Latin *supremus*, mean 'final,' 'consummate,' 'which there is nothing beyond'? The prep. ὑπέρ with accus. = beyond in space: Plato, *Critias* 108 *e*, τοῖς θ' ὑπὲρ Ἡρακλείας στήλας ἔξω κατοικοῦσι καὶ τοῖς ἐντός. And in *supr.* 16 οὐδὲν οἶδ' ὑπέρτερον is 'I know nothing beyond.'

1336.   ἀλλ' ὧν *ἐρῶμαι, ταῦτα συγκατηυξάμην.
There is no objection to ἐρῶ μέν (Jebb).

1340-1341. ὅς, ὦ παῖ, σέ τ' οὐχ ἑκὼν *κάκτανον
σέ τ' αὐτάν.

σέ τ' αὖ τάνδ' (Jebb). I cannot help thinking that the demonstrative is rather frigid here, and that αὐτάν, without

ANTIGONE 47

pressing any antithesis, is pathetic. 'Ay, and thee!' The successive calamities are each too great to be taken easily into one view.

1342-1346.
οὐδ' ἔχω
ὅπα πρὸς πότερον ἴδω· *πάντα γὰρ
λέχρια *τἀν χεροῖν, τὰ δ' ἐπὶ κρατί μοι
πότμος δυσκόμιστος εἰσήλατο.

Doubtless πᾶ καὶ θῶ is a corruption of πᾷ κλιθῶ. But it is not so certain that the phrase did not originate in a gloss. Jebb does not observe that in L. there is a dot, equivalent to an obelus, over πᾶ (sic). λέχρια = 'ready to fall,' cp. Eur. *Med.* 1168, λεχρία πάλιν | χωρεῖ τρέμουσα κῶλα. τὰ δ' ἐπὶ κρατί refers rather to the prophecy of Tiresias than to the deaths of Eurydice and Antigone. And τὰ ἐν χεροῖν has also a general reference. The present is out of gear, the future disastrous.

AJAX

In another place[1] I have tried to show that the supposed inferiority of the latter part of the Ajax is not entirely accounted for by the importance of the burial rite, and the hero's apotheosis. It is true that in the Ajax, as in the Antigone, the living presence of the chief person is withdrawn at the culminating point; but, while the tension of expectancy is thus relaxed, the fund of emotion which has been evoked is not dissipated but rather deepened in the sequel,—while the intervention of Odysseus in the catastrophe restores the calm of spirit which befits the conclusion of a tragic action.

Οὐκ ἦν ἄρ' οὐδὲν πῆμ' ἐλευθέρου δάκνων | ψυχὴν ὁμοίως ἀνδρός, ὥς ἀτιμία, *Fr.* adespot. 110.

28.   τήνδ' οὖν ἐκείνῳ πᾶς τις αἰτίαν νέμει.

νέμει is clearly right. For τρέπει—probably due to a prosaic interpreter, cp. [Lys.] c. *Andoc.* § 13, μὴ βούλεσθε εἰς ὑμᾶς τὴν αἰτίαν ταύτην περιτρέψαι, Plato, *Ep.* iii. 315 *e.*, τοὺς δ' ἔξωθεν, εἴ τι γίγνοιτο ἁμάρτημα, πᾶν εἰς ἐμὲ τρέπειν. In both cases it implies a *wrong* assignment of blame.

33.   τὰ μὲν σημαίνομαι,
    τὰ δ' ἐκπέπληγμαι, κοὐκ ἔχω μαθεῖν ὅπου.

ὅπου, 'where Ajax is.' The tracks about the tent door were so confused that Odysseus could not be sure that Ajax

[1] *Tragic Drama in Aeschylus, Sophocles, and Shakespeare,* p. 84.

AJAX 49

had not gone forth again. The v. r. ὅτου, 'whose footprints they are,' seems to me the work of a prosaic interpolator. 'Is the game in its lair or is it stolen away?' That is the question. See note on *O. T.* 924, 925.

40.   καὶ πρὸς τί δυσλόγιστον ὧδ' ᾖξεν χέρα

In defence of taking ᾖξεν intransitively it may be urged:— (1) that ᾄσσω a few lines earlier (32) is intransitive; (2) that the transitive use is rare; (3) that if χέρα is taken in the secondary sense of 'violent action' the accusative (of cognate signification) is not beyond the limits of tragic idiom; cp. βάσιν in 42.

51, 52.   ἐγώ σφ' ἀπείργω, δυσφόρους ἐπ' ὄμμασι
γνώμας βαλοῦσα, τῆς ἀνηκέστου χαρᾶς.

Most editors have followed the Aldine edition in punctuating after ἀπείργω and βαλοῦσα. And this seems to me to harmonise better with the whole context, than to construe the genitive with γνώμας.

For δυσφόρους, cp. *Hamlet*, I. ii. 203, 'their oppressed and fear-surprised eyes.' Pind. *Nem.* i. 55, θάμβει δυσφόρῳ.

54.   λείας ἄδαστα βουκόλων φρουρήματα.

I am still inclined to render λείας ἄδαστα, 'undivided from the spoil.'

64.   ὡς ἄνδρας, οὐχ ὡς εὐκέρων ἄγραν ἔχων.

I still think that εὔκερων applies to the sheep as well as the kine.

72. ἀπευθύνοντα, 'controlling,' even if taken literally, suggests punishment. Cp. Eur. *Bacch.* 884-6, ἀπευθύνει δὲ βροτῶν | τούς τ' ἀγνωμοσύναν τιμῶντας . . . Her. ii. 177, ἰθύνεσθαι θανάτῳ.

50 PARALIPOMENA SOPHOCLEA

75. οὐ σίγ' ἀνέξει μηδὲ δειλίαν ἀρεῖ;
Of Jebb's careful reasoning in favour of ἀρεῖ here, the strongest point is the quantity of ἄρ. His note is convincing.

76. ἔνδον ἀρκείτω μένων.
For the personal construction, cp. also Eur. *Or.* 1592, φησὶν σιωπῶν· ἀρκέσω δ' ἐγὼ λέγων, Aesch. *Prom.* 621, τοσοῦτον ἀρκῶ σοι σαφηνίσαι.

94. For ἐκεῖνο marking strong interest, cp. also Eur. *Bacch.* 771, κἀκεῖνο ... τὴν παυσίλυπον ἄμπελον.

120. Eur. *Androm.* 98, στερρόν τε τὸν ἐμὸν δαίμον' ᾧ συνεζύγην, *Hel.* 255, τίνι πότμῳ συνεζύγην.

131. ὡς ἡμέρα κλίνει τε κἀνάγει πάλιν
ἅπαντα τἀνθρώπεια·

ἡμέρα, *i.e. diuturnitas temporis*, Linwood. Jebb, agreeing with the Scholiast, takes it of a single day, perhaps rightly. Schneidewin, without authority, reads ἦμαρ ἕν, cp. Eur. *Hec.* 285.

135. Σαλαμῖνος ἔχων βάθρον ἀγχιάλου.

Ἀγχίαλος, as an epithet of an island, seems to have special reference to the *town*, which was usually near the shore. The *ancient* city of Salamis was on the seaward coast; Strab. 9, p. 393.

143. τὸν ἱππομανῆ
λειμῶν' ἐπιβάντ'.

ἱππομανῆ. To the parallels adduced by Lobeck should be added καρπομανής, *fr.* 591, Hesych. εἰς κόρον ἐξυβρίζουσα.

AJAX

151.   περὶ γὰρ σοῦ νῦν
            εὔπειστα λέγει.

εὔπειστα. It appears to me on looking at the facsimile that ει is corrected from ι—but probably by the first hand.

154, 155.   τῶν γὰρ μεγάλων ψυχῶν ἱεὶς
                οὐκ ἂν ἁμάρτοι.

Before the obliteration of the σ of ἁμάρτοισ in L. it had been marked as doubtful, with a dot above it. I still prefer ἁμάρτοι.

157.   πρὸς γὰρ τὸν ἔχονθ' ὁ φθόνος ἕρπει.

Cp. Eur. *fr.* 294.

εἰς τἀπίσημα δ' ὁ φθόνος πηδᾶν φιλεῖ.

Fr. adespot. 547, 12, πρὸς γὰρ τὸ λαμπρὸν ὁ φθόνος βιάζεται.

158, 159.   καίτοι σμικροὶ μεγάλων χωρὶς
                σφαλερὸν πύργου ῥῦμα πέλονται.

Cp. Eur. *fr.* 21.

οὐκ ἂν γένοιτο χωρὶς ἐσθλὰ καὶ κακά,
ἀλλ' ἔστι τις σύγκρασις, ὥστ' ἔχειν καλῶς.

159. πύργου ῥῦμα : Jebb says '*protection*, garrison for the city walls': (so the interlinear gloss πόλεως, and Stobaeus). 'Not, "tower of defence."' Hermann likewise rejected the latter interpretation as 'less simple.' To me it still appears more poetical. If this is an error, I am not ashamed to err with Lobeck. Cp. Eur. *Heracl.* 260 :

ἅπασι κοινὸν ῥῦμα δαιμόνων ἕδρα,

and, for a figurative use of πύργος, *O. T.* 1201, θανάτων δ' ἐμᾷ | χώρᾳ πύργος ἀνέστα, Eur. *Med.* 389 :

ἢν μέν τις ἡμῖν πύργος ἀσφαλὴς φανῇ.

52   PARALIPOMENA SOPHOCLEA

169.   μέγαν αἰγυπιὸν *δ' ὑποδείσαντες.

In favour of the insertion of δὲ after αἰγυπιὸν, may be noticed the erroneous doubling of δ in ὑποδείσαντες by the first hand in L.

170.   τάχ' ἂν ἐξαίφνης, εἰ σὺ φανείης,
σιγῇ πτήξειαν ἄφωνοι.

I now agree with Jebb and Hermann in punctuating after ἐξαίφνης.

176.   ἦ πού τινος νίκας ἀκάρπωτον χάριν.

Jebb says 'νίκας ἀκάρπωτον χάριν = νίκας ἀκαρπώτου χάριν.' But is not the enallage rendered somewhat harsh, by the obvious meaning of ἀκάρπωτον χάριν = 'a fruitless favour'? On the other hand, the unusual force of the cognate accusative, implying the cause of an action, may be softened, as suggested in my note, by association with the ordinary adverbial use of χάριν. This idiomatic use is similarly combined with an epithet by Pindar, *Ol.* xi. 78, ἐπωνυμίαν χάριν | νίκας ἀγέρωχον. Cp. also ἄδωρος χάρις in Eur. *fr.* 869.

179.   ἦ χαλκοθώραξ *ἦ τιν' Ἐννάλιος
μομφὰν ἔχων.

Although ἦ is not elsewhere postponed by Sophocles, the particle is so expressive here that I cannot think it 'condemned.' The Platonic instances are undoubted, yet I suspect they are in a less proportion than 1 : 50. And the interrogative ἆρα is thus postponed by Sophocles, *Ant.* 632, *Phil.* 114.

186.   ἥκοι γὰρ ἂν θεία νόσος.

ἥκοι . . . ἄν, 'must come,' Jebb.   Rather 'may have come.' Cp. Aesch. *Ag.* 1509:

πατρόθεν δὲ συλλήπτωρ γένοιτ' ἂν ἀλάστωρ.

194.   ὅπου μακραίωνι
στηρίζει ποτὲ τᾷδ' ἀγωνίῳ σχολᾷ.

ἀγωνίῳ σχολᾷ. I adhere, though not too confidently, to the explanation given in my edition of 1879, viz.: 'a rest which is no rest, but contention fraught with peril.' If understood merely as = 'battle-pause,' the phrase will hardly bear the emphasis which is required.

196.   ἐχθρῶν δ' ὕβρις ὧδ' *ἀταρβής.

If any change is wanted, I should prefer ἀταρβήτως.

— ⏑́ ⏑ ⏑ ⏑́ ⏑ ⏑́ ⏗ —

211.   λέγ', ἐπεί σε λέχος *δουριάλωτον
στέρξας ἀνέχει θούριος Αἴας.

The parallel of *Trach.* 360 is rather in favour of λέχος being an adverbial accusative.

215. Cp. *fr.* 332, ἰσοθάνατον (quoted by Pollux as a strange compound).

221-245.   οἵαν ἐδήλωσας ἀνδρὸς αἴθονος
       . . . ὥρα τιν' ἤδη κάρα καλύμμασι.

Jebb's text involves a slight change both in the str. and antistr. By accepting A's. reading of 221, and κάρα from T. etc. in 245, a probable enough rhythm is obtained—

— ⏑́ ⏑ ⏗ ⏑́ ⏑ — ⏑ — ⏑ ⏘

passing from the trochaic to the logaœdic metre in the following line.

54   PARALIPOMENA SOPHOCLEA

250.   ποντοπόρῳ ναῒ μεθεῖναι.

μεθῆκεν is used absolutely in Eur. *fr.* 779, l. 7—
κρούσας δὲ πλευρὰ πτεροφόρων ὀχημάτων
μεθῆκεν.

257, 258.   λαμπρᾶς γὰρ ἄτερ στεροπᾶς
ἄξας ὀξὺς νότος ὡς λήγει.

λαμπρᾶς ἄτερ στεροπᾶς is certainly predicative with λήγει, and not to be joined with ἄξας. The only doubt is whether the phrase is pregnant (or proleptic)=(1) 'so as to be without the lightning flash,' or simply (2) 'he ceases without lightning'; *i.e.* 'the storm abates without a fatal result.' I agree that the former is more probable on the whole.

264.   Cp. *fr.* 346, μόχθου γὰρ οὐδεὶς τοῦ παρελθόντος λόγος.

285.   Cp. *fr.* adespot. 407, ἐφέσπερον δαίουσα λαμπτῆρος σθένος.

292.   ὁ δ' εἶπε πρός με βαί', ἀεὶ δ' ὑμνούμενα.

Cp. Theodectes, *fr.* Alcmaeon 1 (p. 801 N) :
σαφὴς μὲν ἐν βροτοῖσιν ὑμνεῖται λόγος
ὡς οὐδέν ἐστιν ἀθλιώτερον φυτὸν
γυναικός.

301.   τέλος δ' ὑπάξας διὰ θυρῶν.

For ὑπὸ in ὑπάξας, cp. Eur. *Hec.* 53 :
περᾷ γὰρ ἥδ' ὑπὸ σκηνῆς πόδα.

302.   λόγους ἀνέσπα, τοὺς μὲν 'Ατρειδῶν κάτα.

Cp. *fr.* adespot. 529.
(ὅταν τις . . .)
γλώσσῃ ματαίους ἐξακοντίσῃ λόγους.

319, 320. πρὸς γὰρ κακοῦ τε καὶ βαρυψύχου γόους
τοιούσδ' ἀεί ποτ' ἀνδρὸς ἐξηγεῖτ' ἔχειν.

Jebb adopts the explanation marked (2) in my large edition, which in the smaller edition (CA.) is considered doubtful, viz.: 'that such lamentations belong to a dull-spirited man.' Encouraged by the approval of so skilled a grammarian, I now adhere to this. Those who doubt of it may change ἔχειν to ἄγειν: 'He taught us to esteem.' But see note on *O.T.* 708.

337, 338. ἀνὴρ ἔοικεν ἢ νοσεῖν, ἢ τοῖς πάλαι
νοσήμασι ξυνοῦσι λυπεῖσθαι παρών.

I do not join ξυνοῦσι with πάλαι, nor do I understand it of the haunting memory of his trouble, but rather of the present evidence of what is past. *Vid. supr.* 307, καὶ πλῆρες ἄτης ὡς διοπτεύει στέγος.

339. ἰὼ παῖ παῖ.

I adhere confidently to my former view that ἰώ, παῖ, παῖ, is an apostrophe to Teucer, which Tecmessa, in maternal anxiety, naturally misunderstands. Ajax corrects her by loudly saying Τεῦκρον καλῶ. It is only when Tecmessa (510) has appealed to him on behalf of Eurysakes that he bids him to be brought (530).

351. Cp. *fr.* adespot. 568, κλύδωνα σαυτῷ προσφέρεις αὐθαίρετον.

360, 361. σέ τοι σέ τοι μόνον δέδορκα ποιμένων ἐπαρκέσοντ'·
ἀλλά με συνδάϊξον.

The word understood with συνδάϊξον is clearly τοῖς ποιμνίοις. I still venture to think that the same is to be

56   PARALIPOMENA SOPHOCLEA

supplied with ἐπαρκέσοντα. 'I see in thee the only shepherd to defend' (*i.e.* 'to avenge') 'the flocks.' Ajax still sees in imagination the hirelings whom he had slain. He now invites a friendly hand to give the blow which they had failed to give. I know that this is 'bold'; but it makes a stronger context than the conjectural πημονάν, which must otherwise be accepted *faute de mieux*.

366.   ἐν ἀφόβοις με θηρσὶ δεινὸν χέρας.

Jebb prefers the meaning of ἀφόβοις to which I give the second place: 'fearing no harm from man.' Perhaps he is right.

375, 376.   ἐν δ' ἑλίκεσσι βουσὶ καὶ κλυτοῖς πεσὼν αἰπολίοις ἐρεμνὸν αἷμ' ἔδευσα.

Whether or not, in using Epic words, Sophocles sometimes gives them through association new shades of meaning, is a question worth raising, though difficult to answer with certainty. I have suggested that κλυτοῖς here may mean 'loud,' as one of the Scholiasts thought, and ἐρεμνὸν, 'darkling.' See below 608, 890.

381.   κακοπινέστατόν τ' ἄλημα στρατοῦ.

ἄλημα: I am again guilty of heresy in deriving this word from ἀλᾶν=πλανᾶν and not from ἀλέω. The latter is the meaning given by Hesychius: but the glossator who explains ἄλημα by ἀπάτημα must have agreed with Eustathius, who treats the word as equivalent to πλάνημα.

384.   ἴδοιμι *μήν νιν, καίπερ ὧδ' ἀτώμενος.

ἴδοιμι μήν νιν is a very probable conjecture, and the authority of the Triclinian MS. which reads ἴδοιμι δή is weak.

AJAX

386. Eur. *H. F.* 1244, ἴσχε στόμ' ὡς μὴ μέγα λέγων μεῖζον πάθῃς.

405-425.

405. εἰ τὰ μὲν φθίνει,
φίλοι †τοῖς δ'
ὁμοῦ πέλας†,
μώραις δ' ἄγραις προσκείμεθα,

. . . .

425. ἐξερέω μέγα
οἷον οὔ τινα
Τροία στρατοῦ
δέρχθη χθονὸς μολόντ' ἀπὸ
Ἑλλανίδος.

I may as well state the grounds of my 'guess-work' here. I do not pretend that it deserves a better name.

1. I assume that in 406 one of the two words ὁμοῦ πέλας is superfluous; and I infer that πέλας may have been a corruption of πάλαι, and that τοῖσδ' ὁμοῦ was added to explain the new reading. This makes—

εἰ τὰ μὲν φθίνει, φίλοι, πάλαι·
μώραις δ' ἄγραις προσκείμεθα.

2. Turning now to the antistrophic lines, the expression suffers nothing, but only becomes more terse, if στρατοῦ and ἀπό are ejected. Then we have—

ἐξερῶ μέγ', οἷον οὔ τινα
Τροία χθονὸς δέρχθη μολόνθ'.

(δέρχθη and χθονός being transposed *metri gratia*.) And the sense is further improved by reading εἰ τάδε μέν in 405, and retaining ἐξερέω in 423.

εἰ τάδε μὲν φθίνει gives exactly the meaning desiderated by Jebb.

406. μώραις δ' ἄγραις προσκείμεθα.

προσκείμεθα. Not exactly 'addicted to,' but 'involved in.' I would rather compare *El.* 1040, ᾧ σὺ πρόσκεισαι κακῷ. Eur. *fr.* 418, κακοῖς γὰρ οὐ σὺ πρόσκεισαι μόνη.

408. δίπαλτος: Eur. *I. T.* 323, ὡς δ' εἴδομεν δίπαλτα πολεμίων ξίφη.

420. Perhaps εὔφρονες, cp. Bacchyl. iii. 46, ἐϋκτίτων, etc.

443. κρίνειν ἔμελλε κράτος ἀριστείας τινί.

κρίνειν in L. is corrected by the Scholiast from καίνειν.

447. κεἰ μὴ τόδ' ὄμμα καὶ φρένες διάστροφοι.

ὄμμα. The scribe at first wrote ὄνομα.

450. γοργῶπις. Cp. ὀβριμοδερκής in Bacchyl. xv. 20.

451. ἤδη μ' ἐπ' αὐτοῖς χεῖρ' ἐπευθύνοντ' ἐμήν.

I still prefer ἐπευθύνοντ', the first hand of L., as the more vivid reading. But either is possible, and ἐπεντύνοντ' has strong MS. authority.

465. Cp. Eur. *Suppl.* 315, πόλει παρόν σοι στέφανον εὐκλείας λαβεῖν.

475, 476. τί γὰρ παρ' ἦμαρ' ἡμέρα τέρπειν ἔχει
προσθεῖσα κἀναθεῖσα τοῦ γε κατθανεῖν;

'What of (the certainty of) death can day following day' (or 'one day more') 'either add or withdraw, so as to afford delight?' τί τοῦ γε κατθανεῖν προσθεῖσα καὶ ἀναθεῖσα τέρπειν ἔχει ἡμέρα παρ' ἦμαρ; So I have taken the words, supposing it possible that καὶ may sometimes connect alternatives. See note on *Ant.* 687. This interpretation differs but little from that of Hermann : ' Hoc dicit : *quid potest dies cum die alternans oblectationis afferre, quum nihil nisi de moriendi necessitate aut addat aliquid, aut differat?*' Instead of simply 'by detracting anything from the necessity of death,' the Greek love of antithesis inserts 'or adding to it.' The difficulty here lies, of course, in the use of καί. But if the participles are treated as hypothetical, they might be paraphrased thus : ἐάν τε προσθῇ ἐάν τε ἀναθῇ ; or, by an extension of the idiom, ἐάν τε ... καὶ μὴ (*Ant.* 327), ἐάν τε προσθῇ καὶ ἀναθῇ. Similarly in *Trach.* 952 (κοινὰ δ') ἔχειν τε καὶ μέλλειν might be expanded into εἴτε ἔχοι τις, εἴτε καὶ μέλλοι ἔχειν. Or again, one day may be supposed to add, another to take away. So Hermann says : ''Ημέρα παρ' ἦμαρ *dicit, quia duo deinde infert,* προστιθέναι *et* ἀνατιθέναι.'

Jebb rejects this view, and decides in favour of the first of three other meanings put forward in my note—supplying τῷ κατθανεῖν with προσθεῖσα, and rendering 'now pushing us forward, now drawing us back, on the verge—of death.' This is nearly equivalent to the words in my note : (1) 'since it can only bring a man near to death and then reprieve him from it.' This, if I remember rightly, was James Riddell's explanation.

For the general sense, cp. *fr.* 866.

ὅστις γὰρ ἐν κακοῖσιν ἱμείρει βίου
ἢ δειλός ἐστιν ἢ δυσάλγητος φρένας.

And for παρ' ἆμαρ, cp. Pind. *Pyth.* xi. 63.

496.   *ᾗ γὰρ θάνῃς σὺ καὶ τελευτήσας ἀφῇς.

I now see no objection to the slight change from εἰ to ᾗ.

511.
εἰ νέας
τροφῆς στερηθεὶς σοῦ διοίσεται μόνος.

For διοίσεται = 'he will pass his days,' cp. also Eur. *fr.* 280. διέφερε· διῆγεν (MS. διέφθειρε), Hesych. i. p. 989.

527.
καὶ κάρτ' ἐπαίνου τεύξεται πρὸς γοῦν ἐμοῦ.

καὶ κάρτ'. I prefer to take καὶ as intensive here, strongly (but ironically) confirming the Chorus' αἰνοίης ἄν. Cp. *O. C.* 301, καὶ κάρθ', ὅτανπερ τοὔνομ' αἴσθηται τὸ σόν.

534.
πρέπον γε τἂν ἦν δαίμονος τοὐμοῦ τόδε.

Compare the use of ἑπόμενος with the genitive : *e.g.* Plat. *Polit.* 271 *e*, ὅσα τῆς τοιαύτης ἐστὶ κατακοσμήσεως ἑπόμενα.

572, 573.
καὶ τἀμὰ τεύχη μήτ' ἀγωνάρχαι τινὲς
θήσουσ' Ἀχαιοῖς μήθ' ὁ λυμεὼν ἐμός.

ὁ λυμεὼν ἐμός. In Eur. *Phil.*, according to Dio Chrysostom, Odysseus in disguise described himself to Philoctetes as ὁ κοινὸς τῶν Ἑλλήνων λυμεών.

575, 576.
Cp. Eur. *Tro.* 1196 *f.*

597.
Cp. Eur. *Tro.* 799, 800, Σαλαμῖνος . . . νάσου περικύμονος οἰκήσας ἕδραν.

601-05.
*'Ιδᾷδι μίμνων λειμῶνι πόᾳ *τε μήλων
ἀνήριθμος αἰὲν εὐνῶμαι,
χρόνῳ τρυχόμενος.

So I would now read these lines.

1. In reading 'Ιδᾷδι . . . λειμῶνι I agree with Wolf. The obvious objection is that the adjective has a feminine termination, and that ' λειμών is never feminine.'—(Jebb.)

AJAX

(*a*) But genders in Sophocles are sometimes modified by poetical association. Αἰθήρ is feminine, *O. T.* 866, although masculine in at least four other places: Κιθαιρών is celebrated as the nursing *mother* of Oedipus, *O. T.* 1092: αὐλών is feminine in *Trach.* 100, as well as in *fr.* 505, ἐπακτίας | αὐλῶνας, on which Athenaeus observes καλοῦσι δ' ἀρσενικῶς τοὺς αὐλῶνας ..., οἱ δὲ ποιηταὶ θηλυκῶς. See also *fr.* adespot. 196 :

αὐλῶνά θ' ἦν ἄρδουσι,

quoted by Herodian as a solecism, Carcinus, *Achilles fr.* 1, βαθεῖαν εἰς αὐλῶνα, and Ar. *Aves*, 244, ἐλείας παρ' αὐλῶνας, 'by marshy hollows,' where the feminine termination accentuates the notion of soft luxuriance, which might be equally conceived to affect the use of λειμών here. (The synonym λεῖμαξ is feminine.) Cp. the use of κώδων fem. in line 17, of a *hollow* trumpet, and αἰὼν feminine in Pind. *Nem.* ix. 44, ἐκ πόνων ... τελέθει πρὸς γῆρας αἰὼν ἡμέρα.

(*b*) On the other hand, adjectives with feminine terminations are sometimes attached to masculine nouns: *fr.* 16, 'Ἑλλάς· ὁ ἀνήρ· Σοφοκλῆς Αἴαντι Λοκρῷ (*Antiatt.* p. 97, 4). See Nauck, *Fr. Tr. Gr.* p. 134; Eur. *Phoen.* 1509, τίς Ἑλλὰς ἢ βάρβαρος. See also Eur. *fr.* 958 :

τίς δ' ἐστὶ δοῦλος τοῦ θανεῖν ἄφροντις ὤν.

And in *fr.* 610, ἐθέλων ἐσθίειν τὸν δέλφακα, a noun usually feminine is masculine (δέλφακα δὲ ἀρσενικῶς εἴρηκε Σοφοκλῆς. —Athenaeus).

(*c*) If πόᾳ is right, the 'zeugma' of λειμῶνι πόᾳ τε may have excused the feminine adjective here.

2. I also agree with Wolf in taking ἀνήριθμος as = ἀναρίθμητος in Eur. *Helen.* 1679, where οἱ ἀναρίθμητοι are opposed to οἱ εὐγενεῖς ; also *Ion*, 837, ἀμήτορ', ἀναρίθμητον, ἐκ δούλης

62   PARALIPOMENA SOPHOCLEA

τινὸς | γυναικός, ἐς σὸν δῶμα δεσπότην ἄγει. And I do not see the force of Jebb's *ex cathedrâ* statement that this is quite untenable. Cp. also Eur. *fr.* 519:

δειλοὶ γὰρ ἄνδρες οὐκ ἔχουσιν ἐν μάχῃ
ἀριθμόν, ἀλλ' ἄπεισι κἂν πάρωσ' ὅμως.

The meaning is much the same as *infra* 1206, where Jebb also renders ἀμέριμνος 'uncared for.' So ἀνήριθμος here is 'unregarded.' For a Biblical parallel, see Judges v. 16, 'Why abodest thou among the sheepfolds, to hear the bleatings of the flocks?' In Soph. *Philoctetes at Troy, fr.* 637, one of the speakers complains of the lowing of the herds:

μέλη βοῶν ἄναυλα καὶ ῥακτήρια.

610.   καί μοι δυσθεράπευτος Αἴας
ξύνεστιν ἔφεδρος.

ἔφεδρος. I will not repeat my '*ex cathedrâ* statement' of 1879, that the Scholiast's explanation is untenable, since it has been adopted by Jebb, who renders it 'a fresh trouble in reserve.' But I do think that this figurative sense harmonises less well with the context, than the more direct and simple meaning with reference to the hero's sullen inaction. Instead of being their defence, his continued presence is an oppressive burden to them. Cp. *supr.* 194, ἄνα ἐξ ἑδράνων, ὅπου . . . στηρίζει. For ἔφεδρος='planted near,' cp. Eur. *Tro.* 138, 139, θάκους οἴους θάσσω | σκηναῖς ἐφέδρους Ἀγαμεμνονίαις. Both meanings occur in [Eur.] *Rhes.* 119, 954.

615.   φίλοις μέγα πένθος εὕρηται.

I am still rather inclined to take εὕρηται as perf. mid., 'He has provided great sorrow for his friends.'

634.   δοῦποι καὶ πολιᾶς ἄμυγμα χαίτας.

Note that the verbal noun in -μα here signifies the act and not the result. Cp. *Ant.* 126 and note; Eur. *Androm.* 826, 827, σπάραγμα κόμας ὀνύχων τε δάϊ' ἀμύγματα θήσομαι.

639, 640.   οὐκέτι συντρόφοις
ὀργαῖς ἔμπεδος, ἀλλ' ἐκτὸς ὁμιλεῖ.

The difficulty is hardly removed by Jebb's suggestion: 'From ξυντρόφοις ὀργαῖς we are left to supply ἄλλαις ὀργαῖς (suggested by ἐκτός) with ὁμιλεῖ.' The phrase must remain as an extreme instance of oxymoron. ὁμιλεῖν occurs absolutely with an adverb of place in *Od.* xxi. 156, ἐνθάδ' ὁμιλέομεν, but is there used of several persons (the suitors of Penelope) consorting together. Cp. Eur. *Hipp.* 935, λόγοι παραλλάσσοντες ἔξεδροι φρενῶν: Soph. *Phil.* 691, ἵν' αὐτὸς ἦν πρόσουρος, and the curious metaphor in Her. iii. 155, ἐξέπλωσας τῶν φρενῶν.

For ὀργαῖς cp. Eur. *Tro.* 53, ἐπῄνεσ' ὀργὰς ἠπίους, and frequent uses in Pindar, *Pyth.* ix. 43, etc.

647.   Cp. *fr.* 832, πάντ' ἐκκαλύπτων ὁ χρόνος εἰς τὸ φῶς ἄγει.

649.   χὠ δεινὸς ὅρκος καὶ περισκελεῖς φρένες.

Jebb reads χαί with Brunck, perhaps rightly. But cp. Aesch. *Ag.* 324, τῶν ἁλόντων καὶ κρατησάντων.

651.   βαφῇ σίδηρος ὥς, ἐθηλύνθην στόμα.

βαφῇ σίδηρος ὥς. Here Jebb and I are entirely in accord, as in so many other places—but I may be allowed to call attention to the fact, since a recent editor has assumed that Jebb was the first to punctuate and interpret the passage in this way: 'βαφῇ σίδηρος ὥς, sc. καρτερὸς γίγνεται, supplied from ἐκαρτέρουν.'—(Jebb, 1896.) 'βαφῇ, an instrumental dative, depends on the idea of hardening contained in ἐκαρτέρουν.'—(*L. C.* 1879.) The Laurentian MS. is punctuated thus:

τότε,
βαφῆι. σίδηρος ὥς, ἐθηλύνθην στόμα.

652. οἰκτείρω δέ νιν.

The scribe of L. at first wrote οἰκτείρων.

655, 656. ὡς ἂν λύμαθ' ἁγνίσας ἐμὰ
μῆνιν βαρεῖαν ἐξαλεύσωμαι θεᾶς.

'The thought in the mind of Ajax is that he will purge himself of his stains by death.'—(Jebb.)
ἐξαλεύσωμαι. The Epic examples of ἀλέομαι are rather in favour of this verb as suited for the context here, in preference to ἐξαλύξωμαι. ἐξαλεύσωμαι, the reading of L., ought not to have had an asterisk in *CA*.

668. ἄρχοντές εἰσιν, ὥσθ' ὑπεικτέον. τί μή;
τί μήν; is probably right, but in Aesch. *Ag*. 672, L. reads τί μή; although in *Suppl*. 999, *Eum*. 203, τί μήν; (*sic*) is read.

670. τοῦτο μὲν νιφοστιβεῖς
χειμῶνες ἐκχωροῦσιν εὐκάρπῳ θέρει.

νιφοστιβεῖς. Cp. the lines in Campbell's *Ode to Winter* :

'Save when adown the ravaged globe,
He travels on his native storm,
Deflowering Nature's grassy robe,
And trampling on her faded form.'

675. Cp. Eur. *H. F.* 861, πόντος ... κύμασιν στένων λάβρως.

678. *ἐγῷδ'. ἐπίσταμαι γὰρ ἀρτίως ὅτι.

Porson's ἐγῷδ' is nearer to the lettering of L. But ἔγωγ', which Jebb adopts from Blaydes, is perhaps more probable. It should be noted, however, that the parallels quoted by Jebb (1347, 1365, *Trach.* 1248, to which may be added *supra* 104) are all in *replies.*

687. ὑμεῖς θ', ἑταῖροι, ταὐτὰ τῇδέ μοι τάδε
τιμᾶτε.

ταὐτὰ is of course adverbial.

691. τάχ' ἄν μ' ἴσως
πύθοισθε, κεἰ νῦν δυστυχῶ, σεσωσμένον.

May not τάχα here retain something of its primary meaning? Jebb *renders,* 'Ere long, perchance.'

699. θεῶν χοροποί' ἄναξ.

Is not θεῶν in Pind. *fr.* 75, χορευτὴν τελεώτατον θεῶν, a partitive genitive?

700. ὅπως μοι
Νύσια Κνώσσι' ὀρχήματ' αὐτοδαῆ ξυνὼν ἰάψῃς.

'That with me thou mayest move blithely in the measures that none hath taught thee.' So Jebb renders, perhaps rightly.

709. πάρα λευκὸν εὐάμερον πελάσαι φάος
θοᾶν ὠκυάλων νεῶν.

λευκὸν φάος. Cp. also *fr.* 5, λευκὴν ἡμέραν· τὴν ἀγαθήν. Σοφοκλῆς Ἀθάμαντι.—(Antiatt.)

718.   εὐτέ γ' ἐξ ἀέλπτων
Αἴας μετανεγνώσθη
θυμῶν 'Ατρείδαις μεγάλων τε νεικέων.

It appears that the plural of θυμός occurs nowhere else in Tragedy. But it suits the context here and in the sense of 'fits of passion' agrees also with the words of the chorus, *infr.* 929-933. It may be observed that the prose use in Plato, *Legg.* 633 *d* (quoted by L. and S.), does not mean 'fits of passion,' but the seat or principle of anger in several persons.

719.   ἄνδρες φίλοι, τὸ πρῶτον ἀγγεῖλαι θέλω.

τὸ πρῶτον is rather an accusative than an adverb: 'The first thing I would communicate is this.'

730.   ὥστε καὶ χεροῖν
κολεῶν ἐρυστὰ διεπεραιώθη ξίφη.

I still think that διεπεραιώθη suggests the crossing of weapons. The strife had gone as far as it could without actual bloodshed.

747.   ποῖον; τί δ' εἰδὼς τοῦδε πράγματος πέρι;
Schneidewin's πάρει is very probable, and improves the sense.

755.   εἰ ζῶντ' ἐκεῖνον εἰσιδεῖν θέλοι ποτέ.

ἐκεῖνον is not merely idiomatic, but represents the phrase of Calchas in pointing emphatically to the hero in his absence. He said ἐὰν θέλῃς ποτὲ ἐκεῖνον ('your brother') εἰσιδεῖν ζῶντα.

769.   πέποιθα τοῦτ' ἐπισπάσειν κλέος.

ἐπισπάσειν. Sophocles used the same word in the *Atreus*, *fr.* 137.

AJAX

771-773. διάς Ἀθάνας, ἡνίκ' ὀτρύνουσά νιν
ηὐδᾶτ' ἐπ' ἐχθροῖς χεῖρα φοινίαν τρέπειν,
τότ' ἀντιφωνεῖ δεινὸν ἄρρητόν τ' ἔπος·

διάς Ἀθάνας. It seems to me awkward to connect this genitive directly with ἀντιφωνεῖν, though it may be understood so, as the sentence proceeds. I prefer to take it as continuing the case of πατρός in no definite construction. Cp. O. T. 701.

Κρέοντος, οἷά μοι βεβουλευκὼς ἔχει.

775. καθ' ἡμᾶς δ' οὔποτ' ἐκρήξει μάχη.

I adhere to my note. See especially the commentary in *CA*. The image is that of a river bursting its banks.

780. ὁ δ' εὐθὺς ἐξ ἕδρας
πέμπει με.

Cf. *fr.* adespot. 275, εὐθὺς ἐξ εὐνῆς.

787, 788. τί μ' αὖ τάλαιναν, ἀρτίως πεπαυμένην
κακῶν ἀτρύτων, ἐξ ἕδρας ἀνίστατε;

Cp. Eur. *fr.* 342.

τί μ' ἄρτι πημάτων λελησμένην
ὀρθοῖς;

795. ἐκεῖνον εἴργειν Τεῦκρος ἐξεφίεται.
ἐξεφίεται, 'gives forth the mandate.'

798-802. ΑΓ. πάρεστ' ἐκεῖνος ἄρτι· τήνδε δ' ἔξοδον
Αἴαντος εἰς ὄλεθρον ἐλπίζει φέρειν.
ΤΕ. οἴμοι τάλαινα, τοῦ ποτ' ἀνθρώπων μαθών;
ΑΓ. τοῦ Θεστορείου μάντεως, καθ' ἡμέραν
τὴν νῦν, ὅτ' αὐτῷ θάνατον ἢ βίον φέρει.

The change in 799, proposed by Blaydes and improved upon by Jebb, seems very probable. But in 802 Jebb's proposal to make ἡ ἔξοδος the subject of φέρει does seem rather 'harsh.' Wecklein's θροεῖ is unobjectionable, if φέρει cannot mean 'he announces.'

811. χωρῶμεν, ἐγκονῶμεν, οὐχ ἕδρας ἀκμή.

For ἀκμή, cp. also Eur. *Hec.* 1042.

βούλεσθ᾽ ἐπεισπέσωμεν; ὡς ἀκμὴ καλεῖ
Ἑκάβῃ παρεῖναι Τρωάσιν τε συμμάχους.

Cp. Eur. 1291, οὐχ ἕδρας ἀγών.

815, 816. ὁ μὲν σφαγεὺς ἕστηκεν ᾗ τομώτατος
γένοιτ᾽ ἄν, εἴ τῳ καὶ λογίζεσθαι σχολή.

'If one has leisure *e'en* to reason about it.'—(Jebb.) I still prefer '*also* for reasoning,' *i.e.* as well as for this elaborate preparation. The act is as *deliberate* as possible. And in σφαγεύς may there not be an *association* of sacrifice?

817, 818. δῶρον μὲν ἀνδρὸς Ἕκτορος ξένων ἐμοὶ
μάλιστα μισηθέντος ἐχθίστου θ᾽ ὁρᾶν.

Jebb observes that Hector and Ajax became ξένοι by the interchange of gifts. This is probably right. ξένος=βάρβαρος does not occur in Tragedy.

820. σιδηροβρῶτι θηγάνῃ νεηκονής.

L. pr. had σιδηροβρώτηι.

835. καλῶ δ᾽ ἀρωγοὺς τὰς ἀεί τε παρθένους.

'The maidens who live for ever' (Jebb). Rather, 'who are maidens for evermore.' παρθένους, sc. οὔσας, absorbed in the following participle.

839-842. καί σφας κακοὺς κάκιστα καὶ πανωλέθρους ξυναρπάσειαν, ὥσπερ εἰσορῶσ᾽ ἐμὲ αὐτοσφαγῆ πίπτοντα, τὼς αὐτοσφαγεῖς πρὸς τῶν φιλίστων ἐκγόνων ὀλοίατο.

Jebb, while rejecting 841, 842, gives strong reasons for retaining 839, 840, I do not object to this, although the suppression of ξυναρπασθέντα or the like after ἐμέ is rather abrupt.

849. γέροντι πατρὶ τῇ τε δυστήνῳ τροφῷ.

My suggestion that the word τροφῷ may be applied to Eribœa here with reference to Telamon as = γηροτρόφος seems to be regarded as an idle fancy. I will only plead in extenuation:

(1) That, while τροφὸς and μήτηρ are constantly associated, no place is quoted in which the meaning is identical. (A doubtful instance occurs in Ion, *fr.* 42; and Sophocles appears to have used μήτηρ = τροφός, *fr.* 967.)

(2) That the tender reminiscence of infancy implied in such a use of the word is hardly in character.

(3) That Eriboea's position in the household, after the union with Hesione, was no longer the same. This seems to be implied in *supr.* 569, Ἐριβοίᾳ λέγω, on which Jebb observes, 'Eurysakes is to honour her and not Hesione.' Cp. *Trach.* 550, i.

μὴ πόσις μὲν Ἡρακλῆς
ἐμὸς καλῆται, τῆς νεωτέρας δ᾽ ἀνήρ.

See also the Homeric Hymn to *Aphrodite*, lines 231, 232.

τοῦ δ᾽ ἤτοι εὐνῆς μὲν ἀπείχετο πότνια Ἠώς,
αὐτὸν δ᾽ αὖτ᾽ ἀτίταλλεν, ἐνὶ μεγάροισιν ἔχουσα.

But I must admit that these grounds are hardly sufficient to justify me in maintaining my view against what seems to be the general opinion.

PARALIPOMENA SOPHOCLEA

859, 860. ὦ γῆς ἱερὸν οἰκείας πέδον
Σαλαμῖνος· ὦ πατρῷον ἑστίας βάθρον.

I take the address to Salamis and to his father's hearth, to be separate invocations.

866. πόνος πόνῳ πόνον φέρει.

For πόνος πόνῳ, cp. also *fr.* adespot 7.

πόνῳ πόνον
ἐκ νυκτὸς ἀλλάσσουσα τὸν καθ᾽ ἡμέραν.

869. κοὐδεὶς *ἐφίσταταί με συμμαθεῖν τόπος.

I maintain that my correction of this line, by simply writing φ for π, is at once simpler and more expressive than any other.

874. πᾶν ἐστίβηται πλευρὸν ἕσπερον νεῶν.

'The westward side of the ships' (Jebb). I still prefer, 'the coast to westward of the ships.'

884-886. ἢ τίς Ὀλυμπιάδων θεᾶν, ἢ ῥυτῶν
βοσπορίων ποταμῶν, τὸν ὠμόθυμον
εἴ ποθι πλαζόμενον λεύσσων
ἀπύοι;

I take ποταμῶν to be 'river gods'—the genitive with τίς, though λεύσσων might possibly agree with τίς of a feminine subject.

890. ἀλλ᾽ ἀμενηνὸν ἄνδρα μὴ λεύσσειν ὅπου.

Cp. Eur. *Suppl.* 1116 (in Murray's *Oxford Text*).

γραίας ἀμενοῦς—οὐ γὰρ ἔνεστιν
ῥώμη παίδων ὑπὸ πένθους.

(ἀμενής does not appear in L. and S.)
Also *Troad.* 193, νεκύων ἀμενηνὸν ἄγαλμα.

905. τίνος ποτ' ἄρ' *ἔρξε χειρὶ δύσμορος;

Jebb defends ἔπραξε, reading ὑπερβριθὲς γὰρ in 951, and reasons with some force in favour of this view. I leave the point undetermined.

916. ἀλλά νιν περιπτυχεῖ
φάρει καλύψω τῷδε παμπήδην.

Jebb suggests that the mantle was brought by an attendant. Is this necessary? See my note.

917. οὐδεὶς ἂν, ὅστις καὶ φίλος, τλαίη βλέπειν.

ὅστις καὶ φίλος. Cp. Eur. *Suppl.* 943, 944.

— . . . τὰς τεκούσας οὐ χρεὼν ψαῦσαι τέκνων;
—ὅλοιντ' ἰδοῦσαι τούσδ' ἂν ἠλλοιωμένους.

Those who would take καί='even,' with the Scholiast and Lobeck might quote Aesch. *fr.* 137.

καὶ μὴν, φιλῶ γάρ, ἀβδέλυκτ' ἐμοὶ τάδε,

supposing this to be said in presence of the corpse of Patroclus.

921. ὡς ἀκμαῖος, εἰ βαίη, μόλοι.

ἀκμαῖος is by the first hand in L. (ᕜ is merely the compendium for οσ which the scribe has occasionally employed.) Whether ἄν could be omitted in the immediate neighbourhood of another optative is a point which I will not venture to determine.

926. στερεόφρων ἄρ' ἐξανύσσειν κακάν

I agree with Jebb in reading ἄρ' ἐξανύσσειν.

931, 932.
ἀνεστέναξες
ὠμόφρων ἐχθοδόπ' Ἀτρείδαις
οὐλίῳ σὺν πάθει.

I doubt whether even in *Phil.* 899, a much later passage, πάθους signifies the *feeling* of Neoptolemus. It is rather the unhappy *situation* in which he finds himself.

936. *χρυσοτύπων ὅπλων ἔκειτ' ἀγὼν πέρι.

For my conjecture, cp. Eur. *El.* 470, of the helmet of Achilles,

ἐπὶ δὲ χρυσοτύπῳ κράνει.

938. χωρεῖ πρὸς ἧπαρ, οἶδα, γενναία δύη.

γενναία δύη. I am still inclined to follow the Scholiast in taking γενναία to mean 'great,' or 'intense,' rather than 'genuine.'

945. οἷοι νῷν ἐφεστᾶσι σκοποί.

I prefer to take οἷοι as a second exclamation.

947, 948. ἀναλγήτων
δισσῶν ἐθρόησας ἄναυδον
ἔργον Ἀτρειδᾶν.

ἄναυδον here is taken as = ἀναύδητον, 'unspeakable,' *i.e.* infamous. I still prefer to understand it in the usual sense : Tecmessa has 'voiced the silent deed.' The Atridae would reduce her and Eurysakes to servitude, '*sans phrase,*' '*sans dire mot.*' Cp. adespot, *fr.* 493.

ὁρᾷς Δίκην ἄναυδον οὐχ ὁρωμένην
εὕδοντι καὶ στείχοντι καὶ καθημένῳ.

954. ἦ ῥα κελαινώπαν θυμὸν ἐφυβρίζει πολύτλας ἀνήρ.

It matters little whether θυμόν is accus. of the internal object, or of the sphere of motion figuratively understood. Jebb takes κελαινώπαν to mean 'darkly spying'; but the literal meaning is 'dark-looking,' 'of dark complexion or hue.'

In πολύτλας the old doubt occurs how far Sophocles, in adopting Epic diction, surrounds it with some new association. I still think that here the word suggests one who can bring himself to anything, πάντα τολμῶν (*O. C.* 761).

965. πρίν τις ἐκβάλῃ.

Cp. *Bacchylides*, xvii. 28, Πολυπήμονός τε καρτέραν | σφῦραν ἐξέβαλεν Προκόπτας ἀρείονος τυχὼν | φωτός.

966. ἐμοὶ πικρὸς τέθνηκεν ἢ κείνοις γλυκύς,
αὐτῷ δὲ τερπνός.

For ἤ without a comparative preceding, cp. also *fr.* adespot. 537: κατθανεῖν γὰρ εὐκλεῶς | ἢ ζῆν θέλοιμ' ἂν δυσκλεῶς. For the hypothetical indicative which I suggested as an alternative explanation, see *Ant.* 1168 and note.

986. μή τις ὡς κενῆς
σκύμνον λεαίνης δυσμενῶν ἀναρπάσῃ.

The only objection to taking κενῆς as = 'widowed,' is that, as a fact of natural history, the lioness is well able to defend her young. But Sophocles, as often happens, thinks less of the image than of the thing signified.

998. ὀξεῖα γάρ σου βάξις ὡς θεοῦ τινὸς
διῆλθ' Ἀχαιοὺς πάντας.

A closer parallel for the genitive θεοῦ is *Trach.* 768, ὥστε τέκτονος.

1008, 1009.
ἦ πού με Τελαμών, σὸς πατὴρ ἐμός θ' ἅμα,
δέξαιτ' ἂν εὐπρόσωπος ἵλεώς τ' ἴσως
χωροῦντ' ἄνευ σοῦ.

For the irony, cp. Eur. *Med.* 504.

καλῶς γ' ἂν οὖν
δέξαιντό μ' οἴκοις ὧν πατέρα κατέκτανον.

1010.
ὅτῳ πάρα
μήδ' εὐτυχοῦντι μηδὲν ἥδιον γελᾶν.

I doubt the exactness of the parallel in Eur. *Med.* 658, ὅτῳ πάρεστι | μὴ φίλους τιμᾶν, where παρεῖναι seems to convey an association of harboured guilt, like ξυνεῖναι in *O. C.* 945, 946, ὅτῳ γάμοι

ξυνόντες εὑρέθησαν ἀνόσιοι τέκνων,

and I still prefer the meaning, 'Who smiles no more, yield Fortune what she may,' as in my translation. Cp. Eur. *Alc.* 347.

σὺ γάρ μοι τέρψιν ἐξείλου βίου.

And for πάρα, *supra* 982, *Ant.* 1096, 1097.

ἀντιστάντα δὲ
ἄτῃ πατάξαι θυμὸν ἐν δεινῷ πάρα.

1018.
ἐρεῖ, πρὸς οὐδὲν εἰς ἔριν θυμούμενος.

Cp. Eur. *Cycl.* 328.

Διὸς βρονταῖσιν εἰς ἔριν κτυπῶν.

A doubt occurs whether οὐδὲν εἰς ἔριν may be joined='a thing that is no cause for quarrel.' Cp. Eur. *Phoen.* 598, πρὸς τὸν οὐδὲν ἐς μάχην.

1024, 1025.
πῶς σ' ἀποσπάσω πικροῦ
τοῦδ' αἰόλου κνώδοντος.

I still think that αἰόλου suggests 'discoloured,' as in *Phil.* 1157.

AJAX

1030. ζωστῆρι πρισθεὶς ἱππικῶν ἐξ ἀντύγων.

I still think that πρισθεὶς implies not only a *firm* but a *galling* grip or pressure.

1042. βλέπω γὰρ ἐχθρὸν φῶτα.

Cp. Eur. *fr.* 727, ἐχθροῦ φωτὸς ἔχθιστον τέκος.

1046. ὁρῶ· μαθεῖν γὰρ ἐγγὺς ὢν οὐ δυσπετής.

It is perhaps implied that Menelaus was below the ordinary standard of an Achaean warrior.

1047, 1048. οὗτος, σὲ φωνῶ τόνδε τὸν νεκρὸν χεροῖν
μὴ συγκομίζειν.

It is true, as Jebb remarks, that κομίζειν is often used of caring for the dead. See especially Eur. *Suppl.* 25, νεκρῶν κομιστήν. But the word in this connection does not lose its ordinary meaning. Thus in Eur. *Suppl.* 126, κομίσαι . . . παῖδας Ἀργείων is to *bring* the dead to a place of burial. And, as Teucer is not merely assisting at his brother's funeral, but conducting it, it is at least allowable to give συγκομίζειν here its proper sense of 'to gather in.' In the passage of Plutarch quoted by L. and S. *s. v.* ii., ἔφθη τὸ σῶμα συγκομισθέν, the preposition cannot mean 'to assist.' Cp. Eur. *fr.* 757, l. 5.

ἀναγκαίως δ' ἔχει
βίον θερίζειν ὥστε κάρπιμον στάχυν.

1051. οὔκουν ἂν εἴποις ἥντιν' αἰτίαν προθείς;

For the participle with understood reference, cp. Eur. *H. F.* 1136.

τί φῄς; τί δράσας; *ib.* 1188, τί φῄς; τί δράσας; where the reference is to 4 lines *supra*.

76   PARALIPOMENA SOPHOCLEA

1064.   ἀμφὶ χλωρὰν ψάμαθον ἐκβεβλημένος.

In taking χλωράν as = 'moist,' I felt that the line suggested *discomfort*,—a place where there was no 'snug lying,' as Sir Lucius puts it. Cp. Lycidas, 154, 'Ay me! whilst thee the *shores* and sounding seas | Wash far away, where'er thy bones are hurled.'—Shakespeare, *Rich. III.* v. 3, 266, 267.

'For me, the ransom of my bold attempt
Shall be this cold corse on the earth's cold face.'

But I do not press my view.

1075.   οὔτ' ἂν στρατός γε σωφρόνως ἄρχοιτ' ἔτι.

ἄρχοιτ' in L. is made, not from ἔχοιτ', but from ἄχοιτ' (the reading of L.² pr. ?). And previous to the alteration made by a recent hand, a ρ, now erased, had been written by an early hand above the line (ἄ̔χοιτ').

1083.   ἐξ οὐρίων δραμοῦσαν εἰς βυθὸν πεσεῖν.

I take this to be one of the cases where the same collocation of words in different contexts is to be differently construed. Although ἐξ οὐρίων in late prose means 'with a fair wind,' no one can imagine that Menelaus means 'will run down the wind to the bottom.' And the other possible interpretation, 'after running before favouring winds,' appears to me to involve an irrelevancy. I therefore think that there is a stress on the preposition, as in Eur. *fr.* 420, ἐξ ἐλπίδων πίπτοντας, and that ἐξ οὐρίων is nearly equivalent to ἔξω δρόμου; 'will drift from her right course and founder.' See the note on *O. T.* 1277, οὐδ' ἀνίεσαν, and Jebb's note on *Trach.* 1078, ἐκ καλυμμάτων.

1098.   The correction of the accent is hardly a sufficient reason for rejecting τόνδ' ἄνδρ', the reading of L.

AJAX 77

1117. ὡς ἂν ᾖς οἷός περ εἶ.

For ὡς ἄν in my interpretation ('however you may be—such as you are'), cp. *infr.* 1369 and note on *O. C.* 1361.

1126. δίκαια γὰρ τόνδ' εὐτυχεῖν κτείναντά με;
Cp. Eur. *Ion.* 1291.
ἔκτεινά σ' ὄντα πολέμιον δόμοις ἐμοῖς.
ib. 1300, 1500.

1132. τούς γ' αὐτὸς αὐτοῦ πολεμίους·
αὐτοῦ, not here = ἐμαυτοῦ. The meaning is generalised.

1159, 1160. ἄπειμι. καὶ γὰρ αἰσχρόν, εἰ πύθοιτό τις,
λόγοις κολάζειν, ᾧ βιάζεσθαι παρῇ.

Although παρῇ is the reading of L. pr., I am inclined to agree with Jebb that πάρα is to be preferred.

1166, 1167. Cp. Pind. *Ol.* ix. 112, Αἰάντεόν τ' ἐν δαίθ' ὡς Ἰλιάδα νικῶν ἐπεστεφάνωσε βωμόν.

1177. κακὸς κακῶς ἄθαπτος ἐκπέσοι χθονός.

It is not quite clear whether 'χθονός' is 'from his land,' as Jebb takes it, or 'from earth,' as I took it in my edition.

1180, 1181. ἔχ' αὐτόν, ὦ παῖ, καὶ φύλασσε, μηδέ σε
κινησάτω τις, ἀλλὰ προσπεσὼν ἔχου.

αὐτὸν is more expressive, if referred to the body of Ajax, and also more in harmony with ἔχου. In the scene as acted there would be no difficulty in going back to 1172, ἔφαψαι πατρός.

1190.   ἀν' *ἀερώδεα *Τρωΐαν.

In favour of ἀερώδεα (Hermann's conjecture, adopted by G. Wolff) may be adduced (1) the exact metrical correspondence to 1197; (2) the other allusions to the damp and misty climate of the Troad (601, 1207). For a similar graphic touch, cp. *fr.* 509, ἀνεμώδεα Σκῦρον.

1199-1211.   ἐκεῖνος οὔτε στεφάνων . . .
καὶ πρὶν μὲν *αἰὲν νυχίου.

I now accept Wolff's correction of 1211 (from καὶ πρὶν μὲν ἐννυχίου) instead of changing οὔτε to *οὗ in 1199.

1206.   κεῖμαι δ' ἀμέριμνος οὕτως.

For ἀμέριμνος, cp. Eur. *Heracl.* 343, 344.

εἰσὶν γὰρ οἵ σου, κἂν ἐγὼ θυραῖος ὦ
μέριμναν ἕξουσ' . . .,

But the other meaning, 'listless,' 'without any object of thought or care,' is not impossible.

1214.   νῦν δ' οὗτος ἀνεῖται στυγερῷ
δαίμονι.

I accept Jebb's decision, but would add that as the devoted victim was released from service to mankind, so Ajax's human function of acting as a bulwark to his friends has ceased. That gives point to the complaint. A somewhat similar use occurs in Eur. *Heracl.* 3.

ὁ δ' ἐς τὸ κέρδος λῆμ' ἔχων ἀνειμένον.

1230.   ὑψήλ' ἐφώνεις κἀπ' ἄκρων ὡδοιπόρεις,

Hesych. 1 p. 104 (quoted by Nauck, Tr. Fr. Gr., p. 539, Eur. *fr.* 570), ἀκρίζων· ἄκροις ποσὶν ἐπιπορευόμενος Εὐριπίδης

AJAX 79

Οἰνεῖ. Eur. *El.* 840, ὄνυχας ἐπ' ἄκρους στάς; *Ion.* 1166, ἐν δ' ἄκροισι βὰς ποσὶ | κῆρυξ ἀνεῖπε, *Iph. T.* 266, ἄκροισι δακτύλοισι πορθμεύων ἴχνος.

1237. ποῦ βάντος ἢ ποῦ στάντος, οὗπερ οὐκ ἐγώ;
I still hesitate to change the former ποῦ to ποῖ.

1244, 1245. ἀλλ' αἰὲν ἡμᾶς ἢ κακοῖς βαλεῖτέ που
ἢ σὺν δόλῳ κεντήσεθ' οἱ λελειμμένοι.

I now (*CA.* n.) prefer to take λελειμμένοι as = 'who have been left behind in the race,' with Jebb. In my edition I mentioned this as an alternative. Cp. Eur. *H. F.* 1173, οὔ που λέλειμμαι καὶ νεωτέρων κακῶν | ὕστερος ἀφῖγμαι.

1255. καὶ σοὶ προσέρπον τοῦτ' ἐγὼ τὸ φάρμακον
ὁρῶ τάχ'.

Cp. *O. C.* 714, τὸν ἀκεστῆρα χαλινόν.

1257. ἀνδρὸς οὐκέτ' ὄντος, ἀλλ' ἤδη σκιᾶς.

I am not satisfied that ἀνδρὸς ... σκιᾶς is *merely* gen. abs. For σκιᾶς, cp. *fr.* 12.
ἄνθρωπός ἐστι πνεῦμα καὶ σκιὰ μόνον.

1266, 1267. φεῦ· τοῦ θανόντος ὡς ταχεῖά τις βροτοῖς
χάρις διαρρεῖ.

For ταχεῖα predicative, cp. *fr.* 786.
ταχεῖα πειθὼ τῶν κακῶν ὁδοιπορεῖ.

1268. εἰ σοῦ γ' ὅδ' ἀνὴρ οὐδ' ἐπὶ σμικρῶν λόγων
Αἴας, ἔτ' ἴσχει μνῆστιν.

οὐδ' ἐπὶ σμικρῶν λόγων : I now prefer the meaning which I put second in my edition and for which Jebb (on second thoughts) decides—'not even in brief words.' See my Translation.

80 PARALIPOMENA SOPHOCLEA

1279. πηδῶντος ἄρδην Ἕκτορος τάφρων ὕπερ.

Cp. *fr.* adespot. 569.

Τεῦκρος δὲ τόξου χρώμενος φειδωλίᾳ
ὑπὲρ τάφρου πηδῶντας ἔστησεν Φρύγας.

1280, 1281. οὐχ' ὅδ' ἦν ὁ δρῶν τάδε
ὃν οὐδαμοῦ φῂς οὐδὲ συμβῆναι ποδί.

I admit that the conjecture *οὗ σὺ μή, βῆναι ποδί is very plausible. But I see no reason for harmonising Agamemnon's words with what Teucer really said (see my note); and though συμβῆναι ποδί, in the sense of 'plants his foot beside (thine),' is awkward, I do not see that it is impossible.

1292. ἀρχαῖον ὄντα Πέλοπα βάρβαρον Φρύγα.

'That Pelops was in his origin a barbarian.' Although such a use of ἀρχαῖος may be without an exact parallel, it is not un-Greek, and the antiquity of Pelops is hardly in point. In *Ant.* 593, ἀρχαῖα, 'from of old,' is a 'secondary predicate.'

1324. ἤκουσεν αἰσχρά· δρῶν γὰρ ἦν τοιαῦτά με.

I take δρῶν . . . με = 'he was treating me shamefully.' To understand αἰσχρὰ ἔλεγέ με does away with the opposition of δρᾶν to λέγειν, which is duly preserved in Jebb's translation.

1353. παῦσαι· κρατεῖς τοι τῶν φίλων νικώμενος.

Cp. also *fr.* adespot. 40.

φίλων γὰρ ἄρξεις μὴ κρατῶν ὅσον θέλεις.

1357. νικᾷ γὰρ ἀρετή με τῆς ἔχθρας πολύ.

Cp. *supra*, note on l. 966. But is ἀρετή the valour of Ajax, or the claims of honourable conduct on Odysseus' part? *Noblesse oblige.*

1365. ἔγωγε· καὶ γὰρ αὐτὸς ἐνθάδ' ἵξομαι.

Jebb has traced with fine perception the gradual shades of alteration in the mood of Agamemnon. But I still question his acceptance of the ordinary interpretation of this line. The commonplace sentiment (for which cp. *fr.* 350,

μηδὲ τῷ τεθνηκότι
τὸν ζῶντ' ἐπαρκεῖν αὐτὸν ὡς θανούμενον)

seems to me hardly in keeping with the attitude of Odysseus here, nor could it well occasion the retort in 1366. Odysseus argues on the ground of cool calculation: 'That is the course I mean to take.' 'Ay, says Agamemnon, 'you are speaking for yourself, after all.' This Odysseus is ready to admit. Cp. Eur. *Iph. A.* 1214, ἐνταῦθ' ἂν ἦλθον.

1373. σοὶ δὲ δρᾶν ἔξεσθ' ἃ †χρή.

I am reluctantly constrained to admit that the forms χρῇς, χρῇ for χρῄζεις, χρῄζει, are sufficiently supported here and in the instances adduced by Jebb.

1393. σὲ δ', ὦ γεραιοῦ σπέρμα Λαέρτου πατρός.

'The mode of address is honorific,' Jebb—the more so as meaner spirits believed Odysseus to be the son of Sisyphus.

1401. εἶμ', ἐπαινέσας τὸ σόν.

For τὸ σόν, cp. Eur. *Tro.* 82, σὺ δ' αὖ, τὸ σόν, παράσχες Αἴγαιον πόρον | τρικυμίαις βρέμοντα.

1416, 1417. κοὐδενὶ <δή>πω λῴονι θνητῶν—
Αἴαντος·—ὅτ' ἦν, τότε φωνῶ.

The double paræmiac can of course not be maintained, and Jebb's insertion of δή is the best remedy hitherto proposed. If the phrase in 1416, 'cannot be explained by attraction,' the two lines must be rejected entirely. Yet something is required to round off the system after τῷ πάντ' ἀγαθῷ, and the general meaning is good. If 1417 is sound, Αἴαντος follows the comparative after a pause; then follows another pause, and the final phrase is added in explanation. For the moderation of this cp. Plato, *Phaedo*, s. *f*., ἀνδρός, ὡς ἡμεῖς φαῖμεν ἄν, τῶν τότε ὧν ἐπειράθημεν ἀρίστου. For ὅτ' ἦν, cp. Eur. *fr*. 311,

ἦσθ' εἰς θεοὺς μὲν εὐσεβής, ὅτ' ἦσθ', ἀεί.

H. F. 443-444,

τοῦ μεγάλου
δήποτε παῖδας τὸ πρὶν Ἡρακλέους.

OEDIPUS TYRANNUS

The impiety of Jocasta appears to me to be regarded by the poet in a very serious light. The great central stasimon shows clearly that the chorus are profoundly moved by it. They had themselves questioned the infallibility of human prophecy; but now they fear that Apollo's honours are growing pale and things divine are coming to nought. In spite of Jocasta's admission that the oracle did not proceed direct from Phœbus himself, and notwithstanding her cold speculation about the power of God apart from his ministers (compare Creon's attitude in the Antigone), she is clearly intended to be irreligious, and hardened by the impunity which had followed the act in which, from fear of the gods, she had done violence to her best affections.

In her extremity, from the force of early habit, she does think of worship, and for the moment appeals once more to Apollo. But the news from Corinth immediately dissipates any such resolve, and she triumphantly exclaims—

'See what has come of that solemn prophecy *of the God*.'

1. Ὦ ΤΈΚΝΑ, Κάδμου τοῦ πάλαι νέα τροφή.

I now agree with Jebb that Κάδμου is not genitive of origin but of possession. Cadmus, as τοῦ γένους ἀρχηγέτης, is master of the flock, which is tended by Oedipus. But I still think that Oedipus is τροφεύς.

2. τίνας ποθ' ἕδρας τάσδε μοι θοάζετε.

I do not believe that θοάζειν = θάσσειν belongs to tragic Greek. Even in Empedocles σοφίης ἐπ' ἄκροισι θόαζε may mean 'speed onwards' (not 'to' but) 'on the heights of wisdom.' Compare the career of the disembodied souls in Plato's *Phaedrus*, 247 BC. In Aesch. *Suppl.* 595,

ὑπ' ἀρχᾶς δ' οὔτινος θοάζων
τὸ μεῖον κρεισσόνων κρατύνει

the meaning is 'he hurries not at bidding of a lord, nor is his rule subordinate to higher powers.' If this be so, θοάζειν = θάσσειν may be only an invention of Alexandrian grammarians. It is objected that here the notions of sitting or kneeling and of hastening are incongruous. But surely the ants on an ant-hill, or bees swarming, might be said θοάζειν τὴν συνοικίαν (or συνεδρίαν). I imagine some of the suppliants to be already placed, and others hastening to join them, while they are marshalled by the priests and the young men.

7. Cp. Eur. *H. F.* 912, μάντιν οὐχ ἕτερον ἄξομαι.

10, 11. τίνι τρόπῳ καθέστατε δείσαντες ἢ στέρξαντες;

For καθέστατε with δείσαντες following, cp. *Her.* vii. 138, § 3, ἐν δείματι μεγάλῳ κατέστασαν. Eur. *Bacch.* 1262, εἰ δὲ διὰ τέλους | ἐν τῷδ' ἀεὶ μενεῖτ', ἐν ᾧ καθέστατε. Andoc. 2, § 8, ἐν οἵῳ κινδύνῳ τε καὶ ἀμηχανίᾳ καθέστατε.

It makes little difference whether the force of the interrogative is continued with the participles, or τι (indefinite) is supplied.

31, 32. Cp. Eur. *Tro.* 59, 60, ἦ πού νιν . . . ἐς οἶκτον ἦλθες;

35.   ὅς *τ' ἐξέλυσας, ἄστυ Καδμεῖον μολών,
σκληρᾶς ἀοιδοῦ δασμόν.

Elmsley's ὅς τ' is not a mere conjecture, as it is implied in the *lemma* of the scholiast, ὥστε μολὼν ἄστυ Καδμεῖον. The forward reference answered by νῦν, τ' (40) is plausible. Cp. *infr.* 694-696. I doubt if ἐξέλυσας contains any allusion to the solution of the riddle. The notion is simply that of removing a burden, as in *Trach.* 653, ἐξέλυσ' ἐπίπονον ἁμέραν; *Aj.* 706, ἔλυσεν αἰνὸν ἄχος ἀπ' ὀμμάτων Ἄρης.

44, 45.   ὡς τοῖσιν ἐμπείροισι καὶ τὰς ξυμφορὰς
ζώσας ὁρῶ μάλιστα τῶν βουλευμάτων.

On Jebb's masterly and exhaustive treatment of these lines in his Appendix, I have only a very few remarks to offer:—

1. The first scholar to *suggest* the new meaning for ξυμφοράς, so fiercely upheld by Dr. Kennedy, was Musgrave, whose note in the edition published posthumously in 1800 ran thus: ' De voce ξυμφορὰ, *vid.* Aesch. *Pers.* 436 *et* 439. Aristoph. *Acharn.* 1202, Eurip. *Iph. Aul.* 1346, Thucydides, i. 140, τὰς ξυμφορὰς τῶν πραγμάτων, ubi Scholiastes τὰς ἀποβάσεις. Sed neque ξυμβολάς spreverim pro ξυμφοράς.' It had not occurred to him that ξυμφοράς could have this meaning, which, however, he thought suitable to the context.

2. In the same year (1800) appeared a new edition of Dalzell's *Collectanea Graeca Majora*, in which he acknowledges the help received from his friend Dr. Thomas Young, a Fellow of the Royal Society, whose acquaintance he had made in Edinburgh, and who had sent him from London various corrections and suggestions which he now embodied in his *Commentary*. As the book seems to be a rare one, it may be worth while to transcribe the terms of this acknowledgment from the Preface to the Notes (*In Notas Prooemium*):—

' In hac sequentium annotationum novâ editione plurimum

debeo doctrinae atque spectatae amicitiae THOMAE YOUNG' (*sic.*), M.D., S.R.S., qui, cum Edinburgi tunc temporis degens etc., ... suumque exemplar, cum multis erratis typographicis correctis, et variis novis annotationibus locupletem, Londino ad me nuper remisit.' Amongst these was the note, which Jebb quotes from a later edition, to which are appended the initials T. Y. The same initials appear likewise in many other places of the work. Jebb's informant, then, was (not unnaturally) mistaken in supposing that 'T' was a misprint for 'J,' and that Dalzell's friend was the contemporary Glasgow Professor, John Young, who is chiefly known as having encouraged Thomas Campbell, when a student, in his verse translations. Although Thomas Young was by this time concentrating his versatile and ingenious mind on physical inquiry, he retained his keen interest in classical study as well as in the decypherment of Egyptian Hieroglyphics.—See the article about him in the *Dictionary of National Biography*. Those were not the days of specialism. The Natural and Mathematical Sciences were still at the stage which produced afterwards such men as Clerk Maxwell, Sir William Rowan Hamilton, and Henry Smith. Glasgow and Edinburgh were then several hours apart.

3. It deserves to be recorded that the new interpretation, which Jebb agrees with me in rejecting, obtained the adherence of so sound a scholar as the late Edward Poste.

4. Jebb omits to notice one place in which ξυμφορά is referred to ξυμφέρω='to bring together,' viz. the *pun* in Plato, *Philebus*, 64 e, οὐδὲ γὰρ κρᾶσις, ἀλλά τις ἄκρατος, ξυμπεφορημένη ἀληθῶς, ἡ τοιαύτη γίγνεται ἑκάστοτε ὄντως τοῖς κεκτημένοις ξυμφορά. This may have been in Mr. Poste's mind when he made the remark above referred to: see his notes *in loco*. But, like the passage in Lucian, it is of course an exception that proves the rule.

For the sense, cp. also *Her.* vii. 157, τῷ δὲ εὖ βουλευθέντι πρήγματι τελευτὴ ὡς τὸ ἐπίπαν χρηστὴ ἐθέλει ἐπιγίγνεσθαι.

56. Cp. also Eur. *fr.* 828, αἱ γὰρ πόλεις εἶσ' ἄνδρες, οὐκ ἐρημία.

82. Cp. Chaeremon, *fr.* 6, στεφάνους τεμόντες ἀγγέλους εὐφημίας; 11, στεφάνους ἑτοιμάζουσιν, οὓς εὐφημίας | κήρυκας εὐχαὶ προυβάλοντο δαιμόνων.

93, 94. τῶνδε γὰρ πλέον φέρω
τὸ πένθος ἢ καὶ τῆς ἐμῆς ψυχῆς πέρι.

I prefer to take πλέον as an adj. in agreement with πένθος, than as adverbial here. And καὶ seems to me not emphatic, ('even'), but idiomatic. It merely adds a slight emphasis to the antithesis. 'I am less concerned for myself than for them.'

95. λέγοιμ' ἄν οἵ' ἤκουσα τοῦ θεοῦ πάρα.

λέγοιμ' ἄν. 'Then I will tell': not 'with thy leave'—inferential, not 'deferential.'

104. πρὶν σὲ τήνδ' ἀπευθύνειν πόλιν.

Cp. *Ant.* 167, ἡνίκ' Οἰδίπους ὤρθου πόλιν.

107. τοὺς αὐτοέντας χειρὶ τιμωρεῖν τινάς.

The active voice in τιμωρεῖν divests the notion of punishment of any personal intention. It is the duty of the state. Cp. ἐπισκήπτειν.

115. πρὸς οἶκον οὐκέθ' ἵκεθ', ὡς ἀπεστάλη.

For ὡς = ἐπεί, cp. Aesch. *S. ad T.* 980, οὐδ' ἵκεθ' ὡς κατέκτανεν.

132. ἀλλ' ἐξ ὑπαρχῆς αὖθις αὖτ' ἐγὼ φανῶ.

αὖθις, 'as he had done in the case of the Sphinx' (Jebb). I doubt. Rather 'recommencing the search.' Cp. *supr.*, δοκοῦντα ταῦτ' ἦν, and *infr.* 567, (ἔρευναν) παρέσχομεν, πῶς δ' οὐχί;

134. πρὸς τοῦ θανόντος τήνδ' ἔθεσθ' ἐπιστροφήν.

Jebb is perhaps right in reading πρό. But I still think that πρός may mean 'on behalf of' (lit. 'towards')—ἐπιστροφήν is *sudden* regard, implying change of attitude, as in *Phil.* 598, 599, quoted in my note.

τίνος δ' Ἀτρεῖδαι τοῦδ' ἄγαν οὕτω χρόνῳ
τοσῷδ' ἐπεστρέφοντο πράγματος χάριν;

138. ἀλλ' αὐτὸς αὐτοῦ, τοῦτ' ἀποσκεδῶ μύσος.

The facsimile of L. shows αὑτοῦ, though the breathing may have been altered by an early corrector.

153. ἐκτέταμαι, φοβερὰν φρένα δείματι πάλλων.

The note in my edition agrees with Jebb, except that 'I am racked' should be read for 'I lie outstretched.' The smaller edition (*CA*) should be corrected accordingly. φρένα ... πάλλων is an instance of the personal construction, like αἴρει θυμόν, *infr.* 914, and the like.

156. Cp. Eur. *Alc.* 449, ἁνίκα ... περινίσσεται ὥρα.

157. ὦ χρυσέας τέκνον Ἐλπίδος, ἄμβροτε Φάμα.

I still think that the phrase is propitiatory, like ἀδυεπές *supra*. The epithet χρυσέας hardly suits with a doubtful expectation.

OEDIPUS TYRANNUS 89

159. πρῶτά σε κεκλόμενος, θύγατερ Διός, ἄμβροτ' Ἀθάνα.
For κεκλόμενος, cp. Aesch. *Suppl.* 40.

νῦν δ' ἐπικεκλομένα | Διὸς πόρτιν ...

resumed in the antistrophe, ὄντ' ἐπιλεξαμένα ...

165. For ὕπερ, cp. also Eur. *Androm.* 317, σῆς ἁμαρτίας ὕπερ.

170.   νοσεῖ δέ μοι πρόπας στόλος, οὐδ' ἔνι φροντίδος ἔγχος.
Here again my large edition agrees with Jebb against *CA*.
φροντίδος ἔγχος — well explained by Jebb as μηχανὴ ἀλεξητηρία.

173.   οὔτε τόκοισιν
            ἰηίων καμάτων ἀνέχουσι γυναῖκες·

τόκοισιν. The scholion ἐν τοῖς τόκοις is supported by τόκοισι, *supr.* 26.

186. For λάμπει, cp. Eur. *Phoen.* 1377, ἀφείθη πυρσὸς ὣς Τυρσηνικῆς | σάλπιγγος ἠχή.

189. Cp. Eur. *El.* 879, ἴτω ξύναυλος βοὰ χαρᾷ.

196.   εἴτ' ἐς τὸν ἀπόξενον ὅρμον.
For ἀπόξενον ὅρμον, cp. *Phil.* 217, ναὸς ἄξενον ὅρμον.

198.   τέλει γὰρ εἴ τι νὺξ ἀφῇ.
I still hold to my defence of the traditional reading, and the explanation of the Scholiast: εἰ γάρ τι ἡ νὺξ ἀφῇ ἐπὶ τῷ ἑαυτῆς τέλει ἀβλαβὲς μὴ φθάσασα αὐτὸ ἀπολέσαι, τοῦτο μεθ'

ἡμέραν ἀνήρπασται, 'For if Night at her close leave anything unharmed, this day assails' (ἐπέρχεται). I do not believe that such a temporal (or quasi-locative) use of the dative is beyond the limits of Sophoclean idiom. For ἐπέρχεσθαι with accus. see *L.* and *S. s. v.*

200. τόν, ὦ [—] πυρφόρων.

In my first edition (1871) I suggested that the interjection might be prolonged in delivery, so as to fill the time of a spondee ⌊⌋. I still think this possible.

214. ἀγλαῶπι — ⌣ —
πεύκᾳ.

For the 'lost Cretic' I have long since suggested μαινόλαν, which may have been dropped through the neighbourhood of μαινάδων.

219-221. ἀγὼ ξένος μὲν τοῦ λόγου τοῦδ' ἐξερῶ,
ξένος δὲ τοῦ πραχθέντος. οὐ γὰρ ἂν μακρὰν
ἴχνευον αὐτό(ς), μὴ οὐκ ἔχων τι σύμβολον.

Jebb makes a valuable contribution in his Appendix to the elucidation of these lines, by disposing of the assumption of the 'suppressed protasis,' according to which οὐ γὰρ ἄν must always be rendered: 'For *else* (if I had not been a stranger) not.' A good example is *Phil.* 867-871.

τό τ' ἐλπίδων
ἄπιστον οἰκούρημα τῶνδε τῶν ξένων.
οὐ γάρ, ποτ', ὦ παῖ, τοῦτ' ἂν ἐξηύχησ' ἐγώ.

On the other hand, the whole sentence, especially μὴ οὐκ in 221, requires a preceding negative expressed or implied, much as in *Phil. l.c.* οὐ γάρ . . . ἐγώ gives the reason for ἐλπίδων ἄπιστον. And this requirement is met by ξένος, 'I was a stranger to the affair, for I could not have traced it.' (οὐ μακράν = 'not at all,' is an idiomatic *litotes*, for which cp.

El. 323, ἐπεὶ τἄν οὐ μακρὰν ἔζων ἐγώ='I could not have lived.') On this view, however, the case in favour of αὐτός (Γ) against αὐτό (sc. τὸ πραχθέν), the reading of L. is less clear than I once thought it. The emphasis on ἴχνευον is sufficient: 'How could I investigate a matter of which I had had no hint?' I should now read αὐτό, which supplies an object for the verb.

227-229.   κεἰ μὲν φοβεῖται, τοὐπίκλημ' ὑπεξελὼν
αὐτὸς καθ' αὑτοῦ· πείσεται γὰρ ἄλλο μὲν
ἀστεργὲς οὐδέν, γῆς δ' ἄπεισιν ἀσφαλής.

ὑπεξαιρεῖν is clearly, as explained by Jebb, 'to remove,' 'take out of the way.' See esp. Plat. *Rep.* viii. 567 *b*, ὑπεξαιρεῖν δὴ τούτους πάντας δεῖ τὸν τύραννον; and Thuc. viii. 70 § 2, ἄνδρας δέ τινας ἀπέκτειναν οὐ πολλούς, οἳ ἐδόκουν ἐπιτήδειοι εἶναι ὑπεξαιρεθῆναι. The language is much condensed, and the most probable construction is indicated by the interlinear gloss (over καθ' αὑτοῦ in L.) 'σημαινέτω' '(Let him act) by removing the guilt (and so informing) against himself.' The remaining words are in connection with ὑπεξελών: 'By taking the guilt away with him. Nothing further shall be done to his annoy. His departure shall be secure from scathe.' ἀσφαλής in poetry has more of the original meaning—'without failure or falling'—than in ordinary prose: *e.g.* Pind. *P.* iii. 153, αἰὼν δ' ἀσφαλής ('unharmed'), οὐκ ἔγεντ' οὔτ' Αἰακίδᾳ παρὰ Πηλεῖ οὔτε παρ' ἀντιθέῳ Κάδμῳ; *O. C.* 1288, ἀσφαλεῖ σὺν ἐξόδῳ. This *nuance* of difference may have lead to the *v.l.* ἀβλαβεῖ, perhaps due originally to a gloss.

230.   εἰ δ' αὖ τις ἄλλον οἶδεν ἐξ ἄλλης χθονὸς
τὸν αὐτόχειρα, μὴ σιωπάτω.

After the general injunction in 224-226, two special cases are indicated: (1) that of the murderer himself; (2) that of one (whether Theban or stranger) who knows that some resident alien is the guilty man. It is rather assumed that such an informant would be himself a foreigner; hence the assurance of reward and of special favour. ἄλλον, *i.e.* 'other than himself,' distinguished from αὐτός *supra*.

258. ἀλλ' ἐξερευνᾶν· νῦν δ', ἐπεὶ κυρῶ τ' ἐγώ.
I would now read κυρῶ τ' with Jebb.

264. ἀνθ' ὧν ἐγὼ τάδ', ὥσπερεὶ τοὐμοῦ πατρός, ὑπερμαχοῦμαι.

ἀνθ' ὧν. The relative resumes the *protasis* in introducing the *apodosis*.

274. ἥ τε σύμμαχος Δίκη.
Cp. Aesch. *Suppl*. 380, ξύμμαχον δ' ἑλόμενος δίκαν.

276. For ἔλαβες, cp. also Her. iii. 74, πίστι τε λαβόντες καὶ ὁρκίοισι.

282. εἰ καὶ τρίτ' ἐστί, μὴ παρῇς τὸ μὴ οὐ φράσαι.
'If there is yet a third course.' So Jebb, with Kennedy, rightly. For δεύτερα, cp. Her. i. 59, and for ἐκ τῶνδε, *ib.* viii. 100, ἄλλην ἔχω καὶ ἐκ τῶνδε βουλήν.

287. ἀλλ' οὐκ ἐν ἀργοῖς οὐδὲ τοῦτ' ἐπραξάμην.
In J.'s note ἐπραξάμην certainly suggests the notion 'I have acted.' But I still think ἐν ἀργοῖς (ἐναργῶς L. pr.) means 'among things not done.' Cp. Eur. *Phoen.* 766, ἓν δ' ἐστὶν ἡμῖν ἀργόν, εἴ τι θέσφατον | οἰωνόμαντις Τειρεσίας ἔχει φράσαι. The phrase is an oxymoron.

288. ἔπεμψα γὰρ Κρέοντος εἰπόντος διπλοῦς πομπούς.
For διπλοῦς, cp. Aesch. *Prom*. 950, διπλᾶς | ὁδούς.

294. ἀλλ' εἴ τι μὲν δὴ *δειμάτων ἔχει μέρος.

δείματός γ' is probable, but δειμάτων, Hartung's conjecture, has something to recommend it. The vague generic plural suits the partitive genitive.

297. ἀλλ' οὐξελέγχων αὐτὸν ἔστιν.

The ξων above the line in L. is certainly not by *p. m.* nor by Σ. The fact that the fut. part. 'agrees with the regular idiom' is rather in favour of the harder reading, in which the present is for a *certain* future, as in Aesch. *Prom.* 513, ὧδε δεσμὰ φυγγάνω.

313. ῥῦσαι δὲ πᾶν μίασμα. Perhaps Professor Kennedy's suggestion, that μίασμα here means what is affected by pollution, deserves more attention than it has received.

317. For τέλη, cp. Eur. *fr.* 639, μάτην δ' ἂν οἴκῳ σὸν τόδ' ἐκβαίη τέλος.

337. ὀργὴν ἐμέμψω τὴν ἐμήν, τὴν σὴν δ' ὁμοῦ
ναίουσαν οὐ κατεῖδες.

Jebb thinks that the words contain an 'undoubted' allusion to Jocasta. The allusion was not intended by Teiresias; whether or not it passed through the mind of the poet is a question like that about Hamlet's 'too much i' the sun,' where Farmer and others have suspected a play of words on 'Son.'

350, 351. ἄληθες; ἐννέπω σὲ τῷ κηρύγματι
ᾧπερ *προεῖπας ἐμμένειν.

I prefer to take ᾧπερ as agreeing by attraction with κηρύγματι. So. *CA.*

360.   οὐχὶ ξυνῆκας πρόσθεν; ἢ 'κπειρᾷ *λόγῳ;

L., as it stands, has [λέγιν]. The scribe had written [λέοι] Correctors had suggested variants, one by writing over οι the compendium for ειν, another by inserting ο above λέ, [λέοι] Finally, some one who approved of

[λέγιν] changed οι to ειν (by adding a down stroke to ο and a curve to ι), and cancelled the compendium, now superfluous [λέγιν]. The forms of ει and ν thus produced do not appear elsewhere in the MS. The archetype probably gave [ ] Cp. *O. C.* 369,

λόγῳ σκοποῦσι τὴν πάλαι γένους φθοράν,

where λόγῳ is not opposed to ἔργῳ, but simply = 'in their talk,' or 'in argument' (*ut dicebant*, Linwood). Also Eur. *Ion,* 1406,

τάδ' οὐχὶ δεινά; ῥυσιάζομαι λόγῳ.

I saw this when consulting the MS. in 1867.

376. The *Oxyrhynchus Papyrus* (vol. i. *n.* xxii.) 'of about the 5th century A.D.,' has με . . . σοῦ—showing this to be an early corruption.

378. *Oxyr. Pap.* shows the variant κρέοντος, ἢ τοῦ.

380.   ὑπερφέρουσα τῷ πολυζήλῳ βίῳ.

I still rather prefer 'the much admired life' (such as mine has been; cp. Trach. 185, and line 1526 in my text). (1) When a rare word occurs twice in the same author, it is safer

OEDIPUS TYRANNUS

to give it the same meaning. (2) The epithet specialises the meaning—not=' life in general,' but 'such a life as mine.' Cp. also *Bacchyl.* i. 74; x. 63.

384. ἣν ἐμοὶ πόλις
δωρητόν, οὐκ αἰτητόν, εἰσεχείρισεν.

'δωρητόν, οὐκ αἰτητόν, feminine' (Jebb). Perhaps rightly, though the neuter is also idiomatic.

401, 402. κλαίων δοκεῖς μοι καὶ σὺ χὡ συνθεὶς τάδε
ἀγηλατήσειν.

ἀγηλατήσειν. The smooth breathing (Jebb) appears to be right.

403. παθὼν ἔγνως ἂν οἷά περ φρονεῖς.

For the meaning given as an alternative in *CA.* ('your punishment should suit with your intents'). Cp. Eur. *Hec.* 330, 331,

ὡς ἂν ἡ μὲν Ἑλλὰς εὐτυχῇ,
ὑμεῖς δ' ἔχηθ' ὅμοια τοῖς βουλεύμασιν.

411. ὥστ' οὐ Κρέοντος προστάτου γεγράψομαι.

Κρέοντος. For the gen., cp. Eur. *Ion.* 311, Λοξίου κεκλήμεθα.

: οὐ :

430. *Oxyr. Pap.*, οὐχὶ θᾶσσον αὖ πάλιν, 433, *Oxyr. Pap.*, ᾔδειν.

434. ἐστειλάμην. Cp. Eur. *Iph. A.* 1355, κἀργόθεν γ' ἐπέμψατο.

96 *PARALIPOMENA SOPHOCLEA*

445, 446. κομιζέτω δῆθ'· ὡς παρὼν σύ γ' ἐμποδὼν
ὀχλεῖς, συθείς τ' ἂν οὐκ ἂν ἀλγύνοις πλέον.

I would now read σύ γ' with the majority of MSS. and Jebb, and ἀλγύνοις with Elmsley.

455, 456. καὶ πτωχὸς ἀντὶ πλουσίου ξένην ἐπὶ
σκήπτρῳ προδεικνὺς γαῖαν ἐμπορεύσεται.

'The order of words is against taking ξένην with γαῖαν' (Jebb). I doubt this. For somewhat similar dislocation, see 644, 645, 1251.

457, 458. φανήσεται δὲ παισὶ τοῖς αὑτοῦ ξυνὼν
ἀδελφὸς αὑτὸς καὶ πατήρ.

It is still not quite certain that αὑτός should be changed to αὐτός. In Jebb's parallels τε ... καί are combined. Cp. Plat. *Polit.* 268 a, αὑτὸς ... τροφός ... αὑτὸς ἰατρός, αὑτὸς ... νυμφευτής ...

466. ὥρα νιν ἀελλάδων
ἵππων σθεναρώτερον
φυγᾷ πόδα νωμᾶν.

ἀελλάδων ἵππων. Cp. *fr.* 626, ἀελλάδες φωναί, Eur. *Bacch.* 873 (νεβρὸς) ἀελλὰς | θρώσκει πεδίον, *Bacchyl.* v. 39, πῶλον ἀελλοδρόμαν.

478. ἀνά τ' ἄντρα καὶ
πέτραισιν *ὕπαυλος.

I still feel that the image of the bull is too violent here, and that ἰσόταυρος—*pace* the ghost of my revered teacher, E. L. Lushington,—is a *vox nihili*. In similar compounds ἴσος implies equality of rank (ἰσόθεος, ἰσόδουλος), or of force (ἰσοθάνατος)—the point here is not fierceness but misery.

OEDIPUS TYRANNUS

I revert to the conjecture which I proposed in 1871, 'and sheltering among rocks' (locative dative). In *Aj.* 796, σκηνῆς ὕπαυλον the genitive is used, but that does not preclude the dative here. Else πέτραισιν ἔναυλος, though less close to the *ductus litterarum*, would do equally well. I must admit, however, that the remainder of the antistrophe, especially l. 482, is in harmony with the figure of the vanquished bull. The word ἀτιμαγέλας in *fr.* 922 is explained, ὁ ἀποστάτης τῆς ἀγέλης ταῦρος, οὕτω Σοφοκλῆς. Is it possible that some early glossator on the present passage was reminded of this compound and brought in ὡς ταῦρος here?

481, 482.   τὰ δ' ἀεὶ
ζῶντα περιποτᾶται.

Cp. Eur. *Hipp.* 563 f.
δεινὰ γὰρ πάντᾳ ποτιπνεῖ (ἁ Κύπρις), μέλισσα δ'
οἷα τις πεπόταται.

490.   τί γὰρ ἢ Λαβδακίδαις ἢ
τῷ Πολύβου νεῖκος ἔκειτ'.

ἔκειτο in plup. passive of τίθημι in the sense of 'to cause' (L. and S. *s. v.* B. iii. 2). Cp. *Od.* 3, 136.

ἥ τ' ἔριν 'Ατρείδῃσι μετ' ἀμφοτέροισιν ἔθηκε.

493, 494.   ἔμαθον, πρὸς ὅτου δὴ ‿ ‿ – – βασάνῳ.

Jebb's emendation is the most probable of those hitherto suggested. But I am inclined to say '*locus nondum sanatus.*' Accepting Jebb's construction, I think that a better word than βασανίζων might be found (προσομιλῶν? *Trach.* 591).

525.   τοῦ πρὸς δ' ἐφάνθη ταῖς ἐμαῖς γνώμαις ὅτι
πεισθεὶς ὁ μάντις τοὺς λόγους ψευδεῖς λέγοι;

Jebb's statement that 'the anastrophe of πρός seems to be confined to instances in which it is immediately followed by an attributive genitive, equivalent to an epithet,' is difficult to refute. In Ar. *Eq.* 32, the reading ποῖον βρέτας πρός; is due to a conjecture of Dindorf's, which is censured by Blaydes and others as 'far from probable.' But may not the unusual inversion be occasioned by the strong emphasis on the interrogative word, which consequently begins the sentence? (Observe that ὅτι is also postponed through emphasis.) Creon's indignation and amazement are thus more naturally expressed than in τοὔπος δ' ἐφάνθη. Creon asks 'from whom came the suggestion?' To which the Chorus reply, 'The thing was said indeed, but I cannot tell you on what ground or authority.'

532.   οὗτος· σὺ πῶς δεῦρ' ἦλθες; ἢ τοσόνδ' ἔχεις

The punctuation of L. was altered by the hand which supplied the accents, perhaps Σ. But I still prefer οὗτος· σὺ πῶς—without denying that οὗτος σύ may be the phrase elsewhere.

557.   καὶ νῦν ἔθ' αὐτός εἰμι τῷ βουλεύματι.

In defence of the rendering, 'I still hold to the advice I gave,' it may be urged that βούλευμα is counsel given, not present opinion. Not 'I am still giving the same advice.' Cp. *Phil.* 521 (μή) . . . τότ' οὐκέθ' αὐτὸς τοῖς λόγοις τούτοις φανῇς.

579.   ἄρχεις δ' ἐκείνῃ ταὐτὰ γῆς, ἴσον νέμων;

Jebb's punctuation is probably right. Cp. Eur. *Phoen.* 547, 548.

σὺ δ' οὐκ ἀνέξει δωμάτων ἔχων ἴσον
καὶ τῷδ' ἀπονεμεῖς;

584-586.   σκέψαι δὲ τοῦτο πρῶτον, εἴ τιν' ἂν δοκεῖς
ἄρχειν ἑλέσθαι ξὺν φόβοισι μᾶλλον ἢ
ἄτρεστον εὕδοντ', εἰ τά γ' αὔθ' ἕξει κράτη.

OEDIPUS TYRANNUS

Cp. Eur. *Hipp.* 1019, 1020.

> πράσσειν τε γὰρ πάρεστι, κίνδυνός τ' ἀπὼν
> κρείσσω δίδωσι τῆς τυραννίδος χάριν.

The parallel thought in Her. v. 106 is obvious.

596.   νῦν πᾶσι χαίρω, νῦν με πᾶς ἀσπάζεται.

νῦν πᾶσι χαίρω. There is little difference between 'in the sight of all,' and 'with the consent of all' (Jebb). The construction is the same in either case, an ethical dative. I agree with Jebb that 'the phrase has been suggested by χαῖρέ μοι, but refers to the meaning, rather than to the form of the greeting,' for which cp. especially Eur. *Hec.* 426, 427.

> — χαῖρ', ὦ τεκοῦσα, χαῖρε Κασάνδρα τέ μοι.
> — χαίρουσιν ἄλλοι, μητρὶ δ' οὐκ ἔστιν τόδε.

Aesch. *Ag.* 538, 539.

> — κῆρυξ Ἀχαιῶν χαῖρε τῶν ἀπὸ στρατοῦ.
> — χαίρω· τεθνᾶναι δ' οὐκ ἔτ' ἀντερῶ θεοῖς.

614, 615.   χρόνος δίκαιον ἄνδρα δείκνυσιν μόνος,
κακὸν δὲ κἂν ἐν ἡμέρᾳ γνοίης μιᾷ.

Cp. *fr.* 59.

> ἀλλ' οὐδὲν ἕρπει ψεῦδος εἰς γῆρας χρόνου.

Eur. *fr.* 60.

> χρόνος δὲ δείξει σ'. ᾧ τεκμηρίῳ μαθὼν
> ἢ χρηστὸν ὄντα γνώσομαι σέ γ' ἢ κακόν.

fr. adespot. 512.

> ἀλλὰ ταῦτα μὲν χρόνος
> δείξει· μόνος γάρ ἐστιν ἀνθρώπων κριτής.

Pind. *Ol.* x (xi.) 66, ὅ τ' ἐξελέγχων μόνος ἀλάθειαν ἐτήτυμον χρόνος.

100 PARALIPOMENA SOPHOCLEA

617.   φρονεῖν γὰρ οἱ ταχεῖς οὐκ ἀσφαλεῖς.

Cp. Eur. *fr.* 1032.

τὸ δ' ὠκὺ τοῦτο καὶ τὸ λαιψηρὸν φρενῶν
εἰς πημονὰς καθῆκε πολλὰ δὴ βροτούς.

622-625.   ΚΡ. τί δῆτα χρῄζεις; ἦ με γῆς ἔξω βαλεῖν;
ΟΙ. ἥκιστα· θνῄσκειν οὐ φυγεῖν σε βούλομαι
ὅταν προδείξῃς οἷόν ἐστι τὸ φθονεῖν.
[*ΚΡ.] ὡς οὐχ ὑπείξων οὐδὲ πιστεύσων λέγεις;

If my interpretation of ὅταν προδείξῃς is rejected as 'straining the sense,' Jebb's ὡς ἄν must be admitted. In every other point we are agreed. But is my interpretation so impossible, if considered in the light of *Ant.* 308, 309? I doubt it. For προδεικνύναι='to show beforehand by an example,' see Thuc. iii. 47, § 3, προδειξάντων ὑμῶν τὴν αὐτὴν ζημίαν... κεῖσθαι. I submit that my *cheville*, [625. *ΟΙΔ. σὺ δ' ὥς γε τἀμὰ πάντ' ἀτιμάσων κράτη] leads up naturally enough to the rejoinder of Creon in 626.

628.   ΚΡ. εἰ δὲ ξυνίης μηδέν; ΟΙ. ἀρκτέον γ' ὅμως.

It makes little difference whether the verbal adjective is considered as 'abstract' (=δεῖ ἄρχειν) or 'impersonal' (=δεῖ ἄρχεσθαι). I make no objection to the former view.

640.   δρᾶσαι δικαιοῖ, δυοῖν ἀποκρίνας κακοῖν.

Jebb's emendation, δυοῖν δικαιοῖ δρᾶν ἀπ. κ., is at least plausible, but not, I think, necessarily required.

657.   σὺν ἀφανεῖ λόγῳ †ἄτιμον βαλεῖν.

For the hiatus, cp. *Ant.* 1319.

ἐγὼ γάρ σ' ἐγὼ ἔκανον, ὦ μέλεος.

666, 667. τάδ' εἰ κακοῖς κακὰ
προσάψει τοῖς πάλαι τὰ πρὸς σφῷν.

I do not see the ground for preferring τὰ δ' to τάδ'. Can τὰ δὲ mean 'other' without a preceding τὰ μὲν expressed or implied? Why may not τάδε point to the approaching threatened evil, more fully expressed in τὰ πρὸς σφῷν? προσάψει seems to me more pathetic if taken actively, continuing γῇ as subject. It is an instance of *personal* expression. τὰ πρὸς σφῷïν in *CA*. is indefensible. The flaw is probably in the antistrophe.

673. Cp. Eur. *Med*. 38, βαρεῖα γὰρ φρήν, οὐδ' ἀνέξεται κακῶς | πάσχουσα.

691. πεφάνθαι μ' ἄν, εἴ σε νοσφίζομαι.

Jebb accepts Hermann's conjecture εἴ σ' ἐνοσφιζόμαν. I cannot think this necessary. πεφάνθαι μ' ἄν may surely be oblique for πεφασμένος ἄν εἴην (not ἦν).

696. τὰ νῦν τ' εὔπομπος αὖ γένοιο.

Thus I would try to improve upom Blaydes' emendation of this line. The wish is less tame than the assertion. But Meineke's expedient of reading πρὸς φίλων for πρὸς σφῷν in the strophe, also deserves consideration.

707. σύ νυν ἀφεὶς σεαυτὸν ὧν λέγεις πέρι.

'Absolve thyself of the things whereof thou speakest,' Jebb. I do not think there is any allusion to the legal sense of ἀφίεναι. I believe the phrase to be equivalent to ἀφεὶς σεαυτοῦ (ταῦτα) ὧν λέγεις πέρι, 'Dismissing these thoughts from thy mind.' (Eur. *Or*. 1022, ἀφεῖσα τοὺς γυναικείους γόους), or more literally, 'casting thyself loose from them.'

For such inversion, see above, Introd. p. x.

709.   μάθ' οὕνεκ' ἐστί σοι
βρότειον οὐδὲν μαντικῆς ἔχον τέχνης.

Jebb rejects the view held by many previous scholars in accordance with an early gloss in L., that ἔχον was here used exceptionally as nearly = ἐχόμενον: ('Non pendent res humanae a vaticiniis,' Linwood). Yet if this were admissible, it would, I think, yield a better sense. The parallels quoted from Herodotus (including vii. 143, § 2) and Aeschylus are not exactly in point, but they show a singular freedom in the use of ἔχειν. And the use in *Aj.* 320 as interpreted by Jebb comes very near to this. The instinct of a scholar may sometimes recognise an unique expression. So Brunck here says 'inusitatum locutionis genus.' Dindorf's note runs 'hoc dicit, res humanas nihil commune habere cum arte vatum, *i.e.* non pendere ab eâ.' Is the meaning 'nothing in mortality *holds* of divination' after all impossible? Several uses of the active voice, where the middle would be more natural, occur in Sophocles: *e.g.* ἄξοντα (*O.C.* 134), μηχανᾶν (*Aj.* 754) τιμωρεῖν, *supr.* 140.

717.   παιδὸς δὲ βλάστας οὐ διέσχον ἡμέραι

L. has a point after βλάστας· (*sic*) with an interlinear gloss by Σ διῆλθον. Another hand has added a different gloss διεδέξαντο, implying a transitive use. It is clear that the ancient interpreters were puzzled. I believe that διέχειν is here used transitively, in a sense corresponding to the intransitive Homeric use (cp. Her. vii. 122), and that βλάστας means not 'birth' but 'growth,' as of a seedling plant. 'Three days had not continued the budding life of the child, when,' etc. Otherwise (2) with the same meaning, and a comma after βλάστας, 'as for the young child, three days had not run their course, when.' The other meaning of διέχειν, 'to hold apart,' is scarcely possible here.

OEDIPUS TYRANNUS

741. τίνα δ' ἀκμὴν ἥβης ἔχων.

(Sc. τοιαύτην φύσιν εἶχε). I do not think that Nauck's conjecture τίνος ἀκμὴν ἥβης is really required. The return to the participle is idiomatic: cp. *infr.* 933, 935; and Her. vi. 13, § 2; vii. 89, § 2; περὶ μὲν τῇσι κεφαλῇσι κυνέας εἶχον, . . ., ἐνδεδυκότες δὲ θώρηκας λινέους, *ib.* 91, λαισήϊα δ' εἶχον ἀντ' ἀσπίδων ὠμοβοέης πεποιημένα, καὶ κιθῶνας εἰρινέους ἐνδεδυκότες. The alteration rather spoils the grace of the implied compliment: ('He was young and vigorous of course.') Dante in the *Convito* sub. init. sets the limit of youth at 45. Oedipus hopes to hear of one far different from the feeble greybeard whom he remembers.

763. κἄπεμψ' ἐγώ νιν. ἄξιος γὰρ *ὥς γ' ἀνήρ.

The σ of ὥς might easily be dropped before γ.

770. ἀξία δέ που μαθεῖν
κἀγὼ τά γ' ἐν σοὶ δυσφόρως ἔχοντ', ἄναξ.

I rather doubt ἐν σοί meaning simply 'in thy breast.' The parallels from Plato are not convincing.

780. καλεῖ παρ' οἴνῳ πλαστὸς ὡς εἴην πατρί.

Cp. Sositheus, *fr.* 2, l. 4 (Nauck p. 822).

οὗτος δ' ἐκείνου παῖς πατρὶ πλαστὸς νόθος.

790. καὶ δεινὰ καὶ δύστηνα προὐφάνη λέγων.

προὔφηνεν is perhaps more in keeping with the restraint of Sophoclean style; but προὐφάνη = 'announced with startling suddenness and clearness,' is more expressive of the agitation of Oedipus.

803. ἀνὴρ ἀπήνης ἐμβεβώς, οἷον σὺ φῄς.

οἷον, 'referring to Jocasta's whole description; not accusative masculine, referring to the person of Laius as described by her,' Jebb. I cannot agree. It was the description in 742-743, that wrung from Oedipus the exclamation οἴμοι τάλας. A point is lost, if this is not specially referred to here.

804-807.
κἀξ ὁδοῦ μ' ὅ θ' ἡγεμὼν
αὐτός θ' ὁ πρέσβυς πρὸς βίαν ἠλαυνέτην.
κἀγὼ τὸν ἐκτρέποντα, τὸν τροχηλάτην,
παίω δι' ὀργῆς.

Jebb supposes the herald to be the ἡγεμών. But it seems unlikely that τὸν ἐκτρέποντα should not refer to the man whose action was described in the two preceding lines. And it was the driver's business, more than that of the herald, to know the way. The herald's office was merely to mark the sacred nature of the expedition.

815. τίς τοῦδ' *ἔτ' ἀνδρὸς ἔστιν ἀθλιώτερος;

So *CA*. There is little to choose between this reading and Jebb's τίς τοῦδε νῦν ἔστ' ἀνδρὸς ἀθλιώτερος;

817. ᾧ μὴ ξένων ἔξεστι μηδ' ἀστῶν *τινά.

Jebb's reading here, ὅν . . . τινί, is more strictly logical. But the MS. text, 'For whom it is forbidden that any should receive him,' is more pointed.

832, 833. βαίην ἄφαντος πρόσθεν ἢ τοιάνδ' ἰδεῖν
κηλῖδ' ἐμαυτῷ συμφορᾶς ἀφιγμένην.

Cp. *fr.* adespot. 110.

καί με συμφορᾶς ἀεὶ
βαθεῖα κηλὶς ἐκ βυθῶν ἀναστρέφει.

OEDIPUS TYRANNUS

836. καὶ μὴν τοσοῦτόν γ' ἐστί μοι τῆς ἐλπίδος.

Jebb's comment, 'τῆς ἐλπίδος is hope in the abstract,' is probably right.

863, 864. εἴ μοι ξυνείη φέροντι
μοῖρα τὰν εὔσεπτον ἁγνείαν λόγων.

φέροντι = 'φερομένῳ,' Jebb (in the sense of 'winning'). This may be right, but I still incline to the other view = 'bearing about with me,' or 'within me' which Jebb thinks 'too bold.'

870. οὐδὲ μή ποτε λάθα κατακοιμάσῃ.

Jebb, in his first edition, agreed with mine in reading οὐδὲ μὰν ... κατακοιμάσει. The difference is slight, and I make no objection to his reconsidered judgment.

876, 877. *ἀκρότατον εἰσαναβᾶσ'
ἀπότομον *ἐξώρουσεν εἰς ἀνάγκαν.

Jebb's reading of these lines, adopted from the conjectures of G. Wolff and Schnelle, is very ingenious and plausible; but I hesitate to accept it.

(1) Wolff's ἀκρότατα γεῖσ' ἀναβᾶσ', recalling the fate of Capaneus, appears to me too precise and definite for Sophoclean imagery; see above, note on 478. It takes somewhat from the sublimity of the conception of Pride, falling from a towering height till 'her feet stumble upon the dark mountains' (Jeremiah xiii. 16). For the vagueness of ἀκρότατον, cp. Plat. *Theaet.* 175 *d*, ἀφ' ὑψηλοῦ; *Rep.* vii. 518 *b*, εἰς φανότερον ἰοῦσα ὑπὸ λαμπροτέρου μαρμαρυγῆς ἐμπέπλησται; *Phaedo* 89 *b*, ἐπὶ πολὺ ὑψηλοτέρου.

(2) In the only instance quoted for the superlative of ἄποτμος, it is followed by a genitive, 'most luckless of men.' From that to the absolute use is a doubtful step. Nor does the superlative add to the strength of the expression.

In defence of my conjectural reading I would urge (1) that in a word of four short syllables the ictus may count as lengthening the syllable on which it falls. For the effect of ictus on quantity, see especially Eur. *Phoen.* 796, θίασον, answered by δώματα in the antistrophe; *Bacchyl.* iii. 64, ὦ μεγαίνητε Ἱέρων. (2) That Sophocles' fondness for verbs compounded with ἐξ is well known, and here the correspondence of ἐξ to εἰς is effective. Prof. E. L. Lushington ingeniously conjectured ἀπότομον <ὄρος>, ὤρουσεν, in which, however, the phrasing is somewhat awkward.

890.   καὶ τῶν ἀσέπτων ἔρξεται.

Cp. *fr.* 49, ἄσεπτον· ἀσεβές. Σοφοκλῆς αἰχμαλωτίσιν (Hesych. i. p. 568). And, for ἔρξεται with gen., Her. vii. 197, § 5, Ξέρξης ... ὡς κατὰ τὸ ἄλσος ἐγένετο, αὐτός τε ἔργετο αὐτοῦ.

891.   ἦ τῶν ἀθίκτων ἕξεται ματᾴζων.

Blaydes' conjecture, θίξεται, is ingenious, but I cannot think it 'certain.' At the risk of condemnation for bad taste I prefer ἕξεται as stronger and as calling up the image of perverseness in holding fast by things forbidden. Cp. the figure in *Ant.* 854, 855,

ὑψηλὸν ἐς Δίκας βάθρον
προσέπεσες, ὦ τέκνον, πολύ,

and see Aesch. S. *c.* T. 98, βρετέων ἔχεσθαι: also Eur. *Iph. T.* 799, ἀθίκτοις περιβαλὼν πέπλοις χέρα.

892, 893.   τίς ἔτι ποτ' ἐν τοῖσδ' ἀνὴρ
            θεῶν βέλη ψυχᾶς *ἀμύνοι;

=**906, 907.**   φθίνοντα γὰρ Λαΐου
            θέσφατ' ἐξαιροῦσιν ἤδη.

Jebb's text here agrees with that adopted in *CA*. But I

OEDIPUS TYRANNUS

now revert to the view which I suggested in 1871, to reject ἔρξεται and read ἀμύνοι (potential optative) for ἀμύνειν, adopting, of course, Hermann's θεῶν for θυμῷ. (The gloss τὴν θείαν δίκην appears also, by an early hand, in L.)

For ἐν τοῖσδ', cp. Plat. *Tim.* 42 *b, c*, μὴ παυόμενος δὲ ἐν τούτοις ἔτι κακίας: and for τίς ... ἀμύνοι; Aesch. *Cho.* 594, τίς λέγοι; *Ant.* 605.

902, 903.   εἰ μὴ τάδε χειρόδεικτα
             πᾶσιν ἁρμόσει βροτοῖς.

That I am right in making τὰ φωνηθέντα the subject of ἥρμοσε in Plat. *Soph.* 262 *c*, is shown by the words which follow in 262 *d, e*, ἥρμοττε, ἁρμόττει, ἁρμόττοντα, all intransitive. Jebb's remark here was unnecessary and, I think, wrong.

914.   αἴρει θυμόν.   For the personal constr., cp. Bacchyl. i. 55, σαίνει κέαρ.

917.   εἰ φόβους λέγοι.

I take this to be the reading of L. p. m. The correction from εἰ to ἦν is clumsily made by another hand, but the v. l., ἦν ... λέγῃ, seems to have been previously written above the line.

921.   ὅπως λύσιν τιν' ἡμὶν εὐαγῆ πόρῃς.

For λύσιν, cp. esp. Eur. *Alc.* 214.

τίς ἂν πᾷ πόρος κακῶν
γένοιτο καὶ λύσις τύχας
ἃ πάρεστι κοιράνοις;

Neophron. *fr* 1, l. 1, καὶ γὰρ τιν' αὐτὸς ἤλυθον λύσιν μαθεῖν | σοῦ.

924, 925. ἆρ' ἂν παρ' ὑμῶν, ὦ ξένοι, μάθοιμ' ὅπου
τὰ τοῦ τυράννου δώματ' ἐστὶν Οἰδίπου;

The που of ὅπου is written by a second hand over an erasure.

946. ὦ θεῶν μαντεύματα.

Jebb says: 'Jocasta's scorn is pointed, not at the Gods themselves, but at the μάντεις.' This is hardly borne out by 953, τοῦ θεοῦ μαντεύματα.

954. οὗτος δὲ τίς ποτ' ἐστὶ καὶ τί μοι λέγει;

Jebb is right as to the force of the (ethical) dative (μοι).

957. τί φῄς, ξέν'; αὐτός μοι σὺ σημήνας γενοῦ.

σημάντωρ may be right, and is certainly an early variant. But the authorities quoted for the noun in this meaning are late, and σημήνας γενοῦ = 'Be so good as to inform me' seems idiomatic. Jebb's point, that this periphrasis is only used in prohibition, is at least questionable. If μὴ . . . ἀπαρνηθεὶς γένῃ (Plat. *Soph.* 217) is 'do not be guilty of refusing,' why may not σημήνας γενοῦ mean 'oblige me by telling'?

961. σμικρὰ παλαιὰ σώματ' εὐνάζει ῥοπή.

Cp. *fr.* adespot. 102.

> ἡ γὰρ τύχη βραχεῖαν ἢν λάβῃ ῥοπήν,
> ἢ τοὺς ταπεινοὺς . . .
> ἢ τοὺς ἀφ' ὕψους εἰς ζόφον κατήγαγεν.

975. μή νυν ἔτ' αὐτῶν μηδὲν ἐς θυμὸν βάλῃς.

μή νυν, Jebb. By all means (not μὴ νῦν).

OEDIPUS TYRANNUS

987.   καὶ μὴν μέγας *γ' ὀφθαλμὸς οἱ πατρὸς τάφοι.

ὀφθαλμός. Jebb's explanation combines the two notions which I gave as alternatives '"*a bright sudden comfort.*" . . . Not *merely* (though this notion comes in) "a great help to seeing" that oracles are idle.'

997.   ὧν οὕνεχ' ἡ Κόρινθος ἐξ ἐμοῦ πάλαι
μακρὰν ἀπῳκεῖτ'.

The view adopted by Jebb in his 2nd edition from Whitelaw is the same which I gave as an alternative in 1879: 'Corinth has been avoided (lived away from) by me= ἀπῴκουν Κορίνθου.' See above, Introd. p. x. The use of ἐξ with the passive verb is a little puzzling, but probably conveys the association of action from a distance. Cp. *supra*, 970.

οὕτω δ' ἂν θανὼν εἴη 'ξ ἐμοῦ.

1011.   ταρβῶ γε μή μοι Φοῖβος ἐξέλθῃ σαφής.

I still prefer ταρβῶ. The indicative is more forcible, because it withdraws attention from the fact to the motive.

1025.   σὺ δ' ἐμπολήσας ἢ τεκών μ' αὐτῷ δίδως;

I believe τεκών to be sound, for the reasons given in my note. It may also be said that there is a difference between τεκεῖν, to beget offspring, and γείνασθαι, to beget a son. See above, Introd. p. xi.

1031.   τί δ' ἄλγος ἴσχοντ' ἐν νάπαις με λαμβάνεις;

Of the many conjectures I prefer Wakefield's (and Dindorf's). The words are a natural echo of ἐν ναπαίαις . . . πτυχαῖς (1026). ἀγκάλαισι seems to me (1) irrelevant, (2) sentimental.

1062. θάρσει· σὺ μὲν γὰρ οὐδ' ἂν *εἰ τρίτης ἐγὼ
μητρὸς φανῶ τρίδουλος, ἐκφανεῖ κακή.

As said in my note, I am ready to admit οὐδ' ἐὰν τρίτης. But I am not sure that οὐδ' ἂν εἰ is wrong.

1075. μὴ 'κ τῆς σιωπῆς τῆσδ' ἀναρρήξῃ κακά.

ἀναρρήξῃ. To the gloss of the Scholist ἐργάσηται a somewhat later hand has added ἀναδείξῃ εἰς φῶς κακά. I am convinced that both these early commentators were right. For (1) ῥηγνύναι, present tense, or ῥῆξαι, used intransitively, is without precedent. Yet this would be required in l. 1076, if ἀναρρήξῃ were intransitive; and (2) the fear, as in *Ant.* 767, is what the *person* who is gone forth may *do*. This being so, it seems better to read ἀναρρήξῃ (1 aor. subj.) with L. ἀναρρήξει κακὰ ἔπη would, of course, mean 'she will burst forth into reproaches.' But why should ἀναρρήξει κακά have any such meaning?

1084. Cp. *fr.* 100, τὸ γὰρ καλῶς | πεφυκὸς οὐδεὶς ἂν μιάνειεν λόγος.

1090. ἔσει τὰν αὔριον
πανσέληνον.

αὔριον, which has given some difficulty, is adequately explained by Wolff, as quoted in Jebb's note, with reference to the Pandian festival, which immediately followed the Dionysia.

1091. μὴ οὐ σέ γε καὶ πατριώταν Οἰδίπου
καὶ τροφὸν καὶ ματέρ' αὔξειν.

I do not feel that (ἡμᾶς) αὔξειν σε is 'impossibly harsh,' and the ambiguous collocation of πατριώταν *Οἰδίπουν is a harshness on the other side. There is difficulty either way, and Jebb's emendation is not lightly to be rejected.

1098. τίς σε, τέκνον, τίς σ' ἔτικτε τῶν μακραιώνων ἄρα.

*τᾶν for τῶν is probable.

1100. Πανὸς ὀρεσσιβάτα *που
προσπελασθεῖσ'.

I still think that Heath's conjecture *που προς is more probable than Lachmann's *πατρός. In the readings of 1090-1101, the text of Jebb's second edition agrees with mine.

1110, 1111. εἰ χρή τι κἀμὲ μὴ συναλλάξαντά πω,
πρέσβεις, σταθμᾶσθαι.

I rather prefer πρέσβυ, for the reasons given in my note of 1879. Oed. addresses the Coryphæus, who replies at l. 1117.

1113. ἔν τε γὰρ μακρῷ
γήρᾳ ξυνᾴδει τῷδε τἀνδρὶ σύμμετρος.

I still think that ξυνᾴδει is used absolutely: σύμμετρος, sc. ὤν.

1130. τόνδ' ὃς πάρεστιν· ἦ ξυνήλλαξάς τί πω;

It is true that in replies a previous construction is often continued after an interruption (*infr.* 1155 and note). But it seems more natural here that the question should be repeated with ἦ: '*Had* you ever to do with him?'

1151. λέγει γὰρ εἰδὼς οὐδέν, ἀλλ' ἄλλως πονεῖ.

ἄλλως πονεῖ: 'the theory which he labours to establish is a mere delusion.' Yes, but also 'he labours to a disastrous end'; 'he works against his own desire.'

1155. δύστηνος, ἀντὶ τοῦ; τί προσχρῄζων μαθεῖν;

δύστηνος: 'Hapless that thou art,' points to the coming 'disclosure' (Jebb). I cannot think so. It is a mere exclamation of distress, like τάλαινα in *O. C.* 318, 'Unhappy that I am,' to be tortured! Cp. also *Trach.* 377, ὦ δύστηνος, ἆρ' ἀνώνυμος | πέφυκεν . . . ;

1170. κἄγωγ' ἀκούειν, ἀλλ' ὅμως ἀκουστέον.

I do not think that ἀκούων is to be lightly rejected. 'I, too, in listening, am close on the horror.'

1175. τεκοῦσα τλήμων;

'The wretch' (Jebb) hardly hits the feeling of the passage. 'Had she the heart?'

1182. ἰοὺ ἰού· τὰ πάντ' ἂν ἐξήκοι σαφῆ.

The force of ἂν in the passages quoted by Jebb differs in degrees of probability. Here the inference is certain. For the verb cp. Her. vi. 80, συμβάλλομαι δ' ἐξήκειν μοι τὸ χρηστήριον.

1188. ὡς ὑμᾶς ἴσα καὶ τὸ μηδὲν ζώσας ἐναριθμῶ.

'ζώσας should not be taken as = "while you live." . . . ζώσας is a more forcible substitute for οὔσας' (Jebb). This view might be supported by *Trach.* 1107, 1108, κἂν τὸ μηδὲν ὦ | κἂν μηδὲν ἕρπω. But the other interpretation is not untenable. 'Lebend, aber ein Nichts' (Schneidewin).

OEDIPUS TYRANNUS

1193.   τὸ σόν τοι παράδειγμ' ἔχων.

I see no reason for reading τὸν σόν, or for departing from the explanation in my note. That the Scholiast took τὸ σόν substantively is rendered probable by the marginal gloss τὸ συμβεβηκός.

1198. For the change from 2nd to 3rd person, cp. *Bacchyl.* ix. 10-18.

1205, 1206.   τίς ἄταις ἀγρίαις τίς ἐν πόνοις
    ξύνοικος ἀλλαγᾷ βίου.

I now accept Hermann's transposition τίς ἄταις ἀγρίαις τίς ἐν πόνοις. But I think that the dative in ἄταις anticipates the ξυν of ξύνοικος, and that ἐν is added pleonastically. Cp. *Phil.* 185.

   ἔν τ' ὀδύναις ὁμοῦ
 λιμῷ τ' οἰκτρός.

1210, 1211.   παιδὶ καὶ πατρὶ
    θαλαμηπόλῳ πεσεῖν.

I prefer the old division of the lines, accounting for the 'irrational syllable' in πατρί (⏑) by the verse-ending. The 'cyclic dactyl' here seems questionable. And I still hold to the interpretation given in my note, 'In whose case the same wide harbour sufficed for father and son to enter rashly as a chambering bridegroom.' Laius and Oedipus had both been impetuous in marriage.

1214, 1215.   δικάζει τὸν ἄγαμον γάμον πάλαι
    τεκνοῦντα καὶ τεκνούμενον.

I still prefer: 'Convicts (thee) as all this while (πάλαι) at once begetter and begotten in that unholy wedlock'; the ellipse of σε as well as the asyndeton being excused by the intensity of the language. L. has an early marginal gloss: Τεκνοῦντα ὅθεν ἐγεννώθης (sic).

1216. ἰὼ Λαΐειον [—] τέκνον.

Λαΐήιον τέκνον seems to me *slightly* preferable to Λαΐειον [ὦ] τέκνον.

1218, 1219. δύρομαι γὰρ ὡς
περίαλλ' *ἰακχίων
ἐκ στομάτων.

An early hand in L. has marked περίαλλα as a rare word (Σ περὶ ἄλλα), and a marginal gloss explains it 'ὑπερβολικῶς.'
I revert to Hermann's emendation. See Elmsley's note: ''Ιακχίων post Hermannum Erdfurtius, cum hac annotatione: *Voc.* ἰάκχιος, *formatum ab* ἰαχή (rather from ἴακχος), *Lexicis addendum.*' I am convinced that στομάτων cannot stand without an epithet. Cp. Eur. *Tro.* 829, ἴακχον οἰωνὸς οἷον τεκέων ὕπερ βοᾷ, 1230, στέναζε, μᾶτερ ... νεκρῶν ἴακχόν, *Hec.* 686.

αἰαῖ, κατάρχομαι γόων
βακχεῖον ἐξ ἀλάστορο·
ἀρτιμαθῆ νόμον.

Eur. *fr.* 586.

Θύσαν Διονύσου
κόραν, ὃς ἂν' Ἴδαν
τέρπεται, σὺν ματρὶ φίλᾳ
τυμπάνων ἰάκχοις.

(In various places where Porson or Hermann has restored ἰακχεῖν, the MSS. have ἰαχεῖν, as if from ἰαχή, Eur. *Or.* 826, 965, 1474, ἰακχᾷ.)

Eur. *fr.* 115.

τί ποτ' Ἀνδρομέδα περίαλλα κακῶν
μέρος ἐξέλαχον, θανάτου τλήμων
μέλλουσα τυχεῖν;

ὡς περίαλλα has been commonly explained by the analogy of ὡς μάλιστα, ὡς μέγιστα (*Phil.* 462), etc. And this is allowable, when it is understood that the ellipse in such cases is not of δυνατόν ἐστιν, as L. and S. affirm, but of the participle of the principal verb. So in *O. C.* 563, ὥς τις πλεῖστ᾽ ἀνὴρ ... ἠθέλησα=ὥς τις πλεῖστα ἀθλήσας, and so here δύρομαι ὡς περίαλλα=δύρομαι, ὡς περίαλλα ὀδυρόμενος. For an analogous use, cp. ᾇ τάχιστα (sc. πύθοιτ᾽ ἄν) in Pind. *Ol.* xiii. 791.

1221, 1222.   τὸ δ᾽ ὀρθὸν εἰπεῖν, ἀνέπνευσά τ᾽ ἐκ σέθεν
καὶ κατεκοίμησα τοὐμὸν ὄμμα.

τὸ δ᾽ ὀρθὸν εἰπεῖν: 'prefaces the bold figure of speech' (Jebb). But in lyric verse such a preface is tame and unnecessary. It is a concession, conveying a faint remnant of the loyalty so confidently asserted in 511, 512, 'To say truth of thee.' This coheres with the concluding words, if understood to mean—

'Thou gavest us relief and rest.'

'Und mir, in Wahrheit,
Zu erathmen halfest du,
Gabest dem Aug' endlich
Schlaferquicknung.'—(SOLGER.)

Sleep is often put for death (*El.* 509, Μυρτίλος ἐκοιμάθη, Eur. *Hec.* 473), but hardly for disaster.

1234, 1235.   ὁ μὲν τάχιστος τῶν λόγων εἰπεῖν τε καὶ
μαθεῖν, τέθνηκε θεῖον Ἰοκάστης κάρα.

The sentence τέθνηκε ... κάρα is the subject. Cp. Eur. *Ion*, 1538, ὁ θεὸς ἀληθὴς ἢ μάτην μαντεύεται ... ταράσσει ... φρένα.

1261.   ἐκ δὲ πυθμένων
ἔκλινε κοῖλα κλῇθρα.

Jebb decides in favour of the meaning to which I gave the

second place, 'that the bolts were torn from their staples.' He is probably right.

1269. περόνας.   Cp. Her. v. 87-89.

1276-1279.
φοίνιαι δ' ὁμοῦ
γλῆναι γένει' ἔτεγγον, οὐδ' ἀνίεσαν
φόνου μυδώσας σταγόνας, ἀλλ' ὁμοῦ μέλας
ὄμβρος χαλάζης *αἱματοῦς ἐτέγγετο.

Jebb practically decides in favour of the view taken in my edition, and more briefly expressed in *CA*: 'they did not send forth mere oozing drops of blood, but all at once the dark gory shower of hail was poured.' The only point left open is whether ὁμοῦ in 1276 is 'at the same moment' or 'together,' *i.e.* the pupils of both eyes. The former is stronger and more simple.

A doubt arises from the different meaning of οὐδ' ἀνίεσαν in *O. C.* 1608, 'and cease not from,' and it is accordingly proposed here to render 'they ceased not from wet drops of gore.' I was influenced by this view in my translation (1896). But, as observed in my note on *O. C. l.c.*, 'that οὐδ' ἀνίεσαν has probably a different meaning in *O. T.* 1277 is no objection to the above rendering.' See above, Introd. p. xi.

Cp. Eur. *Her. F.* 625, καὶ νάματ' ὅσσων μηκέτ' ἐξανίετε.

1280. τάδ' ἐκ δυοῖν ἔρρωγεν, οὐ μόνον, κακά.

οὐ μόνον *κάτα, the emendation made independently by Otto and Jebb, is very plausible.

1291. οὐδ' ἔτι
μενῶν δόμοις ἀραῖος, ὡς ἠράσατο.

Jebb is probably right in connecting δόμοις ἀραῖος, 'fraught with a curse for the house.' Cp. Eur. *Iph. T.* 778, ἢ σοῖς ἀραία δώμασιν γενήσομαι.

1293. Cp. Eur. *Hec.* 1107, κρείσσον' ἢ φέρειν κακά.

1294. δείξει δὲ καὶ σοί.

I still hesitate between making δείξει impersonal='you will see,' and taking Oedipus as a personal subject. Jebb decides for the latter, which in my edition is stated as an alternative. Cp. Eur. *Androm.* 822, δείξειν ἔοικεν ἡ τάλαιν' ὅσον στένει.

1303. φεῦ, δύστανος.

Jebb in his 2nd edition writes φεῦ, φεῦ, δύστην'. But the elision is hardly natural before so distinct a pause. And lamenting anapaests admit of more metrical freedom than the ordinary marching rhythm.

1310. *διαπωτᾶται φθογγὰ φοράδην.

So *CA*. I had myself thought independently of διαπωτᾶται, but I prefer the order given above to that in Jebb's edition.

1311. ἰὼ δαῖμον, ἵν' ἐξήλου.

I now read ἐξήλου (*CA*).

1315. ἀδάματόν τε καὶ δυσούριστ' *ἰόν.

Jebb's conjecture (*crit. n.*), δυσούριστ' ἰόν, was adopted in *CA*.

1329-1366.

1329, 1330. Ἀπόλλων τάδ' ἦν, Ἀπόλλων, φίλοι,
ὁ κακὰ, κακὰ τελῶν *ἐμοὶ τάδ' ἐμὰ πάθεα . .

=1349, 1350. ὄλοιθ' ὅστις ἦν ὃς ἀγρίας πέδας
νομάδος ἐπὶ *πόας ἔλυσ' ἀπό τε φόνου ...

Gottfried Hermann, no mean authority, recognised in this whole passage a combination of dochmiac with iambic and trochaic rhythms, extending even to single lines. I agree with Jebb in thinking ἔλυσ' in 1350 better than ἔλαβ'. But I doubt extremely whether ἔλυσ' ἀπό τε φόνου can be scanned as a dochmiac, corresponding to ἐμὰ τάδ' ἐμὰ πάθεα. I therefore propose to read in 1330

$$\breve{o}\ \kappa\breve{a}\kappa\breve{a}\ \kappa\breve{a}\kappa\breve{a}\ \tau\epsilon\lambda\bar{\omega}\nu \qquad | \qquad \breve{\epsilon}\mu o\grave{\iota}\ \bar{\tau}\acute{a}\delta'\ \breve{\epsilon}\mu\grave{a}\ \breve{\pi}\acute{a}\theta\epsilon a$$

a dochmiac combined with an iambic dipody.
And in 1350

$$\nu o\mu\acute{a}\delta o\varsigma\ \epsilon\pi\grave{\iota}\ \pi\acute{o}a\varsigma \qquad | \qquad \breve{\epsilon}\lambda\nu\sigma'\ \bar{a}\pi\acute{o}\ \tau\epsilon\ \phi\acute{o}\nu o\upsilon$$

The flaw in this line seems to me to lie in ἐπιποδίας—a clumsy epithet. Supposing a dittographia of A (ΠΟΑΑΣ), this would easily change to ΠΟΔΑΣ, and the insertion of an ι might follow. Cp. 1026.

ναπαίαις ἐν Κιθαιρῶνος πτυχαῖς.

When ἀπ' in l. 1349 is cancelled πέδας is seen to be accusative with ἔλυσε.

In l. 1341 I now read μέγ' ὀλέθριον with Erfurdt.

1345. τὸν καταρατότατον, *εἴ τις δὲ καὶ θεοῖς.

=1365. εἰ δέ τι πρεσβύτερον ἔφυ κακοῦ κακόν.

In *CA*, by an error perhaps due to collaboration, εἴ τις is marked with an obelisk instead of an asterisk. It is Hermann's emendation for ἔτι, which is the MS. reading. Reading ἔφυ with L in 1365, he regards the line as a combination of a dochmiac with 3 iambi (I refer to the edition of 1839). Cp. *supra*, note on 1330.

1347. ὡς σ' ἠθέλησα μηδ' ἀναγνῶναί ποτ' ἄν.

I retain the MS. reading, while admitting that there is much to be said for Hermann's correction, μηδέ γ' ἂν γνῶναι. I take the meaning of the traditional reading to be, 'How I could wish that you had never made the discovery' (of your birth). Sophocles may have remembered the Homeric uses, esp. *Od.* i. 216, οὐ γάρ πώ τις ἑὸν γόνον αὐτὸς ἀνέγνω. This gives a more poignant sense to τοῦ νοῦ *supra*. This was felt by the author of a later Scholion in L, ἄθλιε κατ' ἴσον ἕνεκα τῆς συμφορᾶς καὶ ἕνεκα τοῦ νοῦ καὶ τῆς ἐπινοίας καὶ ἕνεκα ὧν ἐπενοήσω. It would be easy to emend ὡς ἠθέλησ' ἂν μή σ' ἀναγνῶναί ποτε.

1354, 1355. τότε γὰρ ἂν θανών,
οὐκ ἦν φίλοισιν οὐδ' ἐμοὶ τοσόνδ' ἄχος.

I still take θανών as nom. pendens, and ἦν as 3rd person with ἄχος for subj. Cp. Eur. *Iph. T.* 695-698, and see *Aj.* 615 and note.

1362. ὁμογενὴς δ' ἀφ' ὧν αὐτὸς ἔφυν τάλας.

Jebb truly observes that ὁμογενὴς is not derived from γεννάω but from γένος = 'having a common offspring.' Cp. *supr.* 261, 262.

κοινῶν τε παίδων κοίν' ἄν, εἰ κείνῳ γένος
μὴ 'δυστύχησεν, ἦν ἂν ἐκπεφυκότα.

1365. εἰ δέ τι πρεσβύτερον ἔφυ κακοῦ κακόν.

ἔφυ MSS. See above, note on 1345.

1374. ἔργ' ἐστὶ κρείσσον' ἀγχόνης εἰργασμένα.

κρείσσον' ἀγχόνης: 'too bad for hanging,' Jebb. Rightly.

1388. οὐκ ἂν ἐσχόμην
τὸ μὴ 'ποκλῆσαι τοὐμὸν ἄθλιον δέμας.

μή, not μὴ οὐ, because of the hypothetical sentence.

1394, 1395. καὶ τὰ πάτρια
λόγῳ παλαιὰ δώμαθ'.

'Once called my father's ancient home,' Jebb. Rather, 'Home long ago in name my father's.'
Cp. *supr.* 1282, ὁ πρὶν παλαιὸς ὄλβος.

1401. For τι, cp. Eur. *Hec.* 992, εἰ τῆς τεκούσης τῆσδε μέμνηταί τί μου.

1405. ἀνεῖτε ταὐτὸν σπέρμα.

'It is absurd to suppose that *the seed sown by Oedipus* could be identified with Oedipus himself,' Jebb. I do not accept this criticism, and the emendation, *ταὐτοῦ, seems to me to extenuate the horror. The later offspring of Jocasta came of the same seed which she had formerly conceived by Laius. ἀνιέναι is said of *birth*, not of *begetting*: Aesch. *S. c. T.* 413.

1406. κἀπεδείξατε
πατέρας, ἀδελφούς, παῖδας, αἷμ' ἐμφύλιον.

αἷμ' ἐμφύλιον. I still think that the parricide is thrown in amongst the other horrors arising from the original marriage of Laius with Jocasta.

1413. For the fear deprecated in these words, cp. Eur. *Her. F.* 1161, 1162, 1219.

1433. ἄριστος ἐλθὼν πρὸς κάκιστον ἄνδρ' ἐμέ.

'Having come to me in so noble a spirit,' Jebb. Perhaps rightly.

1438. ἔδρασ᾽ ἂν εὖ τοῦτ᾽ ἴσθ᾽ ἄν.

'Join τοῦτ᾽' with ἴσθι,' Jebb. I think there is an alternation of clauses as in *Ant.* 682.

λέγειν φρονούντως ὧν λέγεις δοκεῖς πέρι.

1444. οὕτως ἆρ᾽ ἀνδρὸς ἀθλίου πεύσεσθ᾽ ὕπερ;

I take οὕτως ἄρα with πεύσεσθ᾽.

1446. καὶ σοί γ᾽ ἐπισκήπτω τε καὶ προτρέψομαι.

Jebb on προτρέψομαι: 'This strain of lofty admonition seems little in accord with the tone of the broken man.' But the speech down to 1457 is just in such a lofty strain. I adhere to my note. Exhortation rather than entreaty is the logical outcome of belief.

For the injunction, cp. Eur. *Her. F.* 1360, 1361, δὸς τούσδε τύμβῳ ... ἐμὲ γὰρ οὐκ ἐᾷ νόμος.

1463. αἷν οὔποθ᾽ ἡμὴ χωρὶς ἐστάθη βορᾶς
τράπεζ᾽ ἄνευ τοῦδ᾽ ἀνδρός.

Jebb's view of this passage, if I understand him rightly, is substantially the same as mine. Perhaps, however, αἷν (or οἷν) should be taken as a *genitive* with χωρίς. 'From whom my table was never set apart (that they should be) separate from me.' Arndt's ἄλλη is very ingenious.

1469. ἴθ᾽ ὦ γονῇ γενναῖε.

Jebb finds a difference between γονῇ γενναῖε and the phrases with which it is compared. There is a deeper feeling expressed, but the idiom is the same.

1482, 1483.   αἳ τοῦ φυτουργοῦ πατρὸς ὑμὶν ὧδ' ὁρᾶν
τὰ πρόσθε λαμπρὰ προὐξένησαν ὄμματα.

ὧδ' ὁρᾶν, 'to look with this sightless gaze.' So I now understand the words. Cp. *supr.* 419.

βλέποντα νῦν μὲν ὄρθ', ἔπειτα δὲ σκότον.

I was long divided between two ways of taking these apparently simple words:—

(1) 'Which have effected to your sorrow that your father's once bright eyes should see thus,' *i.e.* that they should not see. '*Effecerunt ut ita viderent*,' h.e. ut non viderent' (Linwood); and

(2) 'Which have provided for you this spectacle of your father's once bright eyes, that you should behold them thus.'

The objection which I felt to (1) was, that the dative after προξενεῖν ought not to be merely *ethical (dativus incommodi)*. That difficulty is removed by considering that the verb of sight with reference to eyes has in Greek an association of *reciprocity*. 'Which have procured it for you that the once brilliant eyes of your true father should look on you as now they do'—with the blank pathetic gaze of blindness.

1494, 1495.   τοιαῦτ' ὀνείδη λαμβάνων, ἃ τοῖς ἐμοῖς
γονεῦσιν ἔσται σφῷν θ' ὁμοῦ δηλήματα.

I retain the MS. reading. Laïus was involved in the πρώταρχος ἄτη. Jebb's emendation requires that γοναῖσιν should be repeated with σφῷν as genitive. This is surely unsimple. And for the effect of posthumous dishonour on the dead, see *El.* 1066 *f.*

OEDIPUS TYRANNUS

1513.   οὗ καιρὸς ἀεὶ ζῆν,* βίου δὲ λῴονος.

The conjectural οὗ καιρὸς ἐᾷ ζῆν τοῦ β.δ.λ., 'that ye live where occasion suffers,'—a poor prayer at best,—does away with the contrast between what Oedipus had experienced, and the lot which he desired for his daughters. In setting his face away from Corinth, in settling at Thebes, his life had been full of ἀκαιρία. For the omission of ἐστι, cp. *El.* 75 καιρὸς γάρ.

1520.   ἃ μὴ φρονῶ γὰρ οὐ φιλῶ λέγειν μάτην.

ἃ μὴ φρονῶ. Jebb, in his 2nd edition, says, 'I now think that, on the whole, it suits the context better to take them [the words] as expressing consent (ἃ μὴ φρονῶ = what I do not mean to do).' I doubt of this. Creon's attitude is rather that of non-committal.

1526.   *πρῶτος ἐν ζήλῳ πολιτῶν καὶ τύχαις *ἐπιφλέγων.

My conjectural emendation may appear more reasonable if I state how it occurred to me. I found in the Venetian MS. 468 (V) the reading ἐν ζήλῳ, and it struck me that ἐν ζήλῳ πολιτῶν had the ring of a real Greek phrase. Then at
οὐ ζήλῳ
Milan also I found likewise ἐν for οὐ, ἐν βίῳ M, the v. r. by a later hand. In another Ambrosian MS. (M²) οὐ is read, but *over an erasure*, and by a doubtful hand. Shortly afterwards at Paris, I think in E, I found the gloss ἐπαιρόμενος over ἐπιβλέπων. This seemed to give the trace of another reading, and in a sort of flash ἐπιφλέγων occurred to me. Retaining ὅστις, it still appeared necessary either to read ἐπέφλεγεν or to suppose a lacuna. At a later time, the indefinite pronoun seemed unsuitable, and I thought that if in some early MS. the lines had been ill divided (a thing which has occurred) and ΑΝΗΡΠΡῶΤΟΣ had been read, the letters ΠΡ might have been struck out as a dittographia, and the

remaining letters might suggest ὅστις to the mind of a scribe. I have since observed that L. also has a marginal gloss θαρρῶν, which is repeated in a confused scholion by a later hand, ὅστις κράτιστος ἦν δηλόνοτι οὐκ ἐπὶ εὐδαιμονίᾳ πολιτῶν καὶ εὐτυχίαις θαρρῶν ἀλλ' ἐπὶ τῇ ἑαυτοῦ δηλόνοτι ἀρετῇ. Also over ζήλῳ there is an interlinear gloss εὐδαιμονίᾳ.
For ἐπιφλέγων besides Pind. *Pyth.* ii. 45, cp. *Il.* xxi. 462-5, εἰ δὴ σοί γε βροτῶν ἕνεκα πτολεμίζω δειλῶν, οἳ φύλλοισιν ἐοικότες ἄλλοτε μέν τε ζαφλεγέες τελέθουσιν, ἀρούρης καρπὸν ἔδοντες, ἄλλοτε δὲ φθινύθουσιν ἀκήριοι, Pind. *Nem.* 38, χαρίτων ἑσπέριος ὁμάδῳ φλέγεν.

My view then is that the gloss εὐδαιμονίᾳ belongs to ἐν ζήλῳ πολιτῶν, and the glosses θαρρῶν, ἐπαιρόμενος, to ἐπιφλέγων.

1528, 1529. ὥστε, θνητὸν ὄντ', ἐκείνην τὴν τελευταίαν ἰδεῖν
ἡμέραν ἐπισκοποῦντα, μηδέν' ὀλβίζειν.

Jebb speaks of the infinitive ὀλβίζειν as a 'sententious imperative'. It comes to the same thing, if, in the manner of older grammarians, we say that there is an ellipse of δεῖν.

ELECTRA

It has not been sufficiently noted, that the Laurentian or Medicean MS., the earliest authority for the text of Aeschylus and Sophocles, consistently spells the name of Electra's mother Κλυταιμήστρα, not Κλυταιμνήστρα, and that not only in the text but in the scholia—72 times in all. Attention was first called to this fact, with regard to Aeschylus, by Girolamo Vitelli in his collation for Wecklein's edition of 1885, and with regard to Sophocles by M. Papageorgius in his brochure 'Κλυταιμήστρα οὐχὶ Κλυταιμνήστρα,' Constantinople, 1882. The latter scholar defends this orthography, in which both scribes and the writer of the Scholia are agreed, by the evidence of inscriptions and of Latin texts. The explanation given in the Etym. MS. is to the same effect.

21.   ὡς ἐνταῦθ' *ἴμεν,
    ἵν' οὐκέτ' ὀκνεῖν καιρός, ἀλλ' ἔργων ἀκμή.

Although *ἴμεν, Dawes' conjecture for ἐμὲν, is, of course, future in meaning, it may still be defended: 'Since the place whither we are about to go is one where action must be immediate and unhesitating.' The times of action and of deliberation are distinct. For uses of the future where the present might seem natural, see Jebb's note on *O.T.* 1077. And cp. esp. *Od.* 10, 431, ἆ δειλοί, πόσ' ἴμεν; *Il.* 23, 205, οὐχ ἕδος· εἶμι γὰρ αὖτις ἐπ' Ὠκεανοῖο ῥέεθρα; Eur. *Androm.* 627, εἶμι γὰρ κἀνταυθά σοι: *Iph. A.* 480, εἶμι δ' οὗπερ εἶ σὺ νῦν.

47. ἄγγελλε δ'ὅρκῳ προστιθείς.

In the Appendix to his Shakespeare Lexicon, Schmidt (p. 1424) quotes various instances where the 'whole relation of ideas is inverted.' See above, *General remarks*, p. , and cp. Eur. *El.* 894, ὡς δὲ τῷ σάφ' εἰδέναι τάδε | προσθῶμεν. For the conjectural reading *ὅρκον προστιθείς cp. *fr.* 431, ὅρκου δὲ προστεθέντος ἐπεμελεστέρα ψυχὴ κατέστη.

54. τύπωμα χαλκόπλευρον ἠρμένοι χεροῖν.

Jebb rightly points out that it is unnecessary to take ἠρμένοι as middle voice. The following parallels may be added: *Her.* I. 171, § 6, περὶ τοῖσι αὐχέσι τε καὶ τοῖσι ἀριστέροισι ὤμοισι [τελαμῶνας] περικείμενοι: Eur. *El.* 317.

>   Ἰδαῖα φάρη χρυσέαις ἐζευγμέναι
>   πόρπαισιν.

81. μείνωμεν αὐτοῦ κἀνακούσωμεν γόων;

I grant that Nauck's emendation κἀπακούσωμεν is highly plausible, but I do not see that ἀνακούω, following the analogy of ἀναπυνθάνομαι, is an impossible form.

92. τὰ δὲ παννυχίδων ἤδη στυγεραὶ
  ξυνίσασ' εὐναὶ μογερῶν οἴκων.

I should have thought that ἤδη was simply a temporal adverb with παννυχίδων, 'the nightly vigil,' when night comes.'

139. *θρήνοις οὔτε λιταῖσιν ἀνστάσεις.

The reading remains uncertain; but I am not ashamed of my attempted emendation. Perhaps the change from γόοις to θρήνοις was unnecessary.

152. αἰαῖ, δακρύεις.

That αἰαῖ is an echo of 136, the corresponding line of the strophe, makes somewhat in favour of this, the Laurentian reading.

157. οἷα Χρυσόθεμις ζώει καὶ Ἰφιάνασσα.

Does not οἷα imply something more than 'such as Chr. and Iph.'? Rather 'what sort of life is theirs'—an adverbial predicate.

158. κρυπτᾷ τ' ἀχέων ἐν ἥβᾳ.

I admit the doubt, whether ἀχέων is participle or gen. plural (as Hermann took it), but would urge in favour of the latter view, that the others, although bereaved, do not sorrow as Electra does. This, as regards Orestes, is supported by ὄλβιος following. For the genitive, cp. Eur. *Hipp.* 154, κρυπτὰ κοίτα λεχέων σῶν.

170.   τί γὰρ οὐκ ἐμοί
ἔρχεται ἀγγελίας ἀπατώμενον;

'What message that comes to me is not belied?'

Jebb here prefers the interpretation to which I gave the second place.

176. For νέμουσα, cp. Eur. *fr.* 634, ὅστις νέμει κάλλιστα τὴν αὑτοῦ φύσιν.

182. παῖς Ἀγαμεμνονίδας ἀπερίτροπος.

I do not admit that the alternative given in the Scholion is 'clearly erroneous'; nor is 'heedless' or 'regardless' quite equivalent to ἀνεπίστροφος. I believe that the literal and figurative meanings are combined. Orestes is one who will 'turn again' this way both in thought and act, and so is that other 'who rules as a god upon the shores of Acheron.' I am still inclined to understand this phrase of Agamemnon (θεός, predicative). It is an echo of Aesch. *Cho.* 356-8.

κατὰ χθονὸς ἐμπρέπων
σεμνότιμος ἀνάκτωρ
πρόπολός τε τῶν μεγίστων
χθονίων ἐκεῖ τυράννων.

Ib. 106, αἰδουμένῃ σοὶ βωμὸν ὡς τύμβον πατρός.
Amphiaraus, *infra*, 841, ὑπὸ γαίας ... πάμψυχος ἀνάσσει. And if Niobe is held as a goddess, why may not Agamemnon be a god? In Aesch. *Cho.* 475-8, he is certainly included in the phrases θεῶν τῶν κατὰ γᾶς ... μάκαρες χθόνιοι, as παισίν in 478 clearly shows.

187.   ἅτις ἄνευ τοκέων κατατάκομαι.

The reasons for reading *τεκέων are certainly strong.

195-7.   οἰκτρὰ δ' ἐν κοίταις πατρῴαις
ὅτε σοι παγχάλκων ἀνταία
γενύων ὡρμάθη πλαγά.

Without denying that κοίταις may refer to the banquet, at which, according to the Homeric version of the fable, Agamemnon was slain, I retain σοι as ethical dative in 196, and believe the 'voice' to be Electra's, for the reasons given in my note. This renders the epithet πατρῴαις more poignant, by associating it immediately with the fatal moment. On the other hand, for the meaning which I gave to ἐν κοίταις, 'where he lay in death,' cp. Eur. *El.* 158, κοίτᾳ ἐν οἰκτροτάτᾳ θανάτου.

ELECTRA

226.
τίνι γάρ ποτ' ἄν, ὦ φιλία γενέθλα,
πρόσφορον ἀκούσαιμ' ἔπος;

Though the dative of the agent (= πρὸς τίνος) is a rare use, it seems more suited to the context than 'in whose judgment.' Cp. Eur. *El.* 1183, διὰ πυρὸς ἔμολον . . . ματρὶ τᾷδ' ('at the hands of this my mother').

271. ἴδω δὲ τούτων τὴν τελευταίαν ὕβριν.

'Their crowning insult.' I do not see why this is 'weaker.' Cp. *Phil.* 1044,

εἰ δ' ἴδοιμ' ὀλωλότας
τούτους, δοκοῖμ' ἂν τῆς νόσου πεφευγέναι.

272. τὸν αὐτοφόντην ἡμὶν ἐν κοίτῃ πατρός.

τὸν αὐτοέντην, Jebb, with schol. I do not care to insist; but αὐτοφόντην seems to me more suggestive of the 'bloody deed.'

280. ταύτῃ χοροὺς ἵστησι.

Cp. *Bacchyl.* xi. 112, καὶ χοροὺς ἵσταν γυναικῶν.

287. αὕτη γὰρ ἡ λόγοισι γενναία γυνή.

λόγοισι γενναία: 'noble in her professions,' Jebb. Rather 'reputed noble': cp. Eur. *Hec.* 1572, ὅ τ' οὐκέτ' ὢν λόγοισι Μενέλεως πέλας: *El.* 47, τὸν λόγοισι κηδεύοντ' ἐμοί.

293.
πλὴν ὅταν κλύῃ τινὸς
ἥξοντ' Ὀρέστην.

I still incline to think that τινὸς = ἐμοῦ. Cp. 795,

οὐκοῦν Ὀρέστης καὶ σὺ παύσετον τάδε;

which implies former threats on Electra's part.

316. ὡς νῦν ἀπόντος ἱστόρει τί σοι φίλον.

For τί, as practically equivalent to a relative, cp. Eur. *fr.* 773 (Phaethon), l. 2, αἰτοῦ τί χρῄζεις ἕν, where the conjectural emendations are somewhat forced, and so is the punctuation, αἰτοῦ· τί χρῄζεις; ἕν.

323. πέποιθ', ἐπεί τἂν οὐ μακρὰν ἔζων ἐγώ.

'μακρὰν means, "so long as I actually have lived."' Jebb. Rather 'my life would soon have ended.'
See on *O. T.* 220, οὐ γὰρ ἂν μακρὰν | ἴχνευον.

345, 346. ἔπειθ' ἑλοῦ γε θάτερ', ἢ φρονεῖν κακῶς,
ἢ τῶν φίλων φρονοῦσα μὴ μνήμην ἔχειν·

Jebb's note—('Electra is putting the dilemma between imprudent loyalty and prudent disloyalty')—is not convincing. I adhere to the Scholiast's interpretation: Ὁμολόγησον σαύτην ἢ φρονεῖν κακῶς, προστιθεμένην τοῖς ἐχθροῖς· ἢ φρονοῦσαν, τῶν φιλτάτων ἀμνημονεῖν. 'Either your principles are wrong, or in practice you show forgetfulness.' She then presses home the imputation of inconsistency.

351. οὐ ταῦτα πρὸς κακοῖσι δειλίαν ἔχει;

Cp. *supr.* 309, κἀπιτηδεύειν κακά. I am contented with Linwood's version: *Non malam te solum sed timidam etiam arguunt.*

363. τοὐμὲ μὴ λυποῦν.

The ancient Scholiast undoubtedly read λυποῦν, though it has disappeared from the MSS.: he wrote ἐμοί, φησίν, ἔστω τροφή, ἡ τῇ ἀνάγκῃ μόνον ἁρμόζουσα, καὶ τὴν πείνην ἀπελαύνουσα· οὐ δέομαι γὰρ τοιαύτης τροφῆς ἀφ' ἧς ἡδονὴν σχήσω.

The scholion on λυπεῖν *is by a later hand* in L. See the facsimile : τοῦτο μόνον ἐμὲ βοσκέτω, τὸ μὴ λυπεῖν ἐμὲ αὐτήν, εἰ τοῖς φονεῦσι τοῦ πατρὸς πείθεσθαι ἀναγκασθήσομαι. Erfurdt accepted λυποῦν from the Roman scholia. I read λυποῦν, but differ from the scholiast as to the interpretation. I believe the feeling expressed to be like that of Medea in Eur. *Med.* 598.

> μὴ μοὶ γένοιτο λυπρὸς εὐδαίμων βίος
> μηδ' ὄλβος ὅστις τὴν ἐμὴν κνίζοι φρένα.

It is true that μὴ λυπεῖν ἑαυτόν appears elsewhere as a commonplace sentiment. This may possibly have suggested λυπεῖν to a corrector, to whom the accepted explanation of λυποῦν seemed (as it is) intolerably weak.

The use of ἐμέ for ἐμαυτὴν is not unparalleled. But it is strange in this context, and the hyperbole is hardly natural in a *rhesis*. 'Let me have such sustenance alone as does not grieve my heart'—as I should be grieved if I partook of the murderers' table. Cp. *Phil.* 1043.

> ὡς ζῶ μὲν οἰκτρῶς, εἰ δ' ἴδοιμ' ὀλωλότας
> τούτους, δοκοῖμ' ἂν τῆς νόσου πεφευγέναι.

I find that Camerarius (quoted by H. Stephanus in his edition of 1568), while still reading λυπεῖν, thus paraphrased the note of the scholiast: 'modo sic pascar ne cibus me affligat: quod futurum sentit in dissimulatione odii sui, et assentatione illorum.'

366, 367. Cp. also Eur. *fr.* 1064; *Her.* iii. 53, πολλοὶ . . . τὰ μητρώια διζήμενοι τὰ πατρώια ἀπέβαλον.

376. φέρ' εἰπὲ δὴ τὸ δεινόν.

Cp. also *Her.* vii. 11 § 5, ἵνα καὶ τὸ δεινόν, τὸ πείσομαι, τοῦτο μάθω.

424. τοιαῦτα τοῦ παρόντος, ἡνίχ' Ἡλίῳ
δείκνυσι τοὔναρ, ἔκλυον ἐξηγουμένου.

τοῦ πάροντος. As Jebb says, the question between τοῦ and του is nicely balanced. I remain in doubt, but rather prefer τοῦ.

443. δοκεῖ
γέρα τάδ' οὖν τάφοισι δέξασθαι νέκυς.

I leave the MS. reading intact, while admitting that it is open to question. It may perhaps be objected to the future tense that it assumes that, in spite of Electra's prohibition, the offering would after all be made.

446. κηλῖδας ἐξέμαξεν, 'sc. ἡ Κλυταιμνήστρα,'

Jebb. The change of subject is, of course, possible; but with Agamemnon for subject the phrase conveys a deeper notion of indignity, and I do not see that the middle voice is required. The active is preferred as in *O. T.* 914, αἴρει θυμόν.

451. τήνδε †λιπαρῆ τρίχα.

In my translation I adopted a view of λιπαρῆ which may appear fanciful, but which, in the absence of anything satisfying, may be allowed to stand. I would now suggest, as a somewhat desperate remedy, τήνδ' ἀλάμπρυντον τρίχα. See *Hesych.* i., p. 1160, quoted by Nauck on *fr.* 567: ἐλαιοῦται θρίξ. Σοφοκλῆς Τρωίλῳ. Ἀρίσταρχος ῥυπαίνεται· βέλτιον δὲ λαμπρύνεται.

For the feeling cp. Eur. *Tro.* 1200 *f.* κομίζετ' ἀθλίῳ κόσμον νεκρῷ | ἐκ τῶν παρόντων· οὐ γὰρ ἐς κάλλος τύχας | δαίμων δίδωσιν· ὧν δ' ἔχω, λήψει τάδε.

ELECTRA

456. ἐχθροῖσιν αὐτοῦ ζῶντ' ἐπεμβῆναι ποδί.

Is it quite certain that ι of the dat. sing. is never elided in Tragedy? See *fr.* 722, ζῶντι ποδὶ χρώμενον, ὥς φησὶ Σοφοκλῆς (Eustathius); Eur. *Alc.* 1118, γόργον' ὡς καρατόμῳ (so MSS.). The expression is stronger if this is admitted. The *phrasing* is improved.

459. οἶμαί τι κἀκείνῳ μέλον
πέμψαι τάδ' αὐτῇ δυσπρόσοπτ' ὀνείρατα.

My note on this line is in agreement with Paley's view. It supposes a use of the participle analogous to that in Thuc. i. 36 §1, τὸ μὲν δεδιὸς αὐτοῦ ἰσχὺν ἔχον τοὺς ἐναντίους μᾶλλον φοβῆσον· τὸ δὲ θαρσοῦν ... ἀσθενὲς ὂν πρὸς ἰσχύοντας τοὺς ἐχθροὺς ἀδεέστερον ἐσόμενον. I still incline to this interpretation: 'Some care on his part.'

461. σοί θ' ὑπούργησον τάδε
ἐμοί τ' ἀρωγά.

I think that σοί with ἐμοί depends principally on ἀρωγά.

466. τὸ γὰρ δίκαιον οὐκ ἔχει λόγον.

What is given in my note as an alternative is practically the same with the view which Jebb prefers. I rather incline to the less usual but more vivid construction, according to which τὸ δίκαιον is the subject of ἔχει.

476. δίκαια φερομένα χεροῖν κράτη.

φερομένα. Jebb decides in favour of the interpretation to which I gave the second place: φερομένα='winning', 'carrying off'. He is probably right.

484. οὐ γάρ ποτ' ἀμναστεῖ γ' ὁ φύσας Ἑλλάνων ἄναξ.

Against admitting σέ, it may be urged that both Orestes and Electra are in the mind of the chorus.

488. καὶ πολύπους
καὶ πολύχειρ.

'As with the might of a resistless host' (Jebb). In favour of taking the words more literally, it may be remarked that the chorus are not aware of the oracle quoted by Orestes in 36, 37.

491, 492. ἄλεκτρ' ἄνυμφα γὰρ ἐπέβα μιαιφόνων
γάμων ἁμιλλήμαθ' οἷσιν οὐ θέμις.

Jebb seems to take ἐπέβα as governing the antecedent to οἷσιν. I understand it in an absolute sense. Cp. *Trach.* 843, νέων ἀϊσσόντων γάμων, Eur. *Hipp.* 580, τί ποτ' ἔβα κακόν;

495. πρὸ τῶνδέ τοί μ' ἔχει.

If ἔχει = 'the thought possesses me' is impossible, Jebb's conjecture, θάρσος τι μήποθ' ἡμῖν, seems certainly probable. But if it may stand, ἀδυπνόων in 480 may be scanned - ⏑ ⏑ - as in *Bacchyl.* xii. 73 (Jebb's edition).

498. τοῖς δρῶσι καὶ συνδρῶσιν.

According to Jebb Clytemnestra is the principal, Aegisthus the accessory. Perhaps this is right, but in 955 Electra calls Aegisthus τὸν αὐτόχειρα πατρῴου φόνου.

501. κατασχεῖν is used figuratively also in Eur. *Cycl.* 349, ἐς ἀνδρὸς ἀνοσίου | γνώμην κατέσχον ἀλίμενόν τε καρδίαν.

514. ἔλιπεν ἐκ τοῦδ' οἴκους.

Why does the reading ἔλιπεν exclude anacrusis? May not the rhythm be the same as in

παγχρυσέων δίφρων [or παγχρύσων ἐκ δίφρων]
⌣ ⌣́ ⌣ ⌣́ — —
ἔ λιπεν ἐκ τοῦδ' οἴκους.

518. μή τοι θυραίαν γ' οὖσαν αἰσχύνειν φίλους.

αἰσχύνειν φίλους: 'said from an Athenian point of view' (Jebb). This had, of course, occurred to me. But the emphatic γε seems to imply that the offence indoors was hardly less. I therefore took αἰσχύνειν in a more active meaning. She brings disgrace on the family not only by breaking bounds but by *abusing* them in public as well as by her mean appearance. In the *Phoenissae* of Euripides, *sub init.*, Antigone has her mother's leave to go out of doors to see the battle, but her doing so with the Paedagogus is not felt to be disgraceful. Nor is Hermione's errand in Eur. *Or.* 1323.

525. πατὴρ γάρ, οὐδὲν ἄλλο σοὶ πρόσχημ' ἀεί.

I do not think that the comma at ἄλλο removes the 'awkwardness'. It rather breaks the natural flow of the language.

534. τοῦ χάριν τίνων.

Literally 'returning whose kindness' *i.e.* 'For the sake of whom?' The genitive has caused some difficulty, but cp. Eur. *Or.* 453, χάριτας πατρῴους ἐκτίνων, where the adjective is equivalent to a genitive. This seems a more natural interpretation than 'for the sake of what? of whom?' though the double interrogative is common enough.

563, 564. τίνος
ποινὰς τὰ πολλὰ πνεύματ' ἔσχεν Αὐλίδι·

Jebb's view that Sophocles, like Eur. *Iph. A.*, *sub init.*, adopts the notion of a dead calm, has much to recommend it. But in any case I prefer the reading ἔσχεν Αὐλίδι. For ἔσχεν cp. Eur. *Heracl.* 924, ἔσχεν δ' ὕβριν ἀνδρός, *Bacchyl.* xviii. 27 (ed. Kenyon) τάν τε Κερκυόνος παλαίστραν | ἔσχεν; ib. 41, ὅστε τούτων | ἀνδρῶν κρατερὸν σθένος | ἔσχεν. Eur. *Heracl.* 924; Hdt. vii. 171.

569. ἐκκομπάσας ἔπος τι τυγχάνει βαλών.

βαλών, 'after hitting' (Jebb). I took βαλὼν with τυγχάνει as=ἐκβαλών. See L. and S., *s. v.* ἐκβάλλω, and compare *Trach.* 62, μῦθοι καλῶς πίπτουσιν, where πίπτειν has the force of ἐκπίπτειν. 'After hitting' seems hardly to be required in the context. Nor do I see that 'ἐκκομπάσας, combined with βαλὼν in this sense, would be awkwardly redundant.' βαλών, then, serves to mark the almost involuntary nature of the boast. 'Da geschah es, dass er irgend ein Wort fallen liess' (Schneidewin). And so Ellendt, *s. v.* βάλλω, '*Forte vel temere jacere dicta.*'

581. μὴ πῆμα σαυτῇ καὶ μετάγνοιαν τιθῇς.

I agree in preferring τιθῇς to τίθης here.

591. ἦ καὶ τοῦτ' ἐρεῖς.

I agree in deleting the comma, but see no objection to τοῦτο.

593. αἰσχρῶς δ', ἐάν περ καὶ λέγῃς·

I should now retain δ' from L.

ELECTRA 137

606. κήρυσσέ μ' εἰς ἅπαντας, εἴτε χρῇς κακήν.

I doubtfully accede to the general demand for χρῇς, χρῇ in this and similar contexts. But 'if you must' is not inadmissible.

610, 611. ὁρῶ μένος πνέουσαν· εἰ δὲ σὺν δίκῃ
ξύνεστι, τοῦδε φροντίδ' οὐκέτ' εἰσορῶ.

As I have said elsewhere, I do not see 'that πνέουσαν must be Electra.' And I am convinced, not only that φροντίδος in 612 refers to φροντίδ', but that εἰ δὲ σὺν δίκῃ | ξύνεστι refers to 528, ἡ γὰρ Δίκη νιν εἷλε κοὐκ ἐγὼ μόνη. This is not the only instance of 'by-play' in Greek Tragedy (Eur. *Iph. A.* 1142-4; *Or.* 957-9; *Phoen.* 454-9). If I am right in this, it is needless to read ἐμοί in 612.

645. δισσῶν ὀνείρων.

There seems to be sufficient ground for taking δισσῶν to mean 'doubtful', 'ambiguous'.

647. τοῖς ἐχθροῖσιν ἔμπαλιν μέθες.

I take ἔμπαλιν to mean 'the opposite way': and I do not feel that this is weak. 'Let it recoil upon my foes.'

653. τέκνων ὅσων ἐμοὶ
δύσνοια μὴ πρόσεστιν.

'τέκνων is partitive genitive' (Jebb). But is there not some awkwardness in giving to two consecutive genitives a different construction?

659. τοὺς ἐκ Διὸς γὰρ εἰκός ἐστι πάνθ' ὁρᾶν.
Cp. Eur. *Iph. T.* 1232.
τἄλλα δ' οὐ λέγουσ', ὅμως
τοῖς τὰ πλείον' εἰδόσιν θεοῖς σοί τε σημαίνω, θεά.

681. κεῖνος γὰρ ἐλθὼν εἰς τὸ κλεινὸν Ἑλλάδος.

It is not certain that κοινὸν is to be preferred to κλεινὸν here.

686. δρόμου δ' ἰσώσας †τῇ φύσει τὰ τέρματα.

In attempting to explain this difficult line, I seem to have followed the Scholiast and to have agreed most nearly with G. Wolff. But I took τὰ τέρματα not literally as=the end of the race-course, but more generally as='completion' (L. and S., s. v. τέρμα, ii. 2). Jebb adopts Musgrave's very plausible emendation, τάφέσει, but with a different meaning. As the line so emended is interpreted in three several ways, it seems better to leave the matter undecided. 'When he came back to the point from which he started' is intelligible enough, but hardly requires so elaborate a form of expression.

In defence of my view of the meaning let me cite the following passages of Pindar:—*Ol.* vi. 75 *f*, οἷς ποτε πρώτοις περὶ δωδέκατον δρόμον ἐλαυνόντεσσιν αἰδοία ποτιστάξῃ Χάρις εὐκλέα μορφάν: viii. 19, ἔργῳ δ' οὐ κατὰ εἶδος ἐλέγχων: ix. 65, ὑπέρφατον ἄνδρα μορφᾷ τε καὶ | ἔργοισι: *ib.* 94, ὡραῖος ἐὼν καὶ καλὸς κάλλιστά τε ῥέξας: *Isthm.* vii. (vi.) 22, σθένει τ' ἔκπαγλος ἰδεῖν τε μορφάεις· ἄγει τ' ἀρετὰν οὐκ αἴσχιον φυᾶς.

688, 689. χὤπως μὲν ἐν πολλοῖσι παυρά σοι λέγω
οὐκ οἶδα τοιοῦδ' ἀνδρὸς ἔργα καὶ κράτη·

Jebb's rendering of these lines—'to speak briefly where there is much to tell, I know not the man whose deeds and triumphs have matched his' agrees with the explanation which I placed third (3) 'supposing the language to be more than "usually inexact"'. He takes no notice of the meaning which I still prefer: οὐκ οἶδα ὅπως σοι λέγω παυρα ἐν πολλοῖσιν ἔργα καὶ κράτη τοιοῦδ' ἀνδρὸς='I know not how to tell [even] a few amongst many feats achieved by one so valiant'. This gives the required antithesis to what follows: ἓν δ' ἴσθ', etc. If this is rejected, I would read χὤπως μὲν ἐν παύροισι πολλά σοι λέγω. But there is then less point in ἓν δ' ἴσθ'. Jebb's rendering may perhaps derive support from Pind. *Pyth.* ix. 77, βαιὰ δ' ἐν μακροῖσι ποικίλλειν ἀκοὰ σοφοῖς (cf. also *Ol.* xiii. 98). But, according to my view of the passage, even that method was impossible here.

691.   δρόμων διαύλων *ἆθλ' *ἅπερ νομίζεται.

I agree with Jebb that this line is probably interpolated.

710.   κλήροις ἔπηλαν καὶ κατέστησαν δίφρους.

I am still inclined to retain κλήροις (instrumental dative).

716, 717.   ὡς ὑπερβάλοι
χνόας τις αὐτῶν καὶ φρυάγμαθ' ἱππικά.

I have always felt the same hesitation which is implied in Jebb's change of view. On the whole I acquiesce in his decision, chiefly because of γάρ. The object of each is to *get away*, and so not to be harassed by his neighbour's wheels and the foam from the snorting, panting steeds. Cp. *Bacchyl.* v. 43, 44 (of Pherenicus), οὔπω νιν ὑπὸ προτέρων | ἵππων ἐν ἀγῶνι κατέχρανεν κόνις.

721, 722.   δεξιόν τ' ἀνεὶς
σειραῖον ἵππον εἶργε τὸν προσκείμενον.

The purpose is, of course, to bring round the whole equipage evenly. This may be illustrated from the military evolution known as 'left wheel'. The man on the extreme left of a line of infantry 'steps short', merely marking time, and the man on the extreme right steps fully out, while the man in the centre uses 'half step,' and the rest in proportion. Thus the line revolves round the leftward extremity until the semicircle is complete, when all move in full step once more. But here, since not the same but a parallel line is to be traversed in returning, the left-hand trace-horse does not remain quite still, but moves round a much smaller semicircle than his right-hand fellow. The evolution must be completed before the left-hand rein is loosened, and all four steeds keep step again.

727. ἐκ δ' ὑποστροφῆς.

'The Aenian's horses dashed head-foremost into the Libyan's team, *striking it on the left side*' (Jebb). (The italics are mine.) But according to the Greek, the cars collide 'front to front'. (Else would not the verb be προσπαίουσι?) Now, supposing that there is no *spina*, and none is mentioned in Pausanias (*Dict. of Ant.*, vol. I. p. 965 a), the Aenian's horses, when he has lost control of them, may make a complete circle in turning the goal and so collide with one of those approaching it from the other side.

734-736. I read (with Jebb) ὑστέρας ἔχων . . . ὅπως δ', as in my large edition, not as in *CA*.

740. κάρα προβάλλων ἱππικῶν ὀχημάτων.

'Showing his head in front of the two chariots' (Jebb). Rather, I think, 'bringing his equipage in front'. The car and team together are treated as a single unit. Cp. Eur. *Hippol.* 1229, φόβῳ τέτρωρον ἐκμαίνων ὄχον: Eur. *fr.* (*Phaethon*) 779, l. 6.

> κρούσας δὲ πλευρὰ πτεροφόρων ὀχημάτων
> μεθῆκεν, αἱ δ' ἔπταντ' ἐπ' αἰθέρος πτύχας.

743-745. ἔπειτα λύων ἡνίαν ἀριστερὰν
κάμπτοντος ἵππου λανθάνει στήλην ἄκραν
παίσας·

The critical moment is when the chariot, moving from right to left (not 'from left to right'), has all but made the turn. If the left-hand rein is slackened a fraction of a moment too soon, the horse in his eagerness, instead of completing the semicircle, will cut off a corner and bring the axle end against the stone.

Jebb's view is that, when the horse is let go, he springs directly forwards, so giving the car behind him a slight inclination to the left.

But (1) this would only happen if the rein were slackened *before* the turning-point was reached; and (2) not the axle, but the hinder part of the wheel, would be brought into contact with the stone.

748. πῶλοι διεσπάρησαν εἰς μέσον δρόμον.

Jebb thinks διεσπάρησαν implies that the trace-horses had broken loose. That is possible, but hardly, I think, necessary. Cp. Eur. *Rhes.* 701, νησιώτην σποράδα . . . βίον, 'a life here, there, and everywhere'.

752. φορούμενος πρὸς οὖδας.

'With reference to his fall from the chariot' (Jebb). The frequentative form and the continuous tense seem both against this view. And, as violent motion is implied, I can see no objection to the accusative even if we render 'dragged against the ground'.

760. ὅπως πατρῴας τύμβον ἐκλάχοι χθονός.

I adhere to my note. The optative refers to the purpose of the senders.

773. πῶς γὰρ ἂν μάτην λέγοις;

μάτην λέγοις, 'say the word "μάτην"' (Jebb). I much prefer 'how should your report be in vain?'

781. ὁ προστατῶν χρόνος διῆγέ μ'.

The Scholiast wrote ἐπιγενόμενος (see facsimile), not ἐπιγινόμενος (Jebb). 'The time which stood in front of me', *instans tempus*, is certainly the meaning. But that time is personified, and with a notion of authority which is suggested by the word. Cp. *Hamlet*, s. f. 'as this fell Sergeant, Death, is strict in his arrest'.

διῆγε, 'led me along'. By a bold inversion, she implies that instead of *leading* her life as she will, she is *led*, like a devoted victim.

783. νῦν δ' ἡμέρᾳ γὰρ τῇδ' ἀπηλλάγην φόβου.

ἀπηλλάγην: the stroke to the right of the γ is certainly the beginning of an H by the first hand. A second hand has erased what followed this and turned it into the beginning of μαι.

792. ἄκουε, Νέμεσι.

L. p. m. had written νέμεσσιν (see facsimile).

793. ἤκουσεν ὧν δεῖ.

Clytemnestra echoes Νέμεσι, neglecting τοῦ θανόντος. But I do not think she 'turns her retort as if τοῦ θανόντος depended on ἄκουε' (Jebb).

800. ἥκιστ'· ἐπείπερ οὔτ' ἐμοῦ καταξίως.

I now read καταξίως with Jebb.

ELECTRA

826.   εἰ ταῦτ' ἐφορῶντες κρύπτουσιν ἔκηλοι.

κρύπτουσιν, sc. τὸ ἐφορᾶν.   Cp. Eur. *Alc.* 857, ἔκρυπτε (sc. τὸ συμφορᾷ πεπλῆχθαι).

847.   ἐφάνη γὰρ μελέτωρ
        ἀμφὶ τὸν ἐν πένθει·

I erroneously explained τὸν ἐν πένθει as 'the lamented one'. This mistake was corrected in *CA*. (1886). See above, 290.

852.   δεινῶν *τε στυγῶν τ' *ἄχθει.

The emendation adopted in my text was that of Professor E. L. Lushington. Jebb's view of Hermann's reading is attractive. He also gives good reasons for ἀθρήνεις (= ἃ ἐθρήνεις) in 853. The scholion is πάντα σύροντι τὰ κακά.

858.   εὐπατρίδων τ' ἀρωγαί.

With εὐπατριδᾶν the language is less artificial perhaps, but also more complex. See above, Introd. p. ix. (on Condensed expression).

859. For ἔφυ of a destined thing, cp. Eur. *Phoen.* 916, ἅπερ πέφυκε, ταῦτα κἀνάγκη σε δρᾶν.

896.   πάντων ὅσ' ἔστιν ἀνθέων θήκην πατρός.

ἔστιν certainly, not ἐστίν.

903.   ἐμπαίει τί μοι
        ψυχῇ σύνηθες ὄμμα.

ὄμμα in poetry does not always imply a human face. See Pind. *P.* 60 (ὁ Βάττου παλαιὸς ὄλβος)

    πύργος ἄστεος ὄμμα τε φαεννότατον
    ξένοισι.

905. Cp. Eur. *El.* 325, πυρὰ δὲ χέρσος ἀγλαϊσμάτων.

914. οὔτε δρῶσ' ἐλάνθανεν.

'Whichever shade of meaning were given to ἐλάνθανεν, still δρῶσα, in the absence of anything to mark conditionality, would imply, not εἰ ἕδρα, but ὅτε 'ἕδρα' (Jebb). I do not find this rule convincing. In any case εἰ ἕδρα is understood.

915. ἀλλ' ἔστ' Ὀρέστου ταῦτα τἀπιτίμια.

Dindorf's τἀπιτύμβια, if not ' certain ', is extremely probable. But the marginal variant τἀγλαΐσματα is not to be entirely ignored.

918. νῷν δ' ἦν τὰ πρόσθεν στυγνός.

The δ' though absent from L., seem to me more Greek.

920. φεῦ, τῆς ἀνοίας ὥς σ' ἐποικτείρω πάλαι.

I adhere to my punctuation. Nothing is gained by breaking up the expression.

927. Cp. Eur. *Hel.* 1190, ὅ τε παρών, ὅτ' ὤλλυτο.

947. ἄκουε δή νυν ᾗ βεβούλευμαι τελεῖν.

Jebb decides in favour of ποεῖν (against τελεῖν) as simpler. Perhaps he is right. But the emphatic perfect βεβούλευμαι sorts well with a word implying *decisive* action—'to make an end'.

976. δεξιώσεται: 'properly, to give the right hand to one in welcome' (Jebb). Rather, to extend the right hand towards a person in token of honour. See note on Plato, *Rep.* v., 468 B.

1007. Cp. *Lys. ap. Athenaeum*, 12 p. 551 E.

1022. πάντα γὰρ κατειργάσω.

I do not admit that the omission of ἄν here is 'impossible'. See on 914, and cp. Eur. *Phoen.* 1561 f., δι' ὀδύνας ἔβας, εἰ... ἐπενώμας. One cannot always tell what would be harsh to a Greek ear. But πᾶν γὰρ ἄν seems cacophonous.

1040. εἴρηκας ὀρθῶς ᾧ σὺ πρόσκεισαι κακῷ.

Cp. Eur. *fr.* 422, κακοῖς γὰρ οὐ σὺ πρόσκεισαι μόνη.

1066. ὦ χθονία βροτοῖσι φάμα.

βροτοῖσι probably includes the dead with the living = Rumour amongst mortals, extending to the dead. Cp. Pind. *Ol.* vii. 79-84.

κατακρύπτει δ' οὐ κόνις
συγγόνων κεδνὰν χάριν.
Ἑρμᾶ δὲ θυγατρὸς ἀκούσαις Ἰφίων
Ἀγγελίας, ἐνέποι κεν Καλλιμάχῳ λιπαρὸν
κόσμον Ὀλυμπίᾳ, ὅν σφι Ζεὺς γένει
ὤπασεν.

ib. xiv. 20, 21.

μελαντειχέα νῦν δόμον
Φερσεφόνας ἔλθ' Ἀχοῖ, πατρὶ κλυτὰν φέροισ' ἀγγελίαν.

1070. ὅτι σφὶν ἤδη τὰ μὲν ἐκ δόμων νοσεῖ †

For νοσεῖ or νοσεῖ δή (Tricl.), I propose νοσώδη sc. ἐστίν, in which I find that I agree with Erfurdt.

1071. τὰ δὲ πρὸς τέκνων διπλῆ φύλοπις οὐκέτ' ἐξισοῦται.

Without rejecting the view in favour of which Jebb decides, and which is stated first in my note, with (1), I still rather incline to take διπλῇ φύλοπις to mean 'the war-cry of two children', *i.e.* their hoped-for union in a common cause.

1075. τὸν ἀεὶ πατρὸς
δειλαία στενάχουσ'.

I am not convinced that τὸν ἀεὶ cannot stand for τὸν ἀεὶ χρόνον, nor that 'in *O.C.* 1584' (where see note) 'the words τὸν ἀεὶ conceal some corruption' (Jebb).

1085. σὺ πάγκλαυτον αἰῶνα †κοινὸν εἵλου.

I propose αἰῶν' *ἄοικον. See above 818, 819. In Japanese phrase, Electra makes herself a *Rônin*. Cp. *fr.* adespot. 1284.

ἄπολις, ἄοικος, πατρίδος ἐστερημένος,
πτωχὸς, πλανήτης, βίον ἔχων τοὐφήμερον.

Eur. *Hipp.* 1029, ἄπολις, ἄοικος, φυγὰς, ἀλητεύων χθόνα.

A close parallel occurs in *Her.* iii. 52, where the son of Periander, in anger for his mother's death, ἐν τῇσι στοῇσι ἐκαλινδέετο.

1087. τὸ μὴ καλὸν †καθοπλίσασα.

I propose to read *καθαγνίσασα='having purged away.' The deaths of Aeg. and Cly. would be a sacrifice by which the abomination would be removed. Hesychius (i. p. 56) quoted by Nauck, *fr.* 113, says that Sophocles in the *Amphiaraus* made καθαγνίσαι=διαφθεῖραι. And in *Ant.* 1081,

ὅσων σπαράγματ' ἢ κύνες καθήγνισαν
ἢ θῆρες, ἤ τις πτηνὸς οἰωνός,

the word has a similar force. See also Eur. *Or.* 40,

ἐξ ὅτου σφαγαῖς
θανοῦσα μήτηρ πυρὶ καθήγνισται δέμας.

1092.   νῦν ὑπὸ χεῖρα ναίεις·

ὑπόχειρ may be right. But the limits of metrical licence in tragic lyrics are not finally ascertained. See on *O. T.* 199. For the meaning, cp. Pind. *Pyth.* viii. 77, (δαίμων) ἄλλοτ' ἄλλον ὕπερθε βάλλων, ἄλλον δ' ὑπὸ χειρῶν.

1095, 1096.   ἃ δὲ μέγιστ' ἔβλαστε νόμιμα, τῶνδε φερομέναν
ἄριστα τᾷ Ζηνὸς εὐσεβείᾳ.

Jebb practically decides in favour of the view, which I put forth as an alternative (2) φερομέναν, 'carrying off the palm.' Encouraged by his authority, I would now give the first place to this. τῶνδε = 'on account of these' or 'awarded by these.' The latter involves a slight personification which is already implied in ἔβλαστε.

1104.   ἡμῶν ποθεινὴν κοινόπουν παρουσίαν.

For ποθεινήν = 'welcome' cp. Eur. *I. T.* 515,

καὶ μὴν ποθεινός γ' ἦλθες ἐξ "Αργους μολών.

Hel. 540,

ὡς ποθεινὸς ἂν μόλοις.

Theodectes, *fr.* 10,

ὦ καλλιφεγγῆ λαμπάδ' εἰλίσσων φλογὸς
"Ηλιε, ποθεινὸν πᾶσιν ἀνθρώποις σέλας.

1115.   οἲ 'γὼ τάλαινα, τοῦτ' ἐκεῖν' ἤδη σαφές.

There is little to choose between Jebb's punctuation and mine. The figurative sense of ἄχθος takes something from the 'abruptness and obscurity'.

1143. οἴμοι τάλαινα τῆς ἐμῆς πάλαι τροφῆς.

For τροφῆς, cp. Eur. *Troad.* 1187,

οἴμοι, τὰ πόλλ' ἀσπάσμαθ' αἵ τ' ἐμαὶ τροφαὶ
ὕπνοι τ' ἐκεῖνοι φροῦδά μοι.

1152. τέθνηκ' ἐγώ σοι·

I accept Jebb's explanation of the dative here. Although the feeling is different, the use in *Phil.* 1030 is exactly parallel. Cp. also Eur. *Androm.* 334. See note in *CA*. 'I am dead, who lived in thee.'

1160-1162. οἴμοι μοι·
ὦ δέμας οἰκτρόν, φεῦ φεῦ.
ὦ δεινοτάτας, οἴμοι μοι.

Jebb's arrangement of the lines is right.

1173. ποῖ λόγων ἀμηχάνων
ἔλθω;

I prefer to read ἀμηχάνων with L. and most MSS., 'where all words are impossible, to what word shall I betake me?' Cp. τἄπορον . . . ἔπος in *Phil.* 897.

1178. τόδ' ἔστ' ἐκεῖνο, καὶ μάλ' ἀθλίως ἔχον.

It seems to me that καὶ is intensive here also.

1184. τί μοι ποτ', ὦ ξέν', ὧδ' ἐπισκοπῶν στένεις;

(τί δή ποτ', most MSS.). But may not δή have come in from 1180?

1201. μόνος γὰρ ἥκω τοῖς ἴσοις ἀλγῶν κακοῖς.

I still feel that τοῖσι σοῖς 'is less in keeping with the subtle gradations of the recognition scene'.

ELECTRA

1205. μέθες τόδ' ἄγγος νυν.
I agree that νυν, not νῦν, should be read.

1207. πιθοῦ λέγοντι κοὐχ ἁμαρτήσει ποτέ.
πιθοῦ is certainly better than πείθου.

1215. τοῦτο δ' οὐχὶ σόν.
Jebb refers τοῦτο to τήνδε προσφωνεῖν φάτιν. It seems more natural to refer it to the urn, which is in her hands. 'You have no part in this.'

1239. ἀλλ' οὐ τὰν Ἄρτεμιν τὰν αἰὲν ἀδμήταν.
Jebb is probably right in accepting Fröhlich's conjecture as modified by Hermann. ἀλλ' οὐ μὰ τὴν ἄδμητον αἰὲν Ἄρτεμιν.

1246. ἀνέφελον ἐνέβαλες οὖ ποτε καταλύσιμον.
ἐνέβαλες is certainly an improvement.

1254-1256. ὁ πᾶς ἂν πρέποι παρὼν ἐννέπειν
τάδε δίκᾳ χρόνος.
'δίκᾳ goes with ἐννέπειν, not with πρέποι' (Jebb). Why?

1281 f. ὦ φίλαι, ἔκλυον ἂν ἐγὼ οὐδ' ἂν ἤλπισ' αὐδάν.
ἔσχον ὀργὰν
ἄναυδον οὐδὲ σὺν βοᾷ κλύουσα, τάλαινα.

There are obvious difficulties as to the meaning and connexion, and even as to the reading, of these lines. I would observe, (1) that there is obviously a strong antithesis between νῦν δ' ἔχω σε κ.τ.λ. and what precedes; (2) that τάλαινα refers to ἔκλυον ... κλύουσα; (3) that αὐδή is sometimes = φήμη, as it is here taken by the scholiasts, 'an utterance', the *voicing* of something which affects the mind. So in *O. C.* 240, ἔργων ἀκόντων ἀϊόντες αὐδάν, 'hearing the loud rumour of his unwitting deeds'. In Eur. *Hipp.* 565 *f.*, φήμα and φάτις are synonyms for αὐδή. (Similarly 'sound' in Shakespeare often signifies 'something said or uttered'. See Schmidt's *Shakespeare-Lexicon*, s.v.); (4) ὀργή in poetry may signify the access of any strong emotion, *e.g.* ὀργῇ χρωμένη in *O.T.* 1241 is well explained by Ellendt '*furore percita abiectaque spe mens*'; (5) Electra listened in silence to the report of the Paedagogus, and the few words spoken by her before the exit of Clytemnestra would not seem in the retrospect like an outburst of passion. In fact, she did not speak until Clytemnestra had spoken. Much rather it would seem as if she was crushed—πεπαύμεθ' ἡμεῖς, οὐχ ὅπως σε παύσομεν. (6) For ἐλπίζω of suspecting evil, cp. *Trach.* 110, 111; Aristoph. *Av.* 956. Therefore while admitting that some words may be lost, and that the Scholiast seems to have known a different reading, I would venture to render: 'Dear friends, I heard an utterance beyond my thought. In hearing I restrained my passion, and as I listened, did not cry aloud.' In an epode one cannot be very confident about metre, but I should be inclined to print τάλαινα in a separate line, as in the senarii of *O. C.* 318.

1291. Cp. Eur. *Hec.* 28, κεῖμαι δ' ἐπ' ἀκταῖς, ἄλλοτ' ἐν πόντου σάλῳ.

1306.   *ὑπηρετοίην τῷ πάροντι δαίμονι.

While reading ὑπηρετοίην with most editors, I would observe that rare uses of the middle voice occur elsewhere in Sophocles. See esp. *Trach.* 102, ποθουμένᾳ ... φρενί.

1320, 1321. Cp. Eur. *Or.* 1151, 1152; Andoc. i. 120.

ELECTRA

1339. πῶς οὖν ἔχει τἀντεῦθεν εἰσιόντι μοι ;

τἀντεῦθεν, 'the conditions with which he will have to deal as soon as he enters' (Jebb). Rightly.

1342. εἷς τῶν ἐν Ἅιδου μάνθαν' ἐνθάδ' ὢν ἀνήρ.

'Know that here thou art numbered with the shades' (Jebb). I had taken the sense differently—'Understand that you are the only dead man who is here above.' But I do not insist. Cp. however, Eur. *Or.* 385, τίνα δέδορκα νερτέρων ; | OR. εὖ γ' εἶπας, οὐ γὰρ ζῶ κακοῖς· φάος δ' ὁρῶ.

1360. λόγοις ἀπώλλυς, ἔργ' ἔχων ἥδιστ' ἐμοί.

'ἔργ' ἔχων, possessed of them', 'knowing them' (Jebb). I am still inclined to give ἔχων a more active meaning, 'engaged in', 'supporting', 'furthering'.

1364. τοὺς γὰρ ἐν μέσῳ λόγους. Cp. Eur. *Hel.* 630. πολλοὺς δ' ἐν μέσῳ λόγους ἔχων | οὐκ οἶδ' ὁποίου πρῶτον ἄρξωμαι τανῦν.

1365. πολλαὶ κυκλοῦνται νύκτες ἡμέραι τ' ἴσαι.

I take κυκλοῦσιν in *Trach.* 129 as transitive. See note *in loco*.

1370, 1371. τούτοις τε καὶ σοφωτέροις ἄλλοισι τούτων πλείοσιν μαχούμενοι.

'τούτοις refers to ἀνδρῶν in 1369, the male domestics' (Jebb). As there has been no mention of such persons, it seems more natural to understand τούτοις and τούτων as referring to Clytemnestra and her women.

1380. αἰτῶ, προπίτνω, λίσσομαι, γενοῦ πρόφρων.

While admitting that the ι of πίτνω is elsewhere short, I would not venture to change the reading.

1384. ἴδεθ' ὅπου προνέμεται.

My suggestion of a fire was certainly unnecessary, and was only meant as a subsidiary illustration.

1385. τὸ δυσέριστον αἷμα.

I adhere to the view of these words which I put forth in my edition and expressed in my translation. It is in agreement with one of the Scholia: 'Slaughter in an evil' or 'painful feud'. This really turns on a special use of the verbal adjective which appears also *supra*, 219 f, τὰ δὲ τοῖς δυνατοῖς | οὐκ ἐριστὰ πλάθειν. So in *O. C.* 1614, δυσπόνητον ... τροφήν is 'care involving painful labour'. Compare the drift of Aesch. *Cho.* 827-837.

1395. νεακόνητον αἷμα χειροῖν ἔχων.

If the combination of an iambic dipody with a dochmiac, assumed by Hermann in *O. T.* 1345, may be admitted, the right quantity of νεακόνητον may be retained—scanning μετᾰδρομοι in the strophe.

1414. μοῖρα καθαμερία φθίνει φθίνει.

μοῖρα καθαμερία, 'the fate that hath pursued thee day by day'—Jebb (reading νῦν *σοι in 1413). This is very attractive. But would not φθίνει be an inauspicious word to use in such a connexion? The single use of καθημέριος by Euripides is not a sufficient reason for condemning a meaning which satisfied Hermann; who compares *O. C.* 1079, τελεῖ Ζεύς τι κατ' ἆμαρ. The Chorus in the Choephori are

ELECTRA

in entire sympathy with the matricide, yet they express their horror. That the Chorus here should do so at the first moment is a natural and dramatic touch: nor is the supposition of two ἡμιχόρια to be excluded. And the words of Aegisthus in 1498, τά τ' ὄντα καὶ μέλλοντα Πελοπιδῶν κακά, show that Sophocles does not absolutely ignore the sequel. Hermann's φθίνειν is the easiest change.

1420. παλίρρυτον γὰρ αἷμ' ὑπεξαιροῦσι.

παλίρρυτον. Cp. Eur. *H. F.* 739.

δίκα καὶ θεῶν παλίρρους πότμος.

1423. οὐδ' ἔχω λέγειν.

I withdraw the objection which I formerly expressed to ψέγειν. It is on the whole a probable conjecture.

1424. Ὀρέστα, πῶς *κυρεῖ δέ;

Hermann's conjecture πῶς κυρεῖ δέ; seems unobjectionable and harmonises with the reply of Orestes better than Elmsley's πῶς κυρεῖτε;

1435. ᾗ νοεῖς.

I now give ᾗ νοεῖς to Electra. See *CA*. (Greek text).

1448, 1449. συμφορᾶς γὰρ ἂν
ἔξωθεν εἴην τῶν ἐμῶν τῆς φιλτάτης.

It seems to me unlikely that Electra would speak of her mother as τῆς φιλτάτης in addressing Aegisthus, who well knows the hatred between them. I therefore agree with Wecklein in thinking that τῆς φιλτάτης goes with συμφορᾶς in both senses: 'of events affecting my kindred, that which is nearest to my heart'.

1451. φίλης γὰρ προξένου κατήνυσαν.

I adhere to my note, and think that in Electra's hidden meaning, and also in the more obvious interpretation, the genitive is governed by κατα in comp. 'They have found their way to her.' They 'have finished with regard to her'. This seems better than 'supplying a word understood'.

1457. χαίροις ἄν, εἴ σοι χαρτὰ τυγχάνει τάδε.

I should now read τυγχάνει, rather than τυγχάνοι.

1458. σιγᾶν ἄνωγα, κἀναδεικνύναι πύλας.

I still rather incline to make πύλας the subject of ἀναδεικνύναι, the object being supplied by 1460 (sc. ἄνδρα τόνδε νεκρόν).

1464. τελεῖται τἀπ' ἐμοῦ·

Eur. *Tro.* 74, ἕτοιμ' ἃ βούλει τἀπ' ἐμοῦ.

1473. εἴ που κατ' οἶκόν μοι Κλυταιμήστρα, κάλει.

Jebb does not observe that here and everywhere in the Laurentian (or Medicean) MS., both of Aeschylus and Sophocles, Κλυταιμήστρα is the form given. Attention was called to this fact by Pappageorg in 1882 and by Girolamo Vitelli in his Collation of the Medicean (Laurentian) Aeschylus.

1475. τίνα φοβεῖ; τίν' ἀγνοεῖς;

The horrified gaze of discovery need not be too much hurried, but the alarming inference must naturally lead to the look of terror and strangeness implied in Orestes' words. This is another instance of 'by-play'. See above on 610.

ELECTRA

1478. ζῶν τοῖς θανοῦσιν οὕνεκ' ἀνταυδᾷς ἴσα.

I hold rather doubtfully to my former view. The construction of the accusative, if ζῶντας is read, is not clearly accounted for. Aegisthus has not been 'calling names'. 'While yet in life, thou art answering a dead man with accents of the dead', *i.e.* of one doomed to die.

1481. καὶ μάντις ὢν ἄριστος.

'So good a seer too' seems to me to give the force of καί.

1485, 1486. τί γὰρ βροτῶν ἂν σὺν κακοῖς μεμιγμένων
θνῄσκειν ὁ μέλλων τοῦ χρόνου κέρδος φέροι;

I willingly remove the brackets, as is done in *CA*. The case is the same as with 1007 *supra*.

1498. τά τ' ὄντα καὶ μέλλοντα Πελοπιδῶν κακά.

Compare the end of the *Trachiniae*, where the spectators are aware of 'the glory that is to follow', though it is hidden from Hyllus and the rest.

1506. ὅστις πέρα πράσσειν τι τῶν νόμων θέλοι.

I prefer θέλοι here.

TRACHINIAE

THE possible relation of Greek tragedy to historical events has often been over-estimated; yet it would be foolish to deny that the action of the *Eumenides* has some bearing on political relations between Athens and Argos, and on the position of the Areopagus. In my edition of 1881, I ventured upon a conjecture, which I see no reason to retract, that when the maternal heart of Deianira is drawn forth towards Iole, and the wife of Heracles prays that she may not live to see her own seed made captive, the Athenian audience could not fail to be reminded of the men from Pylos, some of whom no doubt claimed to be descended from Heracles through Hyllus, Deianira's son. This supposition is not violently inconsistent with the probable date of the drama, which, according to Professor Jebb, is to be placed at some point between 420 and 410 B.C. The captives were restored at the peace of Nicias in March 421 B.C. If the limits assigned by Professor Jebb were extended backward so as to include this date, Sophocles might be supposed here to express the feeling of the party of Nicias, which was for the time triumphant. Such an hypothesis does not seem extravagant, though it is inconsistent with the notion entertained in some quarters that the *Heracles* of Euripides was the earlier play.

For the Fable, compare Bacchylides v. 165-175, xv. 13-35 (ed. Kenyon).

TRACHINIAE

1.   Λόγος μέν ἐστ' ἀρχαῖος ἀνθρώπων φανείς.

I do not join ἐστὶν ... φανείς, but why should ἔστιν be read here any more than in *El.* 417? That takes something of the emphasis from λόγος.

7.   ναίουσ' ἐνὶ Πλευρῶνι.

I adhere to my note, though of course I do not regard the reading as certain. Erfurdt's ἔτ' ἐν is certainly the best of the conjectures. Note that ποτὶ for πρός *Eum.* 79, *infra* 1214, is equally rare, and cp. *Ant.* 1241.

27.   λέχος γὰρ Ἡρακλεῖ κριτὸν
ξυστᾶσ'.

I adhere to my note, as abridged in *CA.* I do not think that D. would speak of herself in the neuter gender. The accusative in apposition to the sentence is likewise the most probable construction in Eur. *Tro.* 44 (Κασάνδραν) γαμεῖ βιαίως σκότιον Ἀγαμέμνων λέχος. κριτόν 'adjudged' as the result of conquest: Pind. *Nem.* iv. 1, εὐφροσύνα πόνων κεκριμένων | ἰατρός.

29, 30.   νὺξ γὰρ εἰσάγει,
καὶ νὺξ ἀπωθεῖ διαδεδεγμένη πόνον.

I take διαδεδεγμένη πόνον as equivalent to ἐσχηκυῖα διαδοχὴν πόνου, and would supply Ἡρακλῆ as object of both verbs. 'Night brings him home, and night, succeeding to another labour, thrusts him away'. The question remains whether νὺξ καὶ νὺξ mean one and the same night, or two alternate nights. For the turn of expression cp. Sosiphanes, *fr.* 3.

βροτοί, τί σεμνύνεσθε ταῖς ἐξουσίαις,
ἃς ἕν τ' ἔδωκε φέγγος ἕν τ' ἀφείλετο;

Pind. *Nem.* vi. 1, ἓν ἀνδρῶν, ἓν θεῶν γένος. Eur. *Phoen.* 1689, ἓν ἦμαρ μ' ὤλβισ', ἓν δ' ἀπώλετο.

I do not see why ἀπωθεῖ so construed is 'forced'. Cp. Tennyson's *Love and Duty*,

> 'And crying, "Who is this? behold thy bride",
> She pushed me from thee.'

The presents, including τρέφω, are not historical but general. She is describing the course of her married life up to the present hour. And the description with regard to Heracles is resumed in 34. The Scholiast seems to have understood 'Night brings him, and night sends him away, receiving trouble in his room'—a meaning which may commend itself to some.

42.   ὠδῖνας αὐτοῦ προσβαλὼν ἀποίχεται.

There is certainly no objection to αὐτοῦ.

58.   ἐγγὺς δ' ὅδ' αὐτὸς ἀρτίπους θρώσκει δόμους.

ἀρτίπους. In favour of the meaning 'with timely footstep', of which Jebb and Wecklein approve, might also be quoted Pindar's use of ἀρτιεπής, *Ol.* vi. 61, ἀντεφθέγξατο δ' ἀρτιεπὴς | πατρία ὄσσα.

80.   εἰς τὸν ὕστερον.

As I am not convinced that *O. C.* 1584, *El.* 1075 are certainly corrupt, I still read as above, while admitting that εἰς τό γ' ὕστερον (Reiske) is an easy change.

88.   νῦν δ' ὁ ξυνήθης πότμος οὐκ *εἴα πατρός.

I admit that Wakefield's πρὶν for νῦν is not necessary, though it somewhat improves the sense.

TRACHINIAE

92, 93.   καὶ γὰρ ὑστέρῳ τό γ' εὖ
πράσσειν, ἐπεὶ πύθοιτο, κέρδος ἐμπολᾷ.

I do not see that the optative makes it *clear* that τὸ εὖ πράσσειν means 'good fortune'. Cp. *O. T.* 314, 5.

ἄνδρα δ' ὠφελεῖν ἀφ' ὧν
ἔχοι τε καὶ δύναιτο κάλλιστος πόνων.

100.   ἢ ποντίας αὐλῶνας, ἢ δισσαῖσιν ἀπείροις κλιθείς.

Cp. Eur. *Ion*, 1581-7.

οἱ τῶνδε δ' αὖ
παῖδες γενόμενοι σὺν χρόνῳ πεπρωμένῳ
Κυκλάδας ἐποικήσουσι νησαίας πόλεις
χέρσους τε παράλους, ὃ σθένος τἠμῇ χθονί
δίδωσιν· ἀντίπορθμα δ' ἠπείροιν δυοῖν
πεδία κατοικήσουσιν, Ἀσιάδος τε γῆς
Εὐρωπίας τε.

102.   ποθουμένᾳ γὰρ φρενί.

Rare middles in Sophocles accentuate the *personal* nature of the act or feeling denoted by the verb.

107.   βλεφάρων πόθον.

Cp. *fr.* 733, ὀμμάτειος πόθος.

110.   ἐνθυμίοις εὐναῖς ἀνανδρώτοισι τρύχεσθαι.

I grant that the dative is causal (not locative), but agree with the Scholiast in thinking that ἐνθυμίοις = μεριμνητικαῖς, 'haunted by sad thoughts'.

115.   κύματ' *ἂν εὑρέϊ πόντῳ.

I now prefer *ἂν to *ἐν with Jebb.

116, 117. οὕτω δὲ τὸν Καδμογενῆ τρέφει, τὸ δ' αὔξει, βιότου
πολύπονον ὥσπερ πέλαγος Κρήσιον.

Though the text is hard, I do not think it is improved by
*στρέφει. At all events the words ὥσπερ πολύπονον Κρήσιον
πέλαγος βιότου = 'as it were a troublous Cretan sea of circumstance' are to be construed together. As elsewhere, the figurative language is in transition from simile to metaphor. The image and the thing compared to it are fused in one expression. See below on 129 *f*.

I still think that (τὸ μὲν) τρέφει, τὸ δ' αὔξει may mean 'surrounds, and also glorifies'.

122. ἀδεῖα μέν, ἀντία δ' οἴσω.

'Since ἀντία expresses remonstrance against her despair, there is then no proper antithesis with ἀδεῖα (Jebb). I do not understand. 'I will oppose you, but in a comfortable way' is surely pointed enough. αἰδοῖα, though ingenious, seems more commonplace.

129. ἀλλ' ἐπὶ πῆμα καὶ χαρὰν.

(So in *CA.*). L. *primitus* had χαρὰν, which the first hand changed to χαρᾷ. Hermann had conjectured χαράν. Adoptting this, I take ἐπικυκλοῦσιν actively. Here as *supr.* 117 the image blends with the thing signified, and simile is passing into metaphor. 'As it were a circling orbit of the Bear brings sorrow and joy round to every one.' Cf. *Her.* i. 207, κύκλος τῶν ἀνθρωπηΐων ἐστὶ πρηγμάτων, περιφερόμενος δὲ οὐκ ἐᾷ αἰεὶ τοὺς αὐτοὺς εὐτυχέειν.

134, 135. τῷ δ' ἐπέρχεται
χαίρειν τε καὶ στέρεσθαι.

I now agree with Jebb in preferring the meaning which I gave as an alternative (2), 'While joy and the loss of it, come to *another* in his turn.' So in my Translation.

136. ἃ καὶ σὲ τὰν ἄνασσαν ἐλπίσιν λέγω
τάδ' αἰὲν ἴσχειν.

Here also I now agree with Jebb and Hermann in preferring my second alternative (2) as to the construction of ἃ and τάδε. 'In respect of which truth I bid thee ever to be hopeful regarding this,' viz. the present cause of anxiety.

147. ἡδοναῖς ἄμοχθον ἐξαίρει βίον.
Cp. Eur. *Hec.* 20.
τροφαῖσιν, ὥς τις πτόρθος, ηὐξόμην.

149. λαβῇ τ' ἐν νυκτὶ φροντίδων μέρος.

My note agrees with Jebb's in construing ἐν νυκτὶ with the verb, but I explained it of the marriage night, for which cp. Eur. *Tro.* 665. I now understand the words as he does = 'in the watches of the night'.

163. μοῖραν πατρῴας γῆς διαιρετὸν νέμοι.
Cp. Eur. *H. F.* 462.
σοὶ μὲν γὰρ Ἄργος ἔνεμ' ὁ κατθανὼν πατήρ.

169, 170. τοιαῦτ' ἔφραζε πρὸς θεῶν εἱμαρμένα
τῶν Ἡρακλείων ἐκτελευτᾶσθαι πόνων.

My note on these lines is not quite clear; but I seem to have agreed with Jebb in understanding the vague genitive as one of respect (=περί). I take εἱμαρμένα, however, as attributive, not predicative, and the infinitive as governed by ἔφραζε, the present tense being equivalent to a certain future (prophetic). 'Such destined issue, he declared, should be the consummation of the labours of Hercules. Cp. Pind. *Pyth.* iv. 19.

κεῖνος ὄρνις ἐκτελευτάσει μεγαλᾶν πολίων
ματρόπολιν Θήραν γενέσθαι.

And, for the prophetic present, *ib.* 48, 49.

>τότε γὰρ μεγάλας
>ἐξανίστανται Λακεδαίμονος.

172. δισσῶν ἐκ πελειάδων.

Sophocles elsewhere (*fr.* 414) spoke of the priestesses as such.

174. ὡς τελεσθῆναι χρεών.

Instead of taking ὡς as = ὥστε here, and supplying ἐστί, I would treat χρεών as participial. 'The certain truth of this comes to pass at the present hour, according to the destined fulfilment.'

188. See *Her.* vii. 199, where the site of Trachis is said to be the most spacious in the Malian region.

196. τὸ γὰρ ποθοῦν ἕκαστος ἐκμαθεῖν θέλων.

In defence of the interpretation which Jebb condemns as 'impossibly harsh', I will only observe that the boundary between desire and its object is quickly passed in Greek, and the difference between 'to learn what I long for' and 'to learn what I long to learn' would hardly be felt. Cp. Shak., *Tempest* I. 2, 176.

>'I pray you, Sir—
>For still 'tis beating in my mind—your reason
>For raising this sea storm?'

204-215. ἀνολολύξατε δόμοις
ἐφεστίοις ἀλαλαγαῖς
ὁ μελλόνυμφος . . .

I hold to my reading, commentary, and division of lines. The double Cretic, followed by a diiambus and another

Cretic, makes a suitable opening, and the pure iambic line (cp. 211, 217) is a good link of transition to less regular (syncopated) rhythms. On this ground in 206 I prefer ὁ to ἁ, defending it as αὐτοῦ is defended in 151.

209. Ἀπόλλωνα προστάταν.

The rhythm ᴗ ᵕ ᷉ ᴗ – ᴗ – seems not an unsuitable continuation of ᴗ ᵕ ⏑ ᷉ ᴗ – ᴗ – ᷒. For the accusative cp. Eur. *Iph A.* 1469, ἐπευφήμησατ', ὦ νεάνιδες, | παιᾶνα τῇμῇ ξυμφορᾷ Διὸς κόρην | Ἄρτεμιν; *ib.* 1480.

216. ἀείρομ'.

For ἀείρομαι cp. Eur. *Alc.* 346.

οὔτ' ἂν φρέν' ἐξαίροιμι πρὸς Λίβυν λακεῖν
αὐλόν.

218, 219. ἰδοῦ μ' ἀναταράσσει
εὐοῖ μ' ὁ κισσός.

The repetition of μ' after both interjections belongs to the wildness of the hyporchema. It has probably in both cases the same construction.

240. Cp. Bacchyl. xii. 223, 224, ὕμνων τινὰ τάνδε (δόσιν) φαίνω.

243. εἰ μὴ ξυμφορᾷ κλέπτουσί με.

The first hand of L. seems to have written ξυμφορὰ. The S. has added ι, and an early corrector has changed the accent from ` to ῀. The scholion implies the reading ξυμφοραί. It seems to me rather more in accordance with the poetical style of Sophocles that κλέπτουσι should have a personal subject.

250. τοῦ λόγου δ' οὐ χρὴ φθόνον.

Cf. Eur. *fr.* 387, φθόνου μὲν μῦθον ἄξιον φράσω.

267. φωνεῖ δέ, δοῦλος ἀνδρὸς ὡς ἐλευθέρου
ῥαίοιτο.

Jebb's defence of φωνεῖ δέ is plausible; but I am still inclined to read *φύσει δὲ δοῦλος and to make the gen. depend as one of the agent upon ῥαίοιτο (λείπει ἡ ὑπό S.). Cp. Eur. *fr.* 14, θεοῦ μανείς. It is not the construction, nor the meaning of φωνεῖ, but the *tautology* that seems a weakness in the traditional text.

273. ἀπ' ἄκρας ἧκε πυργώδους πλακός.

πυργώδους πλακός. Iphitus was standing on the κλιτύς (*supra*) surmounted as it was with the Cyclopean wall. The phrase calls up this twofold image.

276, 277. οὐδ' ἠνέσχετο
ὁθούνεκ'.

'And would not endure it, because'. So Jebb explains. Rightly.

279. Ζεύς τἂν συνέγνω ξὺν δίκῃ χειρουμένῳ.

χειρουμένῳ, 'middle' (Jebb). And so *CA*.

303. ὦ Ζεῦ τροπαῖε. Cf. Eur. *Heracl.* 867, Eur. *El.* 671.

315. γέννημα τῶν ἐκεῖθεν οὐκ ἐν ὑστάτοις.

τῶν ἐκεῖθεν. Jebb thinks the partitive genitive 'less natural' here. It agrees better with ἐκεῖθεν. On the other hand, 'an offspring of the folk there' (Jebb) agrees better with τῶν τυράννων in 316. But the difference would hardly be felt by a Greek.

316. Εὐρύτου σπορά τις ἦν;

The version 'was she possibly a child of Eurytus' seems to me on the whole more likely and agrees better with οὐκ οἶδα in the reply.

320. εἴπ' ὦ τάλαιν', ἀλλ' ἡμὶν ἐκ σαυτῆς.

ἀλλά is rather to be joined with ἐκ σαυτῆς, which has the chief emphasis.

323. διοίσει γλῶσσαν.

I remain in doubt between διοίσει and διήσει. There is no precise parallel for the former (cp. however Eur. *fr.* 38, τὰ πόλλ' ἀνάγκη διαφέρει (brings to bear) τολμήματα: Pind. *Pyth.* xi. 59, ἅτε τὸν Ἰφικλείδαν διαφέρει Ἰόλαον ὑμνητὸν ἐόντα); but it is hard to set a limit to original uses of words in Sophocles. It is perhaps worth while to observe that διοισει (*sic*) is without an accent in L.; also that there seems to have been a dot over the ο, perhaps marking the word as doubtful. For other special uses of διαφέρειν cp. Eur. *Phoen.* 265, ὄμμα πανταχῇ διοιστέον: Bacch. 1087, διήνεγκαν κόρας: *Iph. A.* 1195, ἢ σκῆπτρά σοι | μόνον διαφέρειν καὶ στρατηλατεῖν σε δεῖ;

331. τοῖς οὖσιν ἄλλην πρός γ' ἐμοῦ λύπην λάβοι.

I am inclined to retain λάβοι. The general wish is the ground of the particular command. The reading ἄλλην may not be a mere conjecture of Triclinius. He had access to MSS. since lost.

333.
σπεύδῃς.   ὡς σύ θ' οἷ θέλεις

Cp. Imogen in Shak. *Cymb.* iii. 2, 54 ('Pisanio,') 'Who long'st, like me, to see thy lord.'

344.   σοὶ ταῖσδέ τ' οὐδὲν εἴργεται.

I take εἴργεται as impersonal and οὐδὲν as adverbial.

356.   οὐ τἀπὶ Λυδοῖς οὐδ' ἐπ' 'Ομφάλῃ πόνων.

ὑπ' 'Ομφάλῃ is certainly a probable emendation.

363.   τὸν Εὔρυτον τόνδ' εἶπε δεσπόζειν θρόνων.

τόνδ' Jebb, and my edition (1881): τῶνδ' *CA*. This Messenger, like the φύλαξ in the *Antigone*, is profuse in demonstratives.

364.   κτείνει τ' ἄνακτα πατέρα τῆσδε.

Lichas in the market place did not conceal the fact that she is the daughter of Eurytus.

371, 372.   πολλοὶ πρὸς μέσῃ Τραχινίων
                    ἀγορᾷ συνεξήκουον.

It is not necessary to suppose the scene to be any longer the summer meadow. Lichas made some progress, though impeded by the crowd.

378, 379.   ἆρ' ἀνώνυμος
πέφυκεν, ὥσπερ οὑπάγων διώμνυτο;
ΑΓ. ἦ *κάρτα λαμπρὰ καὶ κατ' ὄμμα καὶ φύσιν.

I make no doubt that the question is asked in bitter irony. And I see no objection to ὄμμα—though if ὄνομα were the MS. reading it might be upheld.

382. βλάστας ἐφώνει δῆθεν οὐδὲν ἱστορῶν.

By all means delete the comma, as Jebb proposes.

383. Cp. *Phil.* 961, and note.

390. ἡμεῖς δὲ προσμένωμεν; ἢ τί χρὴ ποιεῖν;
Given to the Ἄγγελος by Jebb and *CA*. Perhaps rightly.

394. δίδαξον, ὡς ἕρποντος ὡς ὁρᾷς ἐμοῦ.
I should now read ὡς ὁρᾷς for εἰσορᾷς with Jebb.

396. πρὶν ἡμᾶς καὶ νεώσασθαι λόγους.
*κἀννεώσασθαι is a probable, but not a certain, conjecture. The simple verb is capable of the meaning required.

398. ἦ καὶ τὸ πιστὸν τῆς ἀληθείας νέμεις;

I prefer to read νέμεις with the MSS. rather than νεμεῖς. It continues the present tense of πάρειμι, and the dative is not easily supplied. The personal claim of Deianira is not yet in question. She asks, 'Are you faithful and true in your report?'

404. τόλμησον εἰπεῖν, εἰ φρονεῖς.

Not, I think, 'If thou comprehendest the question', but 'If you are aware of the facts'. Cp. *O. T.* 1038.

ὁ δοὺς δὲ ταῦτ' ἐμοῦ λῷον φρονεῖ.

Eur. *fr.* 205, φρονῶ δ' ὃ πάσχω· καὶ τόδ' οὐ σμικρὸν κακόν.

416. Cp. Eur. *Suppl.* 568.

419. ἣν ὑπ' ἀγνοίας ὁρᾷς.

For ἀγνοεῖν = 'to fail to recognise', cp. *El.* 1475, τίνα φοβεῖ; τίν' ἀγνοεῖς; Eur. *Androm.* 899, μηδὲν ἀγνόει.

422. σοὶ μαρτυρήσει ταῦτ' ἐμοῦ κλύειν παρών.

I see no reason for altering παρών.

431. ὃς σοῦ παρὼν ἤκουσεν.

There is a certain piquancy in the use of the 3rd person by the blunt Messenger.

440. χαίρειν πέφυκεν οὐχὶ τοῖς αὑτοῖς ἀεί.

I now agree with Jebb in preferring the meaning to which I formerly gave the second place : 'mankind do not always delight in the same things'. So in *CA.* and my translation.

443. Cp. Eur. *Hipp.* 1268, σὺ τὰν θεῶν ἄκαμπτον φρένα καὶ βροτῶν ἄγεις Κύπρι, *ff.*

447, 448. τῇ μεταιτίᾳ
τοῦ μηδὲν αἰσχροῦ μηδ' ἐμοὶ κακοῦ τινος.

'Probably Sophocles meant her to be sincere' (Jebb). I think she is dissembling, in order to elicit the truth ; though, as in the speech of Ajax (*Aj.* 646-692) her real feeling is perceptible throughout. See below 543, 544.

460. Cp. Eur. *Or.* 743, ἢ πλείστους Ἀχαιῶν ὤλεσεν γύνη μία.

462, 463. οὐδ' ἂν εἰ
κάρτ' ἐντακείη τῷ φιλεῖν.

I still think Heracles the subject of ἐντακείη, though Jebb

thinks 'it would be "excessively harsh'". Reasons for this are given in my note (1881) and in *CA*.' Another possible view is to take Iole as subj. of ἐντακείη and Her. of φιλεῖν; 'though she were utterly steeped in his love for her'. But this would be still more accused of 'harshness'. It appears that in his *Hippolytus* Sophocles made Phaedra excuse her passion by the number of Theseus' infidelities.

491. κοῦτοι νόσον γ' ἐπακτὸν ἐξαρούμεθα.

In my note of 1881 I understood these words to mean: 'I will at least not aggravate the trouble which would then be of my own seeking'; *i.e.* I took ἐξαίρεσθαι to have the sense of the active with a reflexive force, and ἐπακτόν as proleptic. I am still rather inclined to this view. There seems to be a long step from ἐξαίρεσθαι μίσθον, κῦδος, νίκην, etc., to ἐξαίρεσθαι νόσον. For the general meaning cp. *fr.* 324.

ταῦτ' ἐστὶν ἄλγιστ', ἣν παρὸν θέσθαι καλῶς
αὐτός τις αὐτῷ τὴν βλάβην προσθῇ φέρων.

And for ἐπακτόν cp. εἰσαγώγιμον in Eur. *fr.* 984.

497. μέγα τι σθένος ἁ Κύπρις ἐκφέρεται νίκας ἀεί.

'Great and mighty is the victory which the Cyprian queen ever bears away' (Jebb (with Schneidewin)). The choice seems to me to lie between this (which agrees with the Scholia, cp. also *Her.* vi. 103, ἐξενείκασθαι), and (2) 'advances in mighty conquering force'. The latter gives, to my mind, a better, because a more *vivid* meaning, but the position of νίκας is awkward. It was Hermann who suggested that ἐκφέρεται might be taken passively to mean 'rushes forth', 'careers', 'advances'. I am inclined to adopt his suggestion, but to read *νικῶσ' ἀεί. The meaning given by Linwood and others, 'exerts', 'puts forth', is not really supported by Eur. *Ion* 1012, δύνασιν ἐκφέρει τίνα = 'obtains what power', the subject being the antecedent to ὅστις in the preceding line.

505. *τίνες ἀμφίγυοι κατέβαν πρὸ γάμων.

ἀμφίγυοι. Jebb, again agreeing with Schneidewin, understands 'two stalwart men', the second part of the compound being merely suggestive of strong limbs. I still prefer 'armed at all points', an epic word freely adapted by the poet, like κλυτός, ἀμενηνός, etc. in the *Ajax*, or τετραόρου, *infra* 507. For κατέβαν, cp. κατέδραμεν in Pind. *Nem.* iv. 14. πρὸ γάμων. 'In πρό, just as in "for", the two notions—"for it" and "before it"—are closely linked' (Jebb).

511. παλίντονα.

If παλίντονος meant merely *curved*, the latter part of the epithet would lose its force. When bent, there is an *opposite* tension, as Heracleitus observed, between the bow and the string.

524. τηλαυγεῖ παρ' ὄχθῳ.

τηλαυγεῖ. From the idea of reciprocal action which attends words of sight in Greek, it is possible that the two notions, 'conspicuous', and 'commanding a distant view', are blended here. See note on *O. T.* 1482, ὧδ' ὁρᾶν. There is the same double force in Pind. *Ol.* vi. 4, πρόσωπον ... τηλαυγές, and Ar. *Av.* 1711, ἡλίου τηλαυγὲς ἀκτίνων σέλας ('seen from afar' and 'glancing from afar').

526. ἐγὼ δὲ μάτηρ μὲν οἷα φράζω.

Jebb's conjecture, ἀγὼν δὲ μαργᾷ μέν, οἷα φράζω is extremely plausible and ingenious. But, although Electra's chorus are not young maidens, the parallel of *El.* 233, ἀλλ' οὖν εὐνοίᾳ γ' αὐδῶ | μάτηρ ὡσεί τις πιστά, is not altogether to be despised.

TRACHINIAE

529.   κἀπὸ ματρὸς ἄφαρ βέβακεν.

Is it necessary to harmonise the details of the drama with the 'common account'? ἐρήμα seems to imply that she left her home.

535.   τὰ δ' οἷα πάσχω συγκατοικτιουμένῃ.

συγκατοικτιουμένῃ; 'To bewail my woes along with you' (Jebb). This is certainly the literal meaning. But the middle is reflexive.

540. For χλαίνης cp. Eur. *fr.* 603, ὅταν δ' ὑπ' ἀνδρὸς χλαῖναν εὐγενοῦς πέσῃς.

541.   ὁ πιστὸς ἡμῖν κἀγαθὸς καλούμενος.

I am still inclined to take ἡμῖν with πιστὸς κἀγαθὸς rather than with καλούμενος.

548, 549.   ὧν ἀφαρπάζειν φιλεῖ
ὀφθαλμὸς ἄνθος.

I still think that ὧν refers to those whose youth is advancing. For the general meaning cp. Eur. *fr.* 24, θήλεια δ' ἥβη θᾶσσον ἐκλείπει δέμας.

554.   λυτήριον †λύπημα.

In support of my conjecture λυτήριον νόημα I would urge (1) that, as the corruption is probably due to the eye of the scribe having wandered to the previous word, it is unnecessary to suppose that the lost syllable resembled λυτ; (2) a further cause of confusion may have been the occurrence of the same letters in the same place of the line above, and in the syllable immediately preceding—ον νο : (the νο of νοῦν in

553 is just above λυ in 554); (3) νόημα does not weaken the emphasis in λυτήριον by repeating the same notion in a different form; (4) the thought so expressed is naturally resumed in 578, τοῦτ' ἐννοήσασ', ὦ φίλαι. In editing the text again, I should print νόημα. Cp. Bacchyl. x. 54; στήθεσσι παλίντροπον ἐμβαλεν νόημα, xv. 25, δαίμων | Δαϊανείρᾳ πολύδακρυν ὕφανε | μῆτιν ἐπίφρον' . . .

558. ἐκ φόνων ἀνειλόμην.

I should now read φονῶν. For the whole passage cp. Bacchyl. xv. 34, 35.

> ὅτ' ἐπὶ ποταμῷ ῥοδόεντι Λυκόρμᾳ
> δέξατο Νέσσου πάρα δαιμόνιον τέρας.

564. ἡνίκ' ἦν μέσῳ πόρῳ.

The 1st person is read in *CA*.

577, 578. δόμοις γὰρ ἦν
κείνου θανόντος ἐγκεκλειμένον καλῶς.

δόμοις. 'Simply "in the house"' (Jebb). Perhaps rightly.

592. ἀλλ' εἰδέναι χρὴ δρῶσαν.

'The participle expresses the leading idea ("if thou wouldst know, thou must act")', Jebb. Rightly.

596. Cp. *fr.* 618, τὸ γὰρ | γυναιξὶν αἰσχρὸν ἐν γυναικὶ δεῖ στέγειν.

602. ὅπως φέρῃς μοι τόνδε γ' εὐϋφῆ πέπλον.

The reasons for ταναϋφῆ are decidedly strong. But γε need not be otiose. It may preface the particular statement which confirms l. 600.

TRACHINIAE

608.   πρὶν κεῖνος αὐτὸν φανερὸν ἐμφανὴς σταθεὶς
δείξῃ θεοῖσιν.

The readings of Triclinius are not always due to his conjecture; and φανερὸν ἐμφανὴς is at least a plausible reading.

613.   θυτῆρα καινῷ καινὸν ἐν πεπλώματι.

A close parallel is Eur. *Suppl.* 593, στρατηλατήσω καινὸς ἐν καινῷ δορί, where this reading is preferred by Mr. G. Murray, the Oxford editor, to κλεινὸς ἐν κλεινῷ δ. The 'ironical' meaning suggested by Jebb is doubtful.

614, 615.   ὃ κεῖνος εὐμαθὲς
σφραγῖδος ἕρκει τῷδ' ἐπ' ὄμμα θήσεται.

Billerbeck's conjecture, approved by Jebb, εὐμαθὲς ... ἐπὸν μαθήσεται, will probably retain its place in the text, in preference to the 'harder reading', which, however, may still obtain some suffrages. In any case I think that ἕρκος denotes not the shape, but the function, of the seal, as guarding what is enclosed.

623.   λόγων τε πίστιν ὧν *λέγεις ἐφαρμόσαι.

The reasons for ὧν λέγεις are irresistible.

627.   αὐτήν θ' ὡς ἐδεξάμην φίλως.

The tendency to minute antithesis in Greek makes αὐτήν θ' possible. It keeps the person of Iole vividly before the mind. See above, 307, ὦ δυστάλαινα, τίς ποτ' εἶ νεανίδων . . .

642-645. *ἀχῶν καναχὰν ἐπάνεισιν . . .
. . . .
*σοῦται πάσας ἀρετᾶς
λάφυρ' ἔχων.

I willingly accept *ἀχῶν (for ἰάχων) and *σοῦται (for σεῦται) from Elmsley and Jebb.

647. ὃν ἀπόπτολιν εἴχομεν, πάντα.

The MS. reading πάντα, joined to χρόνον, seems not impossible, though the long syllable in παντᾷ gives more perfect metrical correspondence to the antistrophe. But there is a natural pause.

649. πελάγιον.

πελάγιον of course literally means 'on the open sea', but I prefer to take it figuratively = 'out of sight of land', and so 'beyond our ken'.

655. ἐξέλυσ' ἐπίπονον ἀμέραν. For the construction cp. also Eur. *Phoen.* 695, μόχθον ἐκλύει.

658. ἔνθα κλῄζεται θυτήρ. Cf. Eur. *Hel.* 132, θανὼν δὲ κλῄζεται καθ' Ἑλλάδα.

660-662. ὅθεν μόλοι πανάμερος
τᾶς πειθοῦς παγχρίστῳ
συγκραθεὶς ἐπὶ προφάσει θηρός.

These lines are confessedly difficult; and I do not see that the difficulties have been completely removed. (1) So far as the metres are concerned, I venture to assume some retardation of the rhythm in the antistrophe. This may be partially avoided by reading συντακείς for συγκραθείς answering ἐξέλυσ. But for θηρόσ=μέραν one may quote *Phil.* 1151, ἀλκάν answering to φίλων. See below on lines 846 and 857. (2) The text of Bacchylides shows that in lyric poetry there sometimes occur forms and uses of words which are either unique or only known to us from late writers (see also Jebb's note on καινοποηθὲν, *infr.* 873 and χειροποιηθέν in 891).

(*a.*) On this ground I would defend πανάμερος as a compound of ἥμερος='quite docile',—'with passion subdued',— a meaning with which the word occurs in ecclesiastical writers. Cp. also εὐήμερος in Aristoph. *Av.* 1321, Plato, *Tim.* 71 D. (*mansuetus*, Ast's Lex.), and δυσήμερος in Strabo, 155. Ἀνήμερος is a more familiar derivative. For ἄμερος in Lyric poetry, cf. also Pind. *Nem.* viii. 3; ix. 44. Πανίμερος seems to me too strong a word. Deianira's friends can hardly expect that Heracles' passionate love-longing (ἵμερος) will be transferred from Iole to her.

(*b.*) Πρόφατος in the sense of 'proclaimed' occurs as a ἅπαξ λεγόμενον in Pindar, *Ol.* viii. 16. Then why may not πρόφασις in lyrics mean 'forespeaking' or 'foreshowing'?

(*c.*) If παγχρίστῳ is retained, it seems necessary to join it as an adj. with προφάσει. But 'a pretext of anointing' gives a poor sense, while 'a prescription of anointing' puts no more strain on the use of the verbal adjective. Cp. 357, ὁ ῥιπτὸς Ἰφίτου μόρος.

(*d.*) συγκραθεὶς (or συντακείς) must then be taken absolutely ='reunited', 'reconciled', *i.e.* to Deianira. Cp. Aesch. *Cho.* 344, νεοκρᾶτα φίλον κομίσειεν.

673. ὑμῖν θαῦμ' ἀνέλπιστον μαθεῖν.
For the alleged 'harshness', cp. Eur. *fr.* 907.

ἄμουσ' ὑλακτῶν ὥστε βαρβάρῳ μαθεῖν.

675. ἀργῆτ' οἰὸς εὐείρῳ πόκῳ.

I am not convinced that the elision of the dative does not occur exceptionally in Tragedy. I am even inclined to defend it in *El.* 456, where, however, it is of course easily avoided. See note there.

678. καὶ ψῆ κατ' ἄκρας σπιλάδος.

If σπιλάς cannot mean the pavement of the court, I should be inclined to agree with Jebb that there is some corruption.

687. ἕως ἂν ἀρτίχριστον ἁρμόσαιμί που.

I am not careful to defend ἄν, and νιν is of course an easy change.

701. τοιόνδε κεῖται προπετές.

προπετές, 'As it fell' (Jebb). Rather, I still think, 'on the point of vanishing'. See below 976 and note.

703. γλαυκῆς ὀπώρας ὥστε πίονος ποτοῦ.

Jebb here decides for the construction to which I gave the second place (2), taking the genitive as in regimen with ποτοῦ. Perhaps he is right.

705. ὥστ' οὐκ ἔχω τάλαινα ποῖ γνώμης πέσω.

For πέσω, cp. Eur. *Iph. T.* 1172.

εἰς ἔρον γὰρ τοῦ μαθεῖν πεπτώκαμεν.

715. χὤσπερ ἂν θίγῃ
φθείρει τὰ πάντα κνώδαλ'.

I retain χὤσπερ='even as', 'as sure as', a meaning which Jebb thinks 'possible but forced'. It seems to me to give a more pointed meaning.

720. ταύτῃ σὺν ὁρμῇ κἀμὲ συνθανεῖν ἅμα.

I now agree in preferring ταύτῃ.

724. τὴν δ' ἐλπίδ' οὐ χρὴ τῆς τύχης κρίνειν πάρος.

The neutral meaning of ἐλπίδ' hardly suits line 726, and there is no reason for rejecting the usual meaning here.

730. ᾧ μηδέν ἐστ' *οἴκοι βαρύ.

Cp. also Eur. *fr.* 102, τύχας τὰς οἴκοθεν: *Med.* 239: *Suppl.* 182, οὔτοι δύναιτ' ἂν οἴκοθέν γ' ἀτώμενος τέρπειν ἂν ἄλλους: *Iph. A.* 1000.

766. κἀπὸ πιείρας δρυός.

It is hardly necessary to take δρυός as=πεύκης here. In *Il.* xxiii. 118, δρῦς is *oak*, as appears from *ib.* 328, ἢ δρυὸς ἢ πεύκης.

768. ὥστε τέκτονος.

'Like something *from* (the hand of) a τέκτων': 'like (a work of) his'(Jebb). This is really what I meant, only better expressed.

776. ὥσπερ ἦν ἐσταλμένον.

Jebb takes these words as part of what Lichas said. But although Hyllus was not present at *supra* 603, he may have heard the report of it on his return journey.

782. διασπαρέντος. Cp. Eur. *Phoen.* 1159, ξανθὸν δὲ κρᾶτα διεπάλυνε καὶ ῥαφὰς | ἔρρηξεν ὀστέων.

790. ῥιπτῶν ἑαυτόν.

I should now read ῥιπτῶν, not ῥίπτων.

799. μάλιστα μὲν μέθες.

I do not see that 'drop me' is 'too gentle' an expression here. Cp. *Phil.* 816. Φ. μέθες μέθες με. Ν. ποῖ μεθῶ; Φ. μέθες ποτέ. H.'s present wish is to be carried out of Euboea and then left alone in his agony. Cp. *O.T.* 1451. ἀλλ' ἔα με ναίειν ὄρεσιν, and *infr.* 1005, 1006. The case of 1254, ἐς πυράν με θῇς, is quite different.

810. ἐπεί μοι τὴν θέμιν σὺ προὔβαλες.

I still prefer 'you have thrown this right in my way'. Cp. the use of προβάλλειν in Plat. *Phaedr.* 241 E τῶν Νυμφῶν, αἷς με σὺ προὔβαλες ἐκ προνοίας.

According to the other view, 'has cast from thee, spurned' (Jebb), there is a transition from the particular to the general notion of θέμις, as of Νέμεσις in *El.* 792, 793.

823, 824. τᾶς παλαιφάτου προνοίας
**ἅ τ' ἔλακεν.

Though ὅ τ' is defensible in metre, **ἅ τ'*, besides corresponding perfectly with the antistrophe, is otherwise preferable, because the 'prophetic wisdom' is more naturally personified than the 'word'. If ὅ is retained, it may be construed as accusative, with πρόνοια as subject.

825. ἀναδοχὰν τελεῖν πόνων.

I prefer to take τελεῖν as absolute with ἀναδοχὰν for subject in the sense of 'undertaking' (not 'succession').

829, 830=839, 840.

The best solution of this corrupt passage—made more suspicious by the blanks in L (see the facsimile)—appears to be Schneidewin's.

829, 830. ἔτι ποτ' ἔτι πόνων ἔχοι θανὼν λατρείαν.

839, 840. φόνια δολιόμυθα κέντρ' ἐπιζέσαντα.

The omission of the proper name is in the manner of Sophocles, and, if I am not mistaken, has given rise to interpolation elsewhere, *e.g.* in *Philoctetes* 671, Ἰξίονα.
On 839 see below.

832, 833. χρίει δολοποιὸς ἀνάγκα,
πλευρὰ προστακέντος ἰοῦ.

The text reads more smoothly with a comma after ἀνάγκα, taking πλευρὰ as an accusative of respect (προστακέντος αὐτῷ πλευρά).

834. ὃν τέκετο θάνατος, ἔτεκε δ' αἰόλος δράκων.

I think it just worth while to copy Hermann's note (ed. 1839): '"Ετρεφε δ' Lobeckius ad *Aj.* 327. Injuria, ut puto, haerent interpretes in verbis τέκετο et ἔτεκε : quae etsi promiscue usurpantur, tamen proprie medii verbi potestas patri magis quam matri convenit: et sic videtur hic Sophocles distinxisse : *quem genuit mors, peperit autem draco.*' The reading ἔτρεφε is a plausible emendation, if emendation is required. But if Hermann's view may be accepted, the language is more forcible.

839, 840. φόνια δολιόμυθα κέντρ' ἐπιζέσαντα.

The rejection of Νέσσου in which many editors agree requires that μελαγχαίτα should be taken substantively.

180 PARALIPOMENA SOPHOCLEA

This may be supported by the following instances: Aesch. *Pers.* 578, τᾶς ἀμιάντου (sc. θαλάσσης): Aesch. *fr.* 253, φαγέδαιναν (sc. νόσον): Soph. *fr.* 435, ὑπὲρ ἀτρυγέτου (sc. πόντου or θαλάσσης): *fr.* 694, νηὸς ἰσχάδα (sc. ἄγκυραν): *fr.* 923, τὴν μακρὰν αὐλῶπιν (sc. λόγχην): *fr.* adespot. 199, ἀργῆν ἔπεφνεν (sc. ὄφιν): perhaps also Eur. *Cycl.* 707, δι' ἀμφιτρῆτος (sc. ἄντρου or πέτρας). See also the omission of the name of Capaneus in *Ant.* 133 *f.*

If νέσου θ' arose from νέσσου θηρός, a gloss (or twofold gloss) on μελαγχαίτα, ὕπο may have arisen independently from an interlinear gloss intended to account for the genitive.

841, 845. ὧν ἅδ' ἁ τλάμων, ἄοκνον
μεγάλαν προσορῶσα δόμοις βλάβαν
νέων ἀϊσσόντων γάμων, τὰ μὲν †οὔτι
προσέβαλεν· τὰ δ' ἀπ' ἀλλόθρου
γνώμας μολόντα *σκαιαῖσι συναλλαγαῖς.

```
 _ ⏑́ ⎣ _ ⏑́ ⏑ ⏑ _
⏑ ⏑ ⏑́ ⏑ ⏑ _ ⏑ ⏑ _ ⏑ _
⏑ _ ⏑ ⏑́ _ ⏑́ ⏑ ⏑́ ⏑ ⏑ ⎣ ⏑̆
⏒ ⏑ ⏑́ ⏑ ⏑ ⏑́ ⏑ _
_ ⏑́ ⏑ _ _ _ ⏑́ ⏑ ⏑ ⏑́ ⏑ _
```

More than seems necessary has been altered here. Taking ὧν as partitive genitive with τὰ μὲν ... τὰ δέ, I understand ἄοκνον, with the Scholiasts, to mean τὴν ὀξεῖαν καὶ ἀμέλλητον. Nauck's conjecture ἀϊσσουσαν (for ἀϊσσόντων) is attractive, because giving an obvious construction for δόμοις, which, however, can stand alone, 'beholding close at hand a dire misfortune "in" (or "for") "her home."' For ἀϊσσόντων, cp. *El.* 492, ἐπέβα ... γάμων ἀμιλλήματα. On the other hand the Nauck-Blaydes conjecture αὐτά (for οὔ τι—Nauck αὐτή) is difficult to withstand. It gives an intelligible sense to προσέβαλε, which the Scholiasts falsely render συνῄδει, and makes the antitheses more pointed. Lines 841-844 may then be rendered 'Whereof this hapless one,—when she perceived at hand dire mischief in her home, through the rash approach of this new marriage,—in part was herself the cause, but for that other part which came' . . . In the following line there is something wrong, and the corresponding line of the antistrophe is in a worse condition. I take ὀλεθρίαις to be a gloss on some other word, for which I propose σκαιαῖσι='ill-omened'. The scholiasts, followed by modern interpreters, vainly tried to connect συναλλαγαῖς with the attempted reconcilement of H. through the love-charm. It clearly refers to the fatal meeting and brief intercourse with the Centaur: 'that other part which came from an alien mind through ill-starred intercourse'.

846. ἦ που ὀλοὰ στένει.

I took ὀλοά (with Schol.) as fem. sing. Jebb (with Schndw.) prefers the neuter plural. The point is doubtful.

851. ἁ δ' ἐρχομένα μοῖρα προφαίνει δολίαν
καὶ μεγάλαν ἄταν.

Jebb decides in favour of the interpretation of δολίαν to which I gave the second place, referring again to the guile of Nessus. The scholiast imagined that the maidens foresaw the suicide of Deianira. But, such is the art of Sophocles, they only think of her as weeping tender tears!

852, 856. ἔρρωγεν παγὰ δακρύων
κέχυται νόσος, ὦ πόποι, οἷον *οὐκ
ἀναρσίων Ἡρακλέους ἀγάκλειτον
ἐπέμολεν πάθος οἰκτίσαι.
ἰὼ κελαινὰ λόγχα προμάχου δορός.

By a slight transposition, and reading οὐκ for οὔπω, I obtain correspondence with the strophe as read above.

182 PARALIPOMENA SOPHOCLEA

852.   ἔρρωγεν παγὰ δακρύων.

Surely not merely 'we all weep'. Rather 'a cause for weeping has burst forth': O. T. 1280, Eur. *Hipp*. 1338 σοὶ τάδ' ἔρρωγεν κακά.

856, 857.   ἰὼ κελαινὰ λόγχα προμάχου δορός
ἃ τότε θοὰν νύμφαν
ἄγαγες.

The point is that the world-champion spear has this time rashly brought away a bride. There lies the tragic contrast. For θοάν, cp. Eur. *Hipp*. 550 δρομάδα Ναΐδ' ὅπως τε Βάκχαν (said of Iole).
And for κελαινά cp. Eur. *fr*. 373 φασγάνου μελανδέτου.

859.   ἄγαγες ἀπ' αἰπεινᾶς
τάνδ' Οἰχαλίας αἰχμᾷ.

For αἰχμᾷ cp. Eur. *H. F.* 158 θηρῶν ἐν αἰχμῇ.

860.   ἁ δ' ἀμφίπολος Κύπρις ἄναυδος.

I still feel that ἄναυδος may contain an allusion to the silence of Iole, *supr*. 322.

862.   πότερον ἐγὼ μάταιος, ἢ κλύω τινὸς
οἴκτου.

Cp. *fr*. 58 ἀκούετ'; ἢ μάτην ἀλυκτῶ; Eur. *El.* 747, βοῆς ἠκούσατ',—ἢ δοκῶ κενὴ | ὑπῆλθέ μ'.

869.   ἀήθης καὶ συνωφρυωμένη.

Jebb's ἀγηθής is very ingenious, and may possibly be right. The difference of sound would scarcely be perceptible to

Byzantine ears. But for ἀήθης (παρὰ τὸ ἔθος schol.), cp. Eur. *Hel.* 417-419, ὅταν δ' ἀνὴρ | πράξῃ κακῶς ὑψηλός, εἰς ἀηθίαν | πίπτει κακίω τοῦ πάλαι δυσδαίμονος, *fr.* adespot. 283.

γύναι, τί μοι τραχεῖα κοὐκ εἰθισμένως
λαλεῖς;

870. χωρεῖ πρὸς ἡμᾶς γραῖα σημαίνουσά τι.

The τροφός may well be imagined as making signs before she speaks.

879. σχετλιώτατα †πρός γε πρᾶξιν.

The correction is doubtful.

884. τάνδ' αἰχμὰν βέλεος κακοῦ
ξυνεῖλε.

I see no ground for Hermann's αἰχμᾷ. ξυνῄρει in Thuc. ii. 51 marks the *comprehensiveness* of the malady. Here ξυν- may be explained 'assisted in seizing', her passion being regarded as an accomplice. Cp. *O. C.* 438-439.

κἀμάνθανον τὸν θυμὸν ἐκδραμόντα μοι
μείζω κολαστὴν τῶν πρὶν ἡμαρτημένων.

Also *fr.* 790.

τίς ἄρα Κύπρις ἢ τίς ἵμερος
τοῦδε ξυνήψατο;

For the constr., in which ἢ τίνες νόσοι is διὰ μέσου, cp. Eur. *Hel.* 1579, ἔτ' ὦ ξέν', ἐς τὸ πρόσθεν, ἢ καλῶς ἔχει, | πλέωμεν;

893. ἔτεκεν ἔτεκε <δὴ> μεγάλαν.

The insertion of δή (Jebb) certainly improves the metre.

894. ἁ νέορτος ἅδε νύμφα.

For νέορτος, cp. *fr.* 788.

καὶ τὰν νέορτον, ᾶς ἔτ' ἄστολος χιτὼν
θυραῖον ἀμφὶ μηρὸν
πτύσσεται, Ἑρμιόναν.

898. καὶ ταῦτ' ἔτλη τις χεὶρ γυναικεία κτίσαι;

No change is needed, certainly.

904, 905. βρυχᾶτο μὲν βωμοῖσι προσπίπτουσ' ὅτι
γένοιτ' ἐρήμη.

Jebb reads with Nauck γένοιντ' ἔρημοι. This is extremely plausible, but detracts somewhat from the pathos. And would the altars in the house of Ceÿx be rendered desolate?

911. καὶ τὰς ἄπαιδας ἐς τὸ λοιπὸν οὐσίας.

Similarly the transition from her own calamity, to lamenting that the goods and chattels (slaves included) would pass into other hands (ἐπ' ἄλλοις), does seem to me inadequate to the situation. I admit the obscurity and the difficulty of the plural οὐσίας, but do not think that either has been removed. In Eur. *fr.* 354, τὰς οὐσίας seems to mean 'what is actually in possession'.

924, 925. πέπλον, ᾧ χρυσήλατος
προὔκειτο μαστῶν περονίς..

Wakefield's ᾗ is probable, but not certain.

942. ὠρφανισμένος *βίον.

Jebb is right in accepting βίον from Wakefield, who has often been happy in emending Sophocles.

944.   ἢ καὶ πλέους τις ἡμέρας λογίζεται.

I rather prefer the rare form πλέους τις to the emendation τι πλείους.

947.   πότερ' *ἆρα πρότερ' ἐπιστένω, πότερα τέλεα περαιτέρω.

Although it seems improbable that τέλεος should = τελευταῖος, this reading points the antithesis better than μέλεα or πάθεα. The verb ἐπιστένω is probably to be resumed with the second clause. May not the meaning be 'Which shall I mourn first, which most and longest, as completing the sum of misery?' Cp. Eur. *El.* 907-908.

εἶεν· τίν' ἀρχὴν πρῶτά σ' ἐξείπω κακῶν ;
ποίας τελευτάς ; τίνα μέσον τάξω λόγον ;

651.   τάδε δὲ μελόμεν' ἐπ' ἐλπίσιν.

Erfurdt's μένομεν seems the most likely correction.

965.   πᾷ δ' αὖ φορεῖ νιν ;

I do not think that πᾷ means 'in what manner?' The ear does not at once distinguish 'by what path' the sufferer is being brought. The chorus had inferred from the sound of feet that a company from abroad were 'steering this way'. If they caught sight of them on the winding road they may have lost them again. They are bewildered.

976.   ζῇ γὰρ προπετής.

I still think that προπετής here, as προπετές *supr.* 701, has a pregnant force, 'verging on death'. Cp. Eur. *Hipp.* 1163. δέδορκε ... φῶς ἐπὶ σμικρᾶς ῥοπῆς. *Alc.* 143, προνωπής ἐστι καὶ ψυχορραγεῖ.

186 PARALIPOMENA SOPHOCLEA

980. φοιτάδα δεινὴν
νόσον.

I rather prefer the explanation of the Scholiast here. Periodic recurrence is not in question. Cp. *Aj.* 59, φοιτῶντ' ἄνδρα μανιάσιν νόσοις.

981. ἀλλ' ἐπί μοι μελέῳ
βάρος ἄπλετον ἐμμέμονε φρήν.

The reason given for a colon after ἄπλετον seems hardly adequate. The pleonasm of a preposition is not infrequent. Cp. *infr.* 994. For βάρος ἄπλετον as adverbial accusative cp. 497 and *Ant.* 1273.

μέγα βάρος μ' ἔχων
ἔπαισεν.

986. οἴμοι ἐγὼ τλάμων.

οἴμοι <μοι> avoids the concurrence of two paroemiacs. But is this necessary in these irregular (lamenting) anapaests?

988. ἆρ' ἐξῄδης, ὅσον ἦν κέρδος.

I should retain the MS. reading with the explanation of the Scholiast. 'Have you then learned?'=ἔγνως ;

995. μελέῳ χάριν ἠνύσω· ὦ Ζεῦ.

Phil. 1139, quoted by Jebb in support of his punctuation against Hermann's, is a conjectural reading and by no means certain. *L* punctuates after ἱερῶν, making this an attribute of βωμῶν, and Ζεὺς the subject of ἠνύσω. I follow Hermann.

996. οἵαν μ' ἆρ' ἔθου λώβαν, οἵαν.

For my view of λώβαν cp. also Eur. *El.* 165, Αἰγίσθου λώβαν θεμένα (σε).

998. ἦν μήποτ' ἐγὼ προσιδεῖν ὁ τάλας
ὤφελον ὄσσοις.

ἦν is rightly referred to κρηπίς. Linwood, punctuating with Hermann, observes ἦν ad rem remotiorem refertur, sicut supra, v. 358, ὃν νῦν παρώσας οὗτος sc. Ἔρωτα quod trium versuum intervallo disjunctum est.

1005, 1006. ἐᾶτέ μ', ἐᾶτέ με δύσμορον *ὕστατον
ἐᾶθ' ὕστατον *εὐνᾶσθαι.

I willingly accept Jebb's reading, suggested by Wunder and Hermann.

1009.   πόθεν ἔστ', ὦ
πάντων Ἑλλάνων ἀδικώτατοι ἀνέρες.

I agree with Hermann as to πόθεν, and take πάντων Ἑλλάνων, not as partitive but as co-extensive with the nominative, as in *O. T.* 1474, τὰ φίλτατ' ἐκγόνοιν ἐμοῖν. 'Ye men, in every part of Greece, O most unrighteous!' This agrees with the context in what follows.

1013.   οὐκ ἔγχος τις ὀνήσιμον οὐκ ἀποτρέψει;

I see nothing wrong in ἀποτρέψει: cp. ἀποσκήπτειν, *Her.* vii. 10, § 5, ἐς οἰκήματα τὰ μέγιστα αἰεὶ . . . ἀποσκήπτει τὰ βέλεα (ὁ θεός), where some MSS. by a natural error have ἐπισκήπτει.

1015, 1016. οὐδ' *ἀπαράξας κρᾶτα βίου θέλει
*λῦσαι τοῦ στυγεροῦ· φεῦ φεῦ.

So I should now venture to read, partly led by the Scholia. It seems to me that μολὼν might be a corruption of (με) λῦ . . . .

188   PARALIPOMENA SOPHOCLEA

1019.   σοί τε γὰρ ὄμμα
ἔμπλεον ἢ δι' ἐμοῦ σώζειν.

Of the attempts to construe the MS. reading the best is Hermann's, quoted by Jebb (an expedient which had occurred to myself in early days), viz., separating ἐμ from πλέον and understanding it as = ἔν for ἔνι. 'There is more hope in thee than in trying to save him through my efforts.' But even this, it must be admitted, is 'construing through a brick wall.' Jebb's emendation, σοὶ γὰρ ἑτοῖμα (sc. ῥώμη) ἐς πλέον ἢ δι' ἐμοῦ σώζειν, is extremely plausible.

1021, 1022.   λαθίπονον δ' ὀδυνᾶν οὔτ' ἔνδοθεν οὔτε θύραθεν
ἔστι μοι ἐξανύσαι *βίοτον·

I find Jebb's suggestion of ἔστι οἱ for ἔστι μοι, making clearer the reference of βίοτον to Heracles, very acceptable —the more so as I take ἔνδοθεν and θύραθεν differently: 'I am powerless to make the life forgetful of anguish either within or without', *i.e.* in mind or body, cp. *O. T.* 1317, 8.

οἷον εἰσέδυ μ' ἅμα
κέντρων τε τῶνδ' οἴστρημα καὶ μνήμη κακῶν.

Eur. *Or.* 1122.

ὥστ' ἐκδακρῦσαί γ' ἔνδοθεν κεχαρμένην.

1022.   τοιαῦτα νέμει Ζεύς.

'Such is the doom appointed by Zeus' (Jebb, with Schol. and edd.). I still venture to prefer 'of such things' (*i.e.* of healing in such a case as this) 'Zeus is the Dispenser. Cp. 1000-1002; and for νέμει, *O. T.*, 200 *f*, πυρφόρων | ἀστραπᾶν κράτη νέμων | ὦ Ζεῦ πάτερ.

1032. *φύσαντ' οἰκτείρας.

Sc. ἐμέ. The ellipse may be excused by ἐμᾶς following. This seems to me a more pathetic appeal than τὸν *φύτορ' οἰκτίρας. For the participle in agreement, with an accusative understood, cp. *Ant.* 133, νίκην ὁρμῶντ' ἀλαλάξαι.

1041. *ὦ Διὸς αὐθαίμων.

Hades is surely the *brother* of Zeus, as in Jebb's translation.

1045. οἴας οἷος ὧν ἐλαύνεται.

οἴας is at once better authenticated and the harder reading.

1046. ὦ πολλὰ δὴ καὶ θερμὰ *κοὐ λόγῳ κακά.

For οὐ λόγῳ cp. also Eur. *fr.* 57.

 ὦ παγκάκιστοι καὶ τὸ δοῦλον οὐ λόγῳ
 ἔχοντες.

1047. καὶ χερσὶ καὶ νώτοισι μοχθήσας ἐγώ.

νώτοισι: cp. Pind. *Nem.* vi. 51.

 ἑκόντι δ' ἐγὼ νώτῳ μεθέπων
 δίδυμον ἄχθος ἄγγελος ἐσβᾶν.

1055.   πνεύμονός τ' ἀρτηρίας
ῥοφεῖ ξυνοικοῦν.

ῥοφεῖ: cp. *fr.* adespot. 602, ψυχορροφεῖν.

190 *PARALIPOMENA SOPHOCLEA*

1057. ἀφράστῳ τῇδε χειρωθεὶς πέδῃ.

It seems more natural to take ἀφράστῳ as = 'mysterious.' The unaccountableness of the agony is part of the trial. See below 1145, where H. at last understands, and 1104, τυφλῆς ὑπ' ἄτης.

1058. λόγχη πεδιάς.

For the collective singular cp. Eur. *Phoen.* 78, πολλὴν ἀθροίσας ἀσπίδ' Ἀργείων ἄγει.

1062. θῆλυς οὖσα κοὐκ ἀνδρὸς φύσιν.

θῆλυς φῦσα is of course palaeographically probable. But the adverbial φύσιν occurs elsewhere in doubtful constructions, *Her.* viii. 38, § 2 ; *El.* 325, 1125 ; *Ag.* 1259.

1074. ἀλλ' ἀστένακτος αἰὲν εἰπόμην κακοῖς.

εἰπόμην, not ἐσπόμην, should probably be read.

1075. ἐκ τοιούτου.

Jebb decides in favour of the view which I gave as (2) 'From being the strong man I was'. Rightly. For θῆλυς cp. Eur. *fr.* 199, τὸ δ' ἀσθενές μου καὶ τὸ θῆλυ σώματος | κακῶς ἐμέμφθης· εἰ γὰρ εὖ φρονεῖν ἔχω, | κρεῖσσον τόδ' ἐστὶ καρτέρου βραχίονος.

1081. αἰαῖ ὦ τάλας.

The hand which wrote ἒ ἔ over the line in L. is not *much* 'later.'

1091. ὑμεῖς ἐκεῖνοι δὴ καθέσταθ'.

Jebb's explanation of καθέστατε is subtle and ingenious. But is it not a little overdone? Cp. *O. T.* 703.

φονέα μέ φησι Λαΐου καθεστάναι.

1117. μὴ τοσοῦτον ὡς δάκνῃ
θυμῷ δύσοργος.

Jebb, reading δάκνει, interprets, with Hermann and Schneidewin, μὴ τοσοῦτον δύσοργος (ὤν) ὡς δάκνει θυμῷ, and says of my rendering (with δάκνῃ), 'But ὡς should then precede μή'. I do not assent to this. Relatives are elsewhere postponed for the sake of emphasis. Cp. *Phil.* 492, πατρί μ' ὡς δείξῃς φίλῳ. This was observed by so exact a scholar as Linwood, who says, '*h. e.* ὡς μὴ τοσοῦτον δάκνῃ, Vim auget sententiae μὴ τοσοῦτον praepositum.'

1118. οὐ γὰρ ἂν γνοίης ἐν οἷς
χαίρειν προθυμεῖ.

ἐν οἷς, 'under what circumstances' (Jebb). Rightly.

1127. οὐ δῆτα τοῖς γε πρόσθεν ἡμαρτημένοις.

I still think that this means 'In former days there was no error of hers that called for silence'. To which Hyllus replies, 'You will say the same of her error to-day'. A similar phrase occurs in Eur. *Troad.* 1128, ἐπὶ τοῖς πρόσθεν ἡμαρτημένοις.

1131. τέρας τοι διὰ κακῶν ἐθέσπισας.

διὰ κακῶν, 'in ill-omened-words' (Jebb), with Schol., Hermann, Schndw., etc. I have taken τέρας . . . ἐθέσπισας

192 PARALIPOMENA SOPHOCLEA

to mean 'You have oracularly uttered a wonder appearing through the midst of woe'. Cp. *Her.* i. 25, θέης ἄξιον διὰ πάντων τῶν ἐν Δελφοῖσι ἀναθημάτων; viii. 37, § 3, καὶ διὰ πάντων φασμάτων ἄξια θαυμάσαι μάλιστα : 142, καὶ διὰ πάντων ἥκιστα. διὰ = 'conspicuous amongst' or 'above'.

1132.   αὐτὴ πρὸς αὐτῆς, οὐδενὸς πρὸς ἐκτόπου.

ἐκτόπου, 'coming from without into the place where she was' (Jebb). Rightly.

1152.   Τίρυνθι συμβέβηκεν ὅστ' ἔχειν ἕδραν

συμβέβηκεν, 'impers., it has come to pass,' Jebb, who decides against the view which, following Musgrave and Hermann, I preferred (1), 'She has obtained leave to dwell at Tiryns.' For the latter, however, cp. Aristot., *Athen. Pol.* c. 39, § 3, ἐὰν δέ τινες τῶν ἀπιόντων οἰκίαν λαμβάνωσιν Ἐλευσῖνι, συμπείθειν τὸν κεκτημένον· ἐὰν δὲ μὴ συμβαίνωσιν ἀλλήλοις τιμητὰς ἑλέσθαι τρεῖς ἑκάτερον, καὶ ἥντιν' ἂν οὗτοι τάξωσιν, τιμὴν λαμβάνειν. This was Musgrave's view, approved by Hermann.

1160.   †πρὸς τῶν πνεόντων μηδενὸς θανεῖν ὕπο.

A clever conjecture of F. Haverfield (1885), βροτῶν πνεόντων, deserves to be recorded here.

1176.   τοὐμὸν ὀξῦναι στόμα.

Jebb takes ὀξῦναι transitively, 'to wait on so as to sharpen.' Rightly. So Solger translated : 'Und nicht mit Zaudern schärfe mir des Mundes Zorn.'

1179. For στάσιν cp. also Eur. *Bacch.* 925.

TRACHINIAE

1197. ἄγριον ἔλαιον.

The term ἄγριος ἔλαιος is said to have been used by Pindar in a hymn, *fr.* 22 (Bergk).

1203. οἴμοι, πάτερ, τί εἶπας;

I adhere to the reading τί εἶπας, and to my note.

1215. κοὐ καμεῖ τοὐμὸν μέρος.

'Thou shalt have no difficulty' (Jebb). This seems a doubtful sense for κάμνω. I still prefer the 3rd person active, though a singular use. See note on *Aj.* 1037, μηχανᾶν. The peculiarity here may be accounted for by the neuter (*i.e.* impersonal) subject. Cp. Eur. *fr.* 311, ξένοις τ' ἐπήρκεις οὐδ' ἔκαμνες εἰς φίλους.

1225, 1226. μηδ' ἄλλος ἀνδρῶν τοῖς ἐμοῖς πλευροῖς ὁμοῦ
κλιθεῖσαν αὐτὴν ἀντὶ σοῦ λάβοι ποτέ.

I do not feel that λάβοι is wrong. H. says, 'do not disobey me in this: I would not that another should have her'.

1229. σμικροῖς ἀπιστεῖν.

σμικροῖς: 'Dative of respect' (Jebb). Perhaps.

1234. μεταίτιος, σοί τ' αὖθις ὡς ἔχεις ἔχειν.

'σοὶ δ'' is more probable than σοί τ'' here' (Jebb). Perhaps.

1261. χάλυβος
λιθοκόλλητον στόμιον.

Jebb's original note on λιθοκόλλητον is again attractive as well as ingenious. I agree so far as to think that the word, which has the chief emphasis, could not be an epithet of a literal bit. But I doubt the allusion to masonry, and the application to the closed lips. 'An iron bit, framed with marble firmness',—or something like this, is what the words suggest to me.

1262. ἀνάπαυε βοήν.

Cp. also Plato, *Phaed.* 117 D, ὅτι ἐν εὐφημίᾳ χρὴ τελευτᾶν.

1270. τὰ μὲν οὖν μέλλοντ' οὐδεὶς ἐφορᾷ.

Cp. Eur. *Heracl.* 871 (Alcmena loq.):

καὶ παῖδα τὸν ἐμὸν πρόσθεν οὐ δοκοῦσ' ἐγὼ
θεοῖς ὁμιλεῖν νῦν ἐπίσταμαι σαφῶς.

1272. Cp. Eur. *Heracl.* 719 (Alcmena loq.), εἰ δ' ἐστὶν ὅσιος αὐτὸς οἶδεν εἰς ἐμέ (Ζεύς).

1275-1279. λεῖπου μηδὲ σύ, παρθέν', ἀπ' οἴκων.

I admit the doubt, but on the whole adhere to the view given in my edition (1881) and to my note on 1275. The Chorus say this to the maidens from within the palace, the same who were addressed in *supra* 205, 206, as μελλόνυμφος.

1278. For Ζεύς, sc. ἔπραξεν (schol.) cp. [Eur.] *Rhes.* 861, καὶ ταῦτ' Ὀδυσσεύς.

PHILOCTETES

In commenting on the *Philoctetes* I put forward a notion with regard to the machinery of the play which seems to have escaped observation. Neoptolemus, having consented to take Philoctetes on board ostensibly for Scyros and the Maliac Gulf, pleads for delay on the ground that the wind is adverse. The direction of the wind is also alluded to in lines 464, 465 and 1450, and is only ignored at the moment when Neoptolemus gives his final consent to take Philoctetes to Scyros. Either the wind has fallen, or he agrees to sail in spite of it. The place is at the north-eastern extremity of Lemnos. The wind therefore is from the west or south-west, and favourable for Troy. I suggest that the poet intended this to be regarded as a providential circumstance, and I therefore take literally the words of the chorus when urging the abstraction of the bow (855):

'The wind is fair, my son, the wind is fair.'

And this is confirmed by the concluding words of Heracles:

'Bright occasion and fair wind, urge your vessel from behind.'

It is clearly assumed, unless the point is ignored as too external, that Odysseus and Neoptolemus are in command of separate ships.

2. βροτοῖς ἄστιπτος οὐδ' οἰκουμένη.

Sophocles does not commit himself to the view that no part of Lemnos was inhabited. It is enough that Philoctetes had been cast upon a desert shore, where no footprint—even of 'Man Friday'—was to be found.

196   PARALIPOMENA SOPHOCLEA

13. κἀκχέω. Cp. Eur. *fr.* 789, ὀκνῶ δὲ μόχθων τῶν πρὶν ἐκχέαι χάριν.

17, 18. ἡλίου . . . ἐνθάκησις. For ἥλιος='sunshine' cp. Plat. *Phaed.* 116 E, ἔτι ἥλιον εἶναι ἐπὶ τοῖς ὄρεσιν: *Her.* viii. 137.

22, 23. ἅ μοι προσελθὼν σῖγα σήμαιν' εἴτ' ἔχει χῶρον πρὸς αὐτὸν τόνδε γ', εἴτ' ἄλλῃ κυρεῖ.

Jebb decides against the MS. reading chiefly on the ground that πρὸς with the accusative could only mean 'facing towards'. But may not ἔχειν πρὸς χῶρον τόνδε have the sense of 'clinging' or 'adhering to this place'? Cp. *Od.* ii. 340 (πίθοι οἴνοιο ἕστασαν) ποτὶ τοῖχον ἀρηρότες. For ἔχει intransitive or absolute, cp. also *Her.* vi. 39 § 2, εἶχε κατ' οἴκους. Eur. *Cycl.* 407, 408, ἐν μυχοῖς πέτρας πτήξαντες εἶχον. *Iph. T.* 1226, ἐκποδὼν . . . τοῦδ' ἔχειν μιάσματος; Pind. *Pyth.* i. 72, ὄφρα κατ' οἶκον ὁ Φοίνιξ ἔχῃ. If a change is required, that adopted by Jebb is unobjectionable. And Elmsley's τόνδ' ἔτ' is certainly attractive.

45. For νόστον='a journey' cp. also Eur. *Hel.* 428, μόνος δὲ νοστῶ, 474 [Eur.] *Rhes.* 427, νόστον τὸν πρὸς Ἴλιον.

46.   μὴ καὶ λάθῃ με προσπεσών.

Cp. Eur. *Heracl.* 338, μὴ λάθῃ με προσπεσών.

66.   τούτων γὰρ οὐδέν μ' ἀλγυνεῖς.

'In saying none of these things will you cause me pain.' Although the words could bear a different meaning, I believe that they would thus have been understood by a Greek. *τούτῳ γὰρ οὐδέν μ' ἀ. is certainly clearer, but has a less natural emphasis. The condensation, suppressing ποιῶν or λέγων, resembles that in τί ἄλλο ... ἤ, cp. *infra* 100, and see Jebb's notes on *Ant.* 497, 646 *f.*

69. οὐκ ἔστι πέρσαι σοὶ τὸ Δαρδάνου πέδον.

I rather prefer σοί, not as suggesting that some one else would succeed, but Odysseus naturally emphasises the part to be taken by Neoptolemus in the success.

79. ἔξοιδα καὶ φύσει σε μὴ πεφυκότα
τοιαῦτα φωνεῖν.

Erfurdt's παῖ is certainly attractive, and the parallels quoted for καί are insufficient. My feeling was that καὶ gave a special emphasis to the admission, 'I *do* know', etc.; 'while I urge this on you, I am also aware'.

83. νῦν δ' εἰς ἀναιδὲς ἡμέρας μέρος βραχὺ
δός μοι σεαυτόν.

εἰς ἀναιδὲς sc. πρᾶγμα: 'to a shameless course'. The omission of the article or the indefinite pronoun here is hardly more difficult than in 742, κοὐ δυνήσομαι κακὸν κρύψαι. Cp. also Eur. *Phoen.* 21, ἔς τε βακχεῖον πεσών: Plato *Rep.* vii. 518 A, ὑπὸ λαμπροτέρου μαρμαρυγῆς. Jebb's interpretation 'one little roguish day' may be right, but seems to me forced and 'harsh'. For ἡμέρας μέρος βραχύ cp. 480, ἴθ'· ἡμέρας τοι μόχθος οὐχ ὅλης μιᾶς, showing that the whole action of the play is imagined as brief.

90, 91. ἀλλ' εἴμ' ἑτοῖμος πρὸς βίαν τὸν ἄνδρ' ἄγειν
καὶ μὴ δόλοισιν.

'μή is generic (it does not, and could not here, go with the infinitive ἄγειν)' (Jebb). I question this and other applications of 'generic μή'. It seems to me that μή here is deprecatory, and, while to be construed with ἄγειν, to imply μὴ ἄγω (subjunctive).

95.   καλῶς
        δρῶν ἐξαμαρτεῖν μᾶλλον ἢ νικᾶν κακῶς.

ἐξαμαρτεῖν: 'To offend' by disobedience, rather than 'to fail'. Cf. Eur. *Alc.* 709, 710; Lys. *c. Eratosth.* § 49 al.

100.   τί οὖν μ' ἄνωγας ἄλλο πλὴν ψευδῆ λέγειν;

Here and elsewhere I leave the hiatus with τί.

111. Cp. *fr.* 749, τὸ κέρδος ἡδύ, κἂν ἀπὸ ψευδῶν ἴῃ, *Her.* iii. 72.

116.   θηρατέ' *ἂν γίγνοιτ' ἄν.

I prefer Hermann's reading, and for the same reason, that it marks the continued hesitation of Neoptolemus. For ἄν repeated cp. *fr.* 673 :

            πῶς ἂν οὐκ ἂν ἐν δίκῃ
        θάνοιμ' ἄν;

Eur. *Heracl.* 721, φθάνοις δ' ἂν οὐκ ἂν τοῖσδε συγκρύπτων δέμας; *Androm.* 77; *Hec.* 742; *Iph. T.* 244:

        χέρνιβας δὲ καὶ κατάργματα
        οὐκ ἂν φθάνοις ἂν εὐτρεπῆ ποιουμένη.

126, 127.   ἐάν μοι τοῦ χρόνου δοκῇτέ τι
        κατασχολάζειν.

'The use of σχολάζειν in the sense of "to linger", "to delay", permitting a genitive to be used, as after ὑστερεῖν, λελεῖφθαι, etc.' (Jebb). This seems needlessly 'bold'. I adhere to my note.

142. τόδ' ἐλήλυθεν
πᾶν κράτος ὠγύγιον.

I still think that ὠγύγιον is rather attributive than predicative.

147. δεινὸς ὁδίτης τῶνδ' ἐκ μελάθρων.

Jebb thinks that 'no Greek could have written' thus. If so, he is right in changing ἐκ to οὐκ. But I am not convinced of it. The phrase when *spoken* would not leave the meaning doubtful.

151. φρουρεῖν ὄμμ'.

'To bear a watchful eye.' I agree with Dindorf. ὄμμα as subject to φρουρεῖν without τὸ ἐμὸν seems weak.

163. στίβον ὀγμεύει τόνδε πέλας που.

In favour of τόνδε it may be suggested that Neopt. points to the track made by the lame foot in departing from the cave. But the *v.r.* τήνδε certainly helps to make τῇδε probable.

166. στυγερὸν στυγερῶς.

The use of στυγερός = 'wretched', as in *Trach.* 1016, seems to turn upon the fact that, in ordinary Greek feeling, commiseration was mingled with abhorrence. See below 225, 226.

167, 168. οὐδέ τιν' αὐτῷ
παιῶνα κακῶν ἐπινωμᾶν.

Though to Jebb it seems 'forced' and 'strained', I still prefer to take transitively ἐπινωμᾶν here (reading αὐτῷ) and προσενώμα in 717; 'he calls in aid no healer', 'he applies the water to his need.' Cp. 1108, οὐ φορβὰν ἔτι προσφέρων.

200   PARALIPOMENA SOPHOCLEA

171.   μηδὲ σύντροφον ὄμμ' ἔχων.

I see no objection to reading ξύντροφον.

174.   For ἀλύει cp. also Eur. *Cycl.* 434, ὥσπερ πρὸς ἰξῷ τῇ κύλικι λελημμένος πτέρυγας ἀλύει.

176.   ὦ παλάμαι †θνητῶν.

I should now read *θεῶν with Lachmann and Jebb.   Cp. Pind. *Ol.* ix. 26, σύν τινι μοιριδίᾳ παλάμᾳ.

178.   οἷς μὴ μέτριος αἰών.

'Whose life exceeds in misery.' The general maxim 'the great are great in misfortune', though approved by Jebb, seems hardly relevant here.

181.   πάντων ἄμμορος ἐν βίῳ.

Jebb joins ἄμμορος ἐν βίῳ.   Rightly.

186-190.   ἀνήκεστα μεριμνήματ' ἔχων.   *ὀρεί-
α δ' ἀθυρόστομος
ἀχὼ τηλεφανὴς *πικραῖς
οἰμωγαῖς †ὑπόκειται.

Mekler's conjecture ὀρεία is certainly very attractive.   Cp. also Eur. *fr.* 118 (Andromeda):

προσαυδῶ σε τὰν ἐν ἄντροις,
ἀπόπαυσον ἔασον Ἀ-
χοῖ με σὺν φίλαισιν
γόου πόθον λαβεῖν.

In 190 ὑπακούει has been independently conjectured by several critics, and with the change from πικρᾶς οἰμωγᾶς to πικραῖς οἰμωγαῖς has been adopted by Jebb. I do not find it convincing, and would suggest that, while adopting the dative plural, it may be possible to find a meaning for ὑπόκειται. ὑφεστηκέναι, ὑποστῆναι, with dat. following is to 'ambush' or 'waylay' (Eur. *Androm.* 1114, *Her.* viii. 91). May not ὑποκεῖσθαι with dat. be metaphorically 'to lie in wait for'—ready to start forth at every cry? Sophocles (*fr.* 652) uses ὑπόστασις = ἐνέδρα.

206.   φθογγά του στίβου κατ' ἀνάγκαν
             ἕρποντος.

I prefer στίβου, which with the slight pause preceding would be readily understood: στίβον ... ἕρποντος without an epithet seems tautological.

215.   ἀλλ' ἦ που πταίων ὑπ' ἀνάγκας
             βοᾷ.

Jebb joins ὑπ' ἀνάγκας with πταίων, not with βοᾷ. Perhaps he is right.

217.   ναὸς ἄξενον ὅρμον.

I would still join ναὸς with ὅρμον. It does not follow from 467 that the ship was invisible from the cave (see Jebb's note *in loco*): but even if it were so, it might be seen, as Jebb observes, from the point whence Philoctetes is approaching. The chorus doubt whether the cry is one of pain or of astonishment.

220.   ναυτίλῳ πλάτῃ.

The textual point here raised is nice and difficult. Jebb's argument hardly takes account of the fact that the few corruptions in Sophocles have sometimes a remote and complex origin. If ποίας πάτρας had been written by mistake—the eye of the scribe having wandered to 222—καὶ and ἐκ might easily be inserted afterwards. To Jebb's remark that 'the two questions ("who and whence") are habitually combined' it may be rejoined that the second question follows quite naturally in 222.

235. πρόσφθεγμα τοιοῦδ' ἀνδρός.

τοιοῦδ' ἀνδρός : 'Not merely a Greek, but one of such gentle breeding' (Jebb). This seems to me a little overdone.

251. οὐδ' ὄνομά *γ', οὐδὲ τῶν ἐμῶν κακῶν κλέος.

οὐδ' ὄνομ' ἄρ', Erfurdt's conjecture, is probably right.

256. μηδ' Ἑλλάδας γῆς μηδαμοῦ διῆλθέ που.

I adhere to που as explained in my note='methinks'.

267. πληγέντ' ἐχίδνης φοινίῳ χαράγματι·

Though Eustathius is sometimes loose in criticism (or relied on inferior MSS.), I am still inclined to read φοινίῳ.

272. ἐν κατηρεφεῖ *πέτρᾳ.

*πέτρᾳ is certainly an improvement, and it is unlikely that Sophocles would write πέτρῳ here.

278. ποῖ' ἀποιμῶξαι κακά;

'He is speaking rather of his misery than his resentment' (Jebb). True: but I still think that ποῖα is adverbial. 'How loudly do you suppose I lamented over my woes!'

PHILOCTETES

285.   ὁ μὲν χρόνος δὴ διὰ χρόνου προὔβαινέ μοι.

Jebb's explanation seems more elaborate than is necessary. 'Well, after a time (διὰ χρόνου) I found the time advancing' —so that the pressure of necessity was more felt.

291.   δύστηνον ἐξέλκων πόδα.

Canter's correction of δύστηνος to δύστηνον is probably right. It improves the *phrasing*. For ἄν cp. especially Eur. *Phoen.* 401, εἶτ' οὐκ εἶχον ἄν.

297.   ἔφην' ἄφαντον φῶς.

ἄφαντον φῶς: 'the hidden spark' (Jebb). I still think that ἄφαντον suggests (1) the difficulty of producing fire in this way and (2) the faint appearance in daylight of the spark produced by striking stone on stone.

305.   τάχ' οὖν τις ἄκων ἔσχε.

As Jebb is satisfied with the single parallel from Plato (*Legg.* 74 A), I have no objection to τάχα (=it may be, that) and withdraw my conjecture. Cp. also Eur. *Bacch.* 560, τάχα δ' ἐν ταῖς πολυδένδροισιν Ὀλύμπου θαλάμαις (θυρσοφορεῖς).

306.   ἐν τῷ μακρῷ γένοιτ' ἂν ἀνθρώπων χρόνῳ.

I still prefer to take ἐν τῷ μακρῷ . . . ἀνθρώπων χρόνῳ, to mean 'the long time of human history'. Hence, perhaps, once or so in ten years. For the expression cp. *fr.* adespot. 550, μακρὸς γὰρ αἰὼν συμφορὰς πολλὰς ἔχει.

315, 316.   οἷς Ὀλύμπιοι θεοὶ
δοῖεν ποτ' αὐτοῖς ἀντίποιν' ἐμοῦ παθεῖν.

οἷς Ὀλύμπιοι θεοὶ: I do not feel the tameness involved

204 PARALIPOMENA SOPHOCLEA

in retaining the MS. reading. Porson's οἷα is extremely plausible. But familiar parallels are sometimes deceptive.

319.   συντυχών —— 342. ὅτῳ σ' ἐνύβρισαν.

It is with diffidence that I continue to press the force of the prep. in comp. in these phrases against Prof. Jebb's authority. Cp. however προσλαμβάνειν with dative in Eur. *I. A.* 1145, Plat. *Theaet.* 207 C.

324.   Cp. also Eur. *Hipp.* 1328, πληροῦσα θυμόν.

343.   ἦλθόν με νηὶ ποικιλοστόλῳ μέτα.

I agree in rejecting ποικιλοστόμῳ, but remain uncertain whether ποικιλοστόλῳ='with gaily-decked prow' (Jebb) or simply 'gaily adorned'. For the former cp. Bacchyl. i 4, ἤλυθεν, αἰολοπρύμνοις | ναυσί: *fr.* adespot. 272, χαλκόδοντας στόλους.

352.   ἔπειτα μέντοι χὠ λόγος καλὸς προσῆν.

'There was a further charm in the reason suggested' (Jebb). Rightly. So rendered in my translation (1st ed. 1874).

371.   πλησίον γὰρ ὢν κύρει.

The historic present would not be amiss, but there hardly seems sufficient cause for departing from the traditional reading.

379.   ἀπῆσθ' ἵν' οὐ σ' ἔδει.

ἵν' οὐ σ' ἔδει sc. ἀπεῖναι. ἵνα='in circumstances in which'. Cp. *infr.* 429.

394. ἃ τὸν μέγαν Πακτωλὸν εὔχρυσον νέμεις.

I still think that νέμειν here means *to dispense*, and that εὔχρυσον is predicative.

401. λεόντων ἔφεδρε.

Of the two possible meanings of the phrase, that which supposes a chariot drawn by lions seems the more majestic.

401, 402. τῷ Λαρτίου σέβας ὑπέρτατον.

I am inclined to adhere to my note. I do not see why τῷ Λαρτίου σέβας ὑπέρτατον may not mean 'investing Odysseus with supreme reverence'.

405. Cp. *fr.* adespot., 579, εἰς ἀσθενοῦντας ἀσθενῶν ἐλήλυθας, which Nauck supposes to be from the *Philoctetes* of Euripides.

409. μηδὲν δίκαιον. Cp. Eur. *Phoen.* 201, ἡδονὴ δέ τις | γυναιξὶ μηδὲν ὑγιὲς ἀλλήλαις λέγειν.

421. τί δ'; ὃς παλαιὸς κἀγαθὸς φίλος τ' ἐμός.

The ellipse of ἐστίν with ἔστιν following is intelligible, and in Jebb's reading τί δ' οὐ παλαιός ... the article seems required. 'And what of him who is an old and good man, and a friend of mine?'—seems unobjectionable.

425. ὃς παρῆν γόνος.

So Jebb. I quite agree. Cp. however, Eur. *Hel.* 848, 849, Τελαμωνίου δ' Αἴαντος εἰσεῖδον σφαγάς | τὸν Νηλέως τ' ἄπαιδα: Pind. *Pyth.* vi. 28 *f.*

426, 427.
δύ' αὔτως δεῖν' ἔλεξας, οἷν ἐγὼ
ἥκιστ' ἂν ἠθέλησ' ὀλωλότοιν κλύειν.

If emendation is necessary, that of Jebb and Blaydes δύ' αὖ τώδ' ἄνδρ' ἔλεξας is extremely neat and plausible. But a doubt may be suggested (1) as to the reference of αὖ, and (2) whether '*vv*. 416-420 form *merely* a parenthetic contrast suggested by the death of Ajax'. On the other hand, in defence of the MS. reading, I would urge (1) that αὔτως='even so', *i.e.* 'in those few words—without saying more', is in accordance with the Homeric use:—*Od.* xiii. 281; xv. 83; xvi. 143; see Monro's notes *in locis* : (2) that the omission of the antecedent to οἷν, if δύο is taken as neuter, is justified by comparing *Ant.* 1194, *Trach.* 548, and similar passages. For ὀλωλότοιν, cp. *Aj.* 791, μῶν ὀλώλαμεν;

428.
τί δῆτα δεῖ σκοπεῖν, ὅθ' οἵδε μὲν
τεθνᾶσ'.

τί δῆτα δεῖ σκοπεῖν, 'What are we to look for?' (Jebb). '*Quo respicere*, h. e. *cui fidere*, oportet?' (Linwood). The latter interpretation seems nearer to the truth. 'Whither must one look?' Schneidewin compares *Ant.* 922. Solger translates 'Worauf bleibt dann zu schaun?'

οἵδε, 'Ajax and Antilochus; perhaps he thinks of Achilles (331) too' (Jebb). Rightly.

429.
Ὀδυσσεὺς δ' ἔστιν αὖ.

I still prefer to punctuate at αὖ, and to understand 'Odysseus on the other hand is still alive, and that in a conjuncture of affairs in which, etc.'

437.
Cp. also Eur. *fr.* 728, φιλεῖ τοι πόλεμος οὐ πάντων τυχεῖν ἐσθλῶν δὲ χαίρει πτώμασιν νεανιῶν | κακοὺς δὲ μισεῖ.

PHILOCTETES

446.   ἐπεὶ οὐδέπω κακόν γ' ἀπώλετο.

οὐδέν may be received on the authority of Suidas, but I doubt the necessity. See note on 83.

451.   ποῦ δ' αἰνεῖν. Cp. Eur. *Her.* 510, ποῦ τάδ' ἐν χρηστοῖς πρέπει;

452.   τὰ θεῖ' ἐπαινῶν.

'Praising the ways of the gods' (Jebb). I formerly took ἐπαινῶν to mean 'When one goes about to praise'; but I should now take τὰ θεῖα differently: 'In praising divine things', *i.e.* 'justice, faithfulness, truth', etc. Cp. Eur. *Ion*, 253, 254, ποῖ δίκην ἀνοίσομεν, εἰ τῶν κρατούντων ἀδικίαις ὀλούμεθα;

457.   χὠ *δειλὸς κρατεῖ.

'δειλὸς is rightly restored by Brunck for δεινὸς of the MSS.' (Jebb). This is probably right. For, though δεινὸς in Plato is certainly on the way to gather evil associations that would suit this place, no such meaning seems to have found its way into common language. Cp. however Thuc. viii. 68, ὑπόπτως τῷ πλήθει διὰ δόξαν δεινότητος διακείμενος.

467.   πλοῦν . . . σκοπεῖν. Cp. Eur. *Hec.* 901, μένειν ἀνάγκη πλοῦν ὁρῶντ' ἐς ἥσυχον.

473.   ἀλλ' ἐν παρέργῳ θοῦ με.

Jebb takes θοῦ με = 'regard me'. I prefer to understand it literally with the Scholiast as = 'stow me'.

Philoctetes speaks of himself as a valueless piece of goods that forms no part of the regular cargo. Cp. *Il.* iii. 310, ἐς δίφρον ἄρνας θέτο.

208 PARALIPOMENA SOPHOCLEA

481. ἐμβαλοῦ μ' ὅπῃ θέλεις ἄγων.

I prefer to regard this first ἄγων as emphatic=ἐὰν μόνον ἄγῃς. Cp. *infr.* 591, ποιοῦ λέγων.

482. ὅποι
ἥκιστα μέλλω τοὺς ξυνόντας ἀλγυνεῖν.

The slight change from ὅποι to ὅπου is perhaps better than to suppose a 'pregnant' construction here.

491. Τραχινίαν τε *δεράδα καὶ τὸν εὔροον.

δειράδ' *ἠδ' ἐς εὔροον (Jebb's conj.) is possibly right.

493, 494. ὃν δὴ παλαί' ἂν ἐξότου δέδοικ' ἐγὼ
μή μοι βεβήκῃ.

The false reading βεβήκοι is probably due to the preceding ἄν, which is thus shown to belong to an early tradition. It is difficult to set a limit to such phrases as οὐ πολὺς χρόνος ἐπειδή, in which a sentence condensed has the force of an adverb. I should therefore still hesitate to adopt παλαιόν.

496. αὐτόστολον πέμψαντά μ' ἐκσῶσαι δόμους.

I should now read δόμους (for δόμοις) with Jebb.

497. τὰ τῶν διακόνων.

Jebb's note substantially agrees with mine. For the meaning cp. Eur. *Iph. T.* 731, 732, ἐγὼ δὲ ταρβῶ μἀπονοστήσας χθονὸς | θῆται παρ' οὐδὲν τὰς ἐμὰς ἐπιστολὰς | ὁ τήνδε μέλλων δέλτον εἰς Ἄργος φέρειν.

505. Cp. *fr.* adespot. 460, ὅταν καλῶς πράσσῃ τις, ἐλπίζειν κακά.

509. ὅσσα μηδεὶς τῶν ἐμῶν τύχοι φίλων.

Porson's change from ὅσσα to *οἷα, of which the only motive was the rarity of the form in Tragedy, may be right, but is hardly necessary.

514, 515. τὸ κείνων κακὸν τῷδε κέρδος μετατιθέμενος.

I agree with Jebb except in so far as I take τιθέμενος rather in the sense of 'making' or 'causing' than that of 'counting'. I adhere to my note.

520. ὅταν δὲ πλησθῇς τῆς νόσου ξυνουσίᾳ.

I prefer to take the genitive with ξυνουσίᾳ. Else πλησθῇς might mean 'infected'.

527. χἠ ναῦς γὰρ ἄξει κοὐκ ἀπαρνηθήσεται.

Against taking ἀπαρνηθήσεται as active deponent is the position of the former καί, which has to be taken ὑπερβάτως with ἄξει, and not with the whole clause.

536, 537. οἶμαι γὰρ οὐδ' ἂν ὄμμασιν μόνην θέαν
ἄλλον λαβόντα πλὴν ἐμοῦ τλῆναι τάδε.

I do not think, with Jebb, that it would be forced to construe οὐκ ἂν ἔτλη τάδε θεασάμενος = 'He could not have borne this even in beholding it'.

550. σοὶ πάντες εἶεν συννεναυστοληκότες.

It is true that in the MS. reading νεναυστοληκότες is wanting in point.

567. ὡς ταῦτ' ἐπίστω δρώμεν'.

Jebb's note on this idiomatic phrase is well worth consideration.

572. πρὸς ποῖον ἂν τόνδ' αὐτὸς οὐδυσσεὺς ἔπλει;

The change from ἂν to αὖ is slight, and gives a reasonable meaning—'Who was this other?' But I am inclined to retain ἂν (explained as in my notes), both as the harder reading, and as expressing the distraction of Philoctetes, who is at a loss to *conjecture* who can be meant.

587, 588. δεῖ δή σ' ἔμοιγ' ἐλθόντα προσφιλῆ λόγον
κρύψαι πρὸς ἡμᾶς μηδέν' ὧν ἀκήκοας.

The singular (λόγον) is more usual for 'a *thing* spoken of'. *Trach.* 78, τὸν λόγον γὰρ ἀγνοῶ.

630. δεῖξαι νεὼς ἄγοντ'.

νεὼς ἄγοντ', 'Leading me from his vessel', *i.e.* 'Bringing me ashore'. So Jebb with Hermann, Schneidewin, etc. I will not press my former view (joining νεὼς with δεῖξαι) against such a consent of authorities, though it was tempting to take ἄγοντα in the same sense with ἄγοιντο in 613. Cp. 357, ἐκβάντα.

635. Cp. Eur. *fr.* 745, τολμᾶν δὲ χρεών· ὁ γὰρ ἐν καιρῷ | μόχθος πολλὴν εὐδαιμονίαν | τίκτει θνητοῖσι τελευτῶν.

639. The wind seems also to have played some part in the *Philoctetes* of Aeschylus, *fr.* 250, ἔνθ' οὔτε μίμνειν ἄνεμος οὔτε πλεῖν ἐᾷ.

648. τί τοῦθ' ὃ μὴ νεώς γε τῆς ἐμῆς ἔνι;

I am inclined to defend ἔνι, though irregular, taking νεώς to mean 'in some part of my ship'. 'Contained in' rather than 'on board of'.

655. ταῦτ', οὐ γὰρ ἄλλα γ' ἔσθ', ἃ βαστάζω χεροῖν.

There seems to me little to choose between the readings of T, ἀλλ' ἔστ', ἀλλ' ἃ and A ἄλλα γ' ἔσθ' ἅ. If the former is stronger, which I doubt, the latter is smoother and more rhythmical.

671, 673. οὐκ ἄχθομαί σ' ἰδών τε καὶ λαβὼν φίλον·
ὅστις γὰρ εὖ δρᾶν εὖ παθὼν ἐπίσταται,
παντὸς γένοιτ' ἂν κτήματος κρείσσων φίλος.

Jebb's argument in favour of retaining these three lines, so restored (by Döderlein) to Neoptolemus, now appears to me to have substantial force,—though it must be allowed that N. is 'daubing it' rather far.

676-681. λόγῳ μὲν ἐξήκουσ', ὄπωπα δ' οὐ μάλα
*τὸν πελάταν λέκτρων ποτὲ τῶν Διὸς
*ἀν' ἄμπυκα δὴ δρομάδα
δέσμιον ὡς ἔβαλεν
*παγκρατὴς Κρόνου παῖς.

So I read these lines, omitting Ἰξίονα in 677 and ὁ in 681. By reading ἀν' ἄμπυκα with Dindorf and Blaydes, the dactylic run in 677=692 is preserved.

Proper names in mythological allusions are often omitted by Sophocles, where, being naturally supplied by the Scholiasts, they have crept into the text. See on *Trach.* 840.

For the short vowel ending in δρομαδᾰ answered by ἀντιτυπὸν in the antistrophe, cp. *El.* 138, πατέρα answering τίν' ἀεί: Aesch. *Suppl.* 950, γυαλᾰ answering (ἐρεσσ | ομενᾱ of the strophe; and Pind. *Pyth.* vi. 13, χεράδι. (The *v. l.* χεράδει, as if from χέραδος, seems to be an invention of grammarians). Also Eur. *Tro.* 593, Πρίαμέ answering to μελέα, and *Hecuba* 453, πατέρα answered by τε θεᾶς, according to the best supported reading.

682.   οὐδ' ἐσιδὼν μοίρᾳ.

ἐσιδὼν is right (so in my small edition, *CA.* 1886).

684.   οὔτ' ἔρξας τιν', οὔτε νοσφίσας.

The words of Eustathius quoted by Jebb, σιωπᾶται τὸ ῥεχθέν, may possibly refer to the ellipse of οὐδὲν or the like.

685.   ἀλλ' ἴσος *ὢν ἴσοις ἀνήρ.

'Equitable towards the equitable' (Jebb). Rightly. Cp. Eur. *fr.* 692, τοῖς μὲν δικαίοις ἔνδικος, τοῖς δ' αὖ κακοῖς | πάντων μέγιστος πολέμιος κατὰ χθόνα.

686.   ὤλλυθ' ὧδ' ἀναξίως.

The reading here and in the antistrophe is very uncertain. The advantage of Jebb's reading is that it does not alter both strophe and antistrophe.

687.   τόδε θαῦμ' ἔχει με, πῶς* δή ποτε πῶς ποτ' ἀμφιπλήκτων.

Jebb reads with Erfurdt and Dindorf:

τόδε τοι θαυμά μ' ἔχει πῶς ποτε κ.τ.λ.

which secures exact correspondence with the antistrophe. I was contented with inserting δή after the first πῶς, which makes Ionic anaclomena correspond to regular Ionics a minore. *Judicet lector.*

PHILOCTETES 213

693. *f.* I am for once constrained to regard the construction proposed by Jebb as 'too bold'. Reading as above in 680, 681, I read here

> παρ' ᾧ στόνον ἀντίτυπον
> *τὰν βαρυβρῶτ' ἀποκλαύ-
> σειεν αἱματηρόν.

I suppose τὰν to have been dropped, from the resemblance to the last syllable of ἀντίτυπον. The disease is personified, as by Philoctetes himself, who without naming it often uses a pronominal expression. Cp. Heracles in the *Trachiniae*, *e.g.* 987, ἡ δ' αὖ μιαρὰ βρύκει. See note on *Trach.* 837, μελαγχαίτα. Philoctetes in Aeschylus, *fr.* 249, spoke of his disease as

> φαγέδαιναν, ἥ μου σάρκας ἐσθίει ποδός.

See note on *Trach.* 838. Although the division of lines in the MSS. of Sophocles is of slight authority, it gives some colour to the above arrangement that ἀποκλαύ | σειεν is thus divided in L.

696. οὐδ' ὃς θερμοτάταν αἱμάδα κηκιομέναν ἑλκέων.

If the above reading of 694 is right, τὰν may have descended from the previous line. I read οὐδ' ὃς with Erfurdt and the Vatican MS. The absence of the article is supported by the hypothetical clause, εἴ τις ἐμπέσοι.

700. φορβάδος ἔκ τε γᾶς ἑλεῖν.

I make no objection to Nauck's conjectural reading of this line (φ. ἐκ γαίας ἑλών) except that it appears to me unnecessary. The construction οὐκ ἔχων τινὰ ἑλεῖν τὰ φύλλα ἐκ τῆς γῆς is sufficiently Greek, and the substitution of a simple and direct construction for a complex and relative one is common enough.

214 PARALIPOMENA SOPHOCLEA

701. εἷρπε *δ' ἄλλότ' *ἀλλαχᾷ.

I accept Hermann's δ' for γὰρ, for the reason given above (686). ἀλλαχῷ is my conjecture, which is honoured by Jebb's acceptance. The text of this stasimon is unusually corrupt and uncertain.

703 f. ὅθεν εὐμάρει' ὑπάρχοι, πόρον ἀνίκ' *ἐξανείη δακέθυμος ἄτα.

I read πόρον with L. and punctuate as above, understanding εὐμάρεια to mean supply for his needs, and πόρον = possibility of locomotion. '(He crept thither) whence he could obtain means of comfort, at such time (τότε *supra*) as his wearing trouble left him free to move.'

707. οὐ φορβὰν ἱερᾶς σπόρον, οὐκ ἄλλων
αἴρων τῶν νεμόμεσθ'.

My note allows for the 'awkwardness' which Jebb refers to, but is it not more awkward to supply with ἄλλων another word than αἴρων, when the two are in such close proximity?

711. πτανῶν πτανοῖς ἀνύσειε γαστρὶ φορβάν.

If πτανοῖς ἰοῖς had been a MS. variant, might it not have been argued that, πτανῶν having been dropped, ἰοῖς, originally a gloss on πτανοῖς, had found its way into the text? The parechesis seems to me idiomatic and picturesque. I take πτανῶν as genitive of material with φορβάν, 'food consisting of winged things'. If this is objected to, I would read πτανὰν πτανοῖς, as proposed in my note. For πτανά substantively = ὄρνιθες, cp. Eur. *Ion*, 903:

ἔρρει
πτανοῖς ἁρπασθεὶς θοίνα
παῖς μοι.

In *fr.* adespot. 581, an arrow is called φόνου πτερόν.

718. λεύσσων δ' ὅπου γνοίη στατὸν εἰς ὕδωρ
αἰεὶ προσενώμα.

I take προσενώμα absolutely, but in the active sense, 'applied it to his need'. See on 168. The construction λεύσσων . . . εἰς ὕδωρ is admitted by Jebb as 'possible'. Cp. *infra* 1107, προσφέρων.

724. *πατρίαν ἄγει πρὸς αὐλάν.

I accept πατρίαν.

725. Μηλιάδων νυμφᾶν.

I agree with Cavallin in joining these words with ὄχθαις, and I retain the dative which, as thus construed, defines the position of the πατρία αὐλά.

728. πλάθει †πᾶσιν, θείῳ πυρὶ παμφαής.

It is of course uncertain what word is to be substituted for πᾶσι: Hermann's πάλαι was plausible; but, if the present is assumed to be historical, Jebb's πατρός is very attractive.

734. τῆς παρεστώσης νόσου.

'Not' "which is upon thee at this moment"' (Jebb). I agree. The disease is imagined as being always *at hand* and ready to become present at any time.

736. I am now inclined to read with Seyffert, Blaydes, and Wecklein:

    ΦΙ. ὦ θεοί.
    ΝΕ.   τί τοὺς θεοὺς ὧδ' ἀναστένων καλεῖς;

746. ἀπαππαπαῖ, παπαῖ, παπαῖ, παπαππαπαῖ.

Jebb's mode of writing the interjections is very plausible.

747. πρόχειρον εἴ τί σοι, τέκνον, πάρα
ξίφος χεροῖν.

Why should Neoptolemus be imagined as sword in hand? Why not 'ready' (πρόχειρον) 'to your hands' (χεροῖν)?

752. τοσήνδ' ἰυγὴν καὶ στόνον σαυτοῦ ποιεῖς.

ποιεῖ (*mid. v.*) or ποεῖ (Jebb) is certainly more probable.

758. ἥκει γὰρ αὕτη διὰ χρόνου πλάνοις ἴσως
ὡς ἐξεπλήσθη.

Most editors, including Jebb, have taken these words as an argument by which Philoctetes thinks to reassure Neoptolemus. That occurs later, 807 *f.*, but the effect of the present speech is to intensify the pity of Neoptolemus, and it is so intended by the speaker. I do not think that ἥκει here can be a 'gnomic' perfect. In Plat. *Symp.* 188 A, quoted by Jebb, Eryximachus is graphically describing certain processes of nature. Here ἥκει γὰρ αὕτη διὰ χρόνου can only mean, 'This plague is come after an interval'. Cp. 788, προσέρχεται τόδ' ἐγγύς.

The remaining words are more difficult. The Scholiast explains ἥκει ἡ νόσος· ἴσως ὅτε ἐκορέσθη πλανωμένη. This appears to have satisfied interpreters. But it does not seem to me to harmonise with the intensity of Philoctetes' anguish. '*On ne badine pas' avec telle souffrance.* The emphasis should fall, not on the absence, but on the presence, of the malady. I am therefore still inclined to punctuate at πλάνοις, to understand ἴσως in the rare sense of 'equally', and to refer ὡς to it. 'The plague returns in its wandering round, in equal force as when it glutted itself beforetime.'

776. τὸν φθόνον. Cp. also Eur. *Rhes.* 456 *f.* φθόνον ἄμαχον ὕπατος | Ζεὺς ἐθέλοι τὸν ἀμφὶ | σοῖσι λόγοισιν εἴργειν.

PHILOCTETES

782.   ἀλλὰ δέδοικ', ὦ παῖ, μή μ' ἀτελὴς *εὔχῃ.

It seems unlikely that the line as corrupted should have made a dochmiac dimeter by pure accident. And, although μ' cannot be for μοι, the limits of the Attic accusative in tragic verse are wide—as is seen in Euripides. By reading εὔχῃ for εὐχή a certain sense is obtainable. On the other hand, Jebb's ἀτέλεστ' for ἀτελής is very plausible.

789.   ἔχετε τὸ πρᾶγμα.

For ἔχετε, cp. Eur. *Hippol.* 1436, ἔχεις γὰρ μοῖραν ᾗ διεφθάρης, *ib.* 1021, *Hel.* 794, Lys. xii. *c. Eratosth.*, 100, ἀκηκόατε . . . ἔχετε, δικάζετε.

791.   ὦ ξένε Κεφαλλήν, εἴθε σοῦ διαμπερές.

Jebb reads σοῦ (not σου), rightly.

800.   τῷ Λημνίῳ τῷδ' ἀνακαλουμένῳ πυρί.

'Yon fire, famed as Lemnian' (Jebb). Rightly.

805.   ποῦ ποτ' ὤν, τέκνον, κυρεῖς;

ποῦ ποτ' ὤν: 'mentally', Jebb (with Schneidewin). I do not think so. Philoctetes in his distraction loses sight of Neoptolemus.

814.   ΦΙ. ἐκεῖσε νῦν μ', ἐκεῖσε ΝΕ. ποῖ λέγεις; ΦΙ. ἄνω.

Jebb, with Hermann and others, interprets ἐκεῖσε . . . ἄνω of the cave, from which Philoctetes has descended somewhat. But Neoptolemus could hardly have failed to understand him, if that had been his meaning. My view is nearer to that of the Scholiast and Linwood ('*Hoc mentis non compos dicit Philoctetes* . . .' Cf. *infra*, 1092'), and of Matthiae, who connected these words with 799-801.

818. *εἴ τι δὴ πλέον φρονεῖς.

I take these words to mean 'Since, as I suppose (δή), you know better than I do what is good for you'. The words of Phil. in 817 are not like a return to composure.

828. εὐαὴς ἡμῖν ἔλθοις.

I still prefer εὐαής, with Seyffert, and in 844 would read ὧν δ' ἂν κἀμείβῃ, with Hermann. The spondaic movement appears suitable.

831. Cf. Eur. *H. F.* 1048 τὸν εὕδι' ἰαύονθ'.

834. ποῖ δὲ βάσει, πῶς δέ μοι τἀντεῦθεν.

The correction of this line, and of 850, is very uncertain. Jebb's changes, though affecting both strophe and antistrophe, are probable enough.

836. πρὸς τί *μένομεν πράσσειν.

Whether μενοῦμεν or μένομεν is read depends on the treatment of 852. I read ὃν αὐδῶμαι there, consequently μένομεν here.

838. πολὺ παρὰ πόδα κράτος <αἴσιον> ἄρνυται.

Exact correspondence with the antistrophe is obtained by supposing a dactyl lost before ἄρνυται. I proposed αἴσιον, which I still think better than other ways of emending the line. Cp. Eur. *fr.* 745.

τολμᾶν δὲ χρεών· ὁ γὰρ ἐν καιρῷ
μόχθος πολλὴν εὐδαιμονίαν
τίκτει θνητοῖσι τελευτῶν.

839, 840.   ἐγὼ δ' ὁρῶ οὕνεκα θήραν
τήνδ' ἁλίως ἔχομεν τόξων.

θήραν here is 'capture', not 'pursuit'. The use of ἔχειν therefore is different from that in *Aj.* 564, etc.

847. *f.* cp. *fr.* 600 πόλλ' ἐν κακοῖσι θυμὸς εὐνηθεὶς ὁρᾷ.

855.   Οὖρός τοι, τέκνον, οὖρος.

In taking οὖρος literally, it is not supposed (as Jebb infers) that the wind has changed. At 640 the wind is adverse for the voyage *to Trachis*. In other words, it is *fair for Troy*.

861.   ἀλλά *τις ὡς Ἀΐδᾳ πάρα κείμενος.

Ἀΐδᾳ πάρα κείμενος, Jebb. This is an improvement on παρακείμενος.

862.   ὁρᾷ.

Jebb reads ὅρα, with Seyffert. I doubt of this.

864.   πόνος
ὁ μὴ φοβῶν κράτιστος.

'The best strategy is that which gives no alarm'.—Jebb (in his translation). I agree in this, but understand it differently from Jebb's note. I take it to mean, 'The best huntsman (or fisherman) is he who does not scare the game'.

874. ἐν εὐχερεῖ | ἔθου. Cp. also Eur. *Hec.* 981, ἐν ἀσφαλεῖ: *Suppl.* 164, ἐν μὲν αἰσχύναις ἔχω | πίτνων πρὸς οὖδας γόνυ σὸν ἀμπίσχειν χερί.

220   PARALIPOMENA SOPHOCLEA

883. ἀνώδυνον βλέποντα κἀμπνέοντ' ἔτι.

In favour of taking ἀνώδυνον (adverbially) with βλέποντα only, cp. Eur. *Alc.* 773, τί σεμνὸν καὶ πεφροντικὸς βλέπεις; Pind. *Pyth.* ii. 20, δρακεῖσ' ἀσφαλές.

890. Cp. *fr.* 635 (Φιλ. ἐν Τροίᾳ) ὀσμῆς ὅπως <τοι> μὴ βαρυνθήσεσθέ μου.

895.   τί δῆτα δρῶμ' ἐγὼ τοὐνθένδε γε;

The potential use, which Jebb admits to be possible, seems also stronger than τί δρῶμ' ἄν in expressing N.s' distraction. Cp. Eur. *Hipp.* 1181, θᾶσσον ἢ λέγοι τις.

899.   ἀλλ' ἐνθάδ' ἤδη τοῦδε τοῦ πάθους κυρῶ.

Jebb prefers the meaning to which I gave the second place. Perhaps he is right.

933.   τὸν βίον *με μἀφέλῃς.

The middle voice is certainly more usual in the sense required, and the change is slight from ἀφέλῃς to ἀφέλῃ.

942.   ἱερὰ λαβὼν τοῦ Ζηνὸς Ἡρακλέους ἔχει.

It does not seem to me inconsistent with usage to join ἱερὰ ... Ἡρακλέους.

953.   εἴσειμι πρὸς σὲ ψιλός.

Jebb reads πρός σε. But in favour of πρὸς σὲ it may be remarked that Ph. had hoped to be taken home. The emphatic use is supported by τῷδ' ἐν αὐλίῳ in the following line.

959. For ῥύσιον, cp. Eur. *fr.* 190, λύρα βοῶν ... ῥύσι ἐξερρύσατο.

961. ὄλοιο μή πω.

Compare the abrupt transition in *Oed. Col.* 1649, ἐξαπείδομεν | τὸν ἄνδρα, τὸν μὲν οὐδαμοῦ παρόντ' ἔτι, and see *Trach.* 383.

972. νῦν δ' ἄλλοισι δούς.

'Sc. τὰ αἰσχρά, having left the base deeds to others whom they befit (οἷς εἰκός, sc. δοῦναι αὐτά)' (Jebb with Schol. and Schneidewin). Hermann justly says of this 'Contorta est haec et quaesita explicatio'. It is more natural to take δούς as = ἐνδούς, the simple for the compound verb. The participle seems to me equivalent to μοῖραν νείμας or the like; and it is not difficult to supply ἃ εἰκός ἐστιν from οἷς εἰκός (sc. ἐμοί τε καὶ Ἡρακλεῖ).

983. στείχειν ἅμ' αὐτοῖς.

'ἅμ' αὐτοῖς, sc. τοῖς τόξοις' (Jebb). Perhaps rightly.

994. ΦΙ. οὔ φημ' ἔγωγε. ΟΔ. φημί.

'οὐ φήμ'—ἐγὼ δὲ φημί. So Gerhard' (Jebb). This is probably right.

1003. ξυλλάβετέ γ' αὐτόν.

I still incline to ξυλλάβετέ γ' αὐτόν, on the ground that the two attendants, on seeing the intention of Philoctetes, have stepped forward to prevent it.

1020. νέμουσιν. Cp. Eur. *fr.* 702, τόλμα σὺ κἄν τι τραχὺ νείμωσιν θεοί.

222   PARALIPOMENA SOPHOCLEA

1029. τί μ' ἄγετε; cp. *Med.* 736, ἄγουσιν οὐ μεθεῖ' ἄν.

1031.   πῶς θεοῖς εὔξεσθ'.

The objection to εὔξεσθ' does not seem to me convincing. I still take the meaning to be, 'How will you speak confidently before the Gods of sacrificing to them?' etc.

1045. Cp. *Med.* 38 : βαρεῖα γὰρ φρήν· οὐδ' ἀνέξεται κακῶς πάσχουσα.

1049.   οὗ γὰρ τοιούτων δεῖ, τοιοῦτός εἰμ' ἐγώ.

'τοιούτων, "such or such" a man,—"any given kind" of person' (Jebb). Yes, but not euphemistic for 'δολίων',—the meaning is general.

1058, 1059.   οἶμαι σοῦ κάκιον οὐδὲν ἄν
                τούτων κρατύνειν, μηδ' ἐπιθύνειν χερί.

The change from οὐ to μή is occasioned, as it seems to me, by ἄν in 1058, which gives a hypothetical turn to the expression.

1085.   ἀλλά μοι καὶ θνῄσκοντι συνοίσει.

συμφέρεσθαι, in the sense of 'to consort with', occurs in *Her.* iv. 114, § 7 (quoted by L. and S.) οὐκ ἂν ὦν δυναίμεθα ἐκείνῃσι συμφέρεσθαι. Considering the manner in which Philoctetes speaks of, and to, his surroundings (936 *f.*, 952 *f.*, 987 *f.*, 1453 *f.* ὦ μέλαθρον ξύμφρουρον ἐμοί . . .), it does not involve too strong a personification to suppose a similar use of συνοίσει here.

PHILOCTETES

1089.   τί ποτ' αὖ μοι τὸ κατ' ἆμαρ
             ἔσται;

I prefer to retain τί ποτ' αὖ, and to read κρατέραισιν in 1110.

1092, 1094.   εἴθ' αἰθέρος ἄνω
                  πτωκάδες ὀξυτόνου διὰ πνεύματος
                  ἕλωσί μ'.   *οὐκέτ' *ἴσχω.

That there is grave corruption here is evident. But emendation is precarious, and the change from οὐ γὰρ ἔτ' ἰσχύω to οὐκέτ' ἴσχω ('I no longer withstand them') is the only approach to certainty.

1096-1100.   σύ τοι σύ τοι κατηξίωσας,
                 ὦ βαρύποτμ', οὐκ ἄλλοθεν ἔχει *τύχαις ἀπὸ μείζονος,
                 εὖτέ γε παρὸν φρονῆσαι
                 τοῦ λῴονος δαίμονος εἵλου τὸ κάκιον *αἰνεῖν.

The general meaning of these lines is clear: but that there is some corruption is manifest. I can only say that Professor Jebb's constitution of the text is as probable as any other, though I must own to an inclination to cancel τᾷδε.

1110. For the sake of metre, perhaps κραταιαῖσιν should be changed to κρατεραῖσιν.

1125.   γελᾷ μου, *χερὶ πάλλων.

Considering the free handling of the glyconics throughout this passage, and also the free use of cases in Sophocles, I am not convinced that γελᾷ μου is impossible.

1131, 1132.   τὸν Ἡράκλειον
                   ἆθλον *ἔμ' ὧδέ σοι
                   οὐκέτι χρησόμενον τὸ μεθύστερον.

I cannot feel that τὸν Ἡράκλειον ἄρθμιον is a natural phrase in the mouth of Philoctetes here.

1134. *ἄλλου δ' ἐν μεταλλαγᾷ.

I should now write thus, with Jebb and Hermann.

1139. μυρί' ἀπ' αἰσχρῶν ἀνατέλλονθ', ὅσ' ἐφ' ἡμῖν κάκ'
ἐμήσατ' †Ὀδυσσεύς.

Between ὦ Ζεῦ and οὗτος there is not much to choose. If οὗτος were the original reading, it would be natural for a glossator to write Ὀδυσσεύς in margin. In either case, the change from ὅσ' to ὅς is hardly required.

1140. ἀνδρός τοι *τὰ μὲν *ἔνδικ' αἰὲν ἐιπεῖν.

This, Jebb's correction, is extremely probable.

1144. τοῦδ' ὑφημοσύνᾳ.

I still think that τοῦδ' ὑφημοσύνᾳ, 'by the substitution of this man' (Neoptolemus) is quite defensible. The Epic word ὑποθημοσύνη is used by Xenophon, *Mem.* i. 3, 7, Ἑρμοῦ ὑποθημοσύνῃ. The reading τῶνδ' ἐφημοσύνᾳ 'by their command', is tautological after ταχθείς. Cp. ὑφείς in *O. T.* 387.

1149. φυγᾷ *μηκέτ' ἀπ' αὐλίων
†πελᾶτ'.

I gladly accept Wecklein's μηκέτ', with Jebb. As to Jebb's own brilliant conjecture πηδᾶτ', I am more doubtful. I grant the obscurity; but still think that the words as above written *may* signify 'No longer with flight from my cavern— approach!' (πελᾶτ' imperative) the sentence being continued (no doubt with anacoluthon) as if the modal dative had been a participle. This seems to me more *vivid*, and therefore preferable.

1153, 1154. ἀλλ' ἀνέδην ὅδε χῶρος ἐρύκεται,
οὐκέτι φοβητὸς ὑμῖν.

I still think that the oxymoron is not beyond the Sophoclean limit. 'This place is slackly guarded, no longer to be fled from by you.' In Jebb's text, the long parenthesis between the adverb and the verb seems improbable, though it has Porson's authority. The resolution of the long syllable in the lyric iambic ($-\overset{\frown}{\smile\smile}= \smile \overset{\prime}{\smile}$) is not very difficult here.
For the meaning assigned to ἀνέδην = ἀνειμένως, cp. Eur. *Suppl.* 1042, φυλακὰς ἀνῆκα; Thuc. iv. 27, § 1, σφῶν ἀνέντων τὴν φυλακὴν περιγενήσεσθαι τοὺς ἄνδρας. The use of the passive in ἐρύκεται presents some difficulty; but if Sophocles can say (*Trach.* 120) Ἄιδα σφε δόμων ἐρύκει, might he not without straining language too far have said ὁ τοξότης ἐρύκει τὸν χῶρον τῶν πολεμίων? Words admitting of reciprocal signification are often thus inverted. Hesiod's τῶν μὲν . . . ἔεργε θυμόν, *Op.* 335, might be otherwise expressed τὰ μὲν . . . ἔεργε θυμοῦ. 'To keep the town from danger,' is the same thing with 'to keep danger from the town.' The meaning in Hom. *Il.* vii. 342 comes very near to this (τάφρον) ἥ χ' ἵππους καὶ λαὸν ἐρυκάκοι ἀμφὶς ἐοῦσα.

1162, 1163. εἴ τι σέβει ξένον, πέλασσον,
εὐνοίᾳ πάσᾳ πελάταν.

Jebb takes ξένον as masculine.—Rightly.
The acc. πελάταν seems to be drawn into agreement with ξένον, instead of the usual dative after πέλασσον, which would be awkward in combination with εὐνοίᾳ.

1165. εὖ γνῶθ' ὅτι σοὶ
κῆρα τάνδ' ἀποφεύγειν.

Although Jebb thinks this impossible, I still take σοί here, and in *Oed. Col.* 721 (sc. πάρεστιν) as = σὸν ἔργον ἐστίν. Cp. also the ellipse in 753, τί σοί;

226   PARALIPOMENA SOPHOCLEA

1169.   ᾧ ξυνοικεῖ.

ὃ ξυνοικεῖ (Jebb). I prefer ᾧ.

1206.   ὡς τίνα* δὴ ῥέξῃς παλάμαν ποτέ ;

Is it necessary to render παλάμαν here, 'rash' or 'violent deed'? May it not be taken in a more general sense, 'to execute what plan' or 'device'?

1207.   κρᾶτ' ἀπὸ πάντα καὶ ἄρθρα τέμω χερί.

Jebb ridicules my view as impossible. With regard to the prothysteron, I would ask in turn, 'is it supposed that Ajax (*Aj.* 238) first cuts off the head and then the tongue?' Again, is χρῶτα πάντα really equivalent to τὰς σάρκας, and is such a phrase as ἀποτεμεῖν χρῶτα possible except in the sense of removing a portion of the skin? And may not πάντα καὶ ἄρθρα be inserted διὰ μέσου = '—all my limbs too—'? Cp. Eur. *Hel.* 1579:

ἔτ' ὦ ξέν', ἐς τὸ πρόσθεν—ἦ καλῶς ἔχει ;—
πλεύσωμεν.

1212.   οὐ γὰρ ἐν φάει γ' ἔτι . . .

1214.   πῶς ἂν εἰσίδοιμί σ', ἄθλιός γ' ἀνήρ.

Here I accept Jebb's reading and notes, rejecting Dindorf's alteration of 1214.

1243.   ξύμπας Ἀχαιῶν λαός, ἐν δὲ τοῖσδ' ἐγώ.

I hesitate to reject τοῖσδ' for τοῖς. If less idiomatic, it is the more emphatic.

1252. *f.*   *ΝΕ. ἀλλ' οὐδέ τοι σῇ χειρὶ πείθομαι τὸ δρᾶν.

Jebb's account of these lines agrees substantially with mine in 1881. There remains, however, one more alternative, viz. to accept the distribution of the persons in L. and to continue 1257 *f.* as spoken by Odysseus, who suddenly withdraws his threat of immediate aggression. In any case it is observable that N., having the bow in his hand, does not offer to use it. That he knows to be beyond his strength. Wecklein's ἴτω for ἔστω though *vivid* is unnecessary.

1260. Cp. Eur. *Heracl.* 109:

καλὸν δέ γ' ἔξω πραγμάτων ἔχειν πόδα.

1265, 1266.   μῶν τί μοι μέγα
πάρεστε πρὸς κακοῖσι πέμποντες κακόν;

μέγα ... κακόν seems to me more expressive than νέα ... κακά. It assumes that some evil is intended.

1277.   καὶ πέρα γ' ἴσθ' ἢ λέγω.

Jebb treats ἴσθι as parenthetical. I doubt.

1284.   ἀρίστου πατρὸς ἔχθιστος γεγώς.

Against αἴσχιστος it should be noted that αἰσχρός is seldom used, in a *moral* sense, of *persons*. See note on *Ant.* 747.

1290. So in Eur. *Ion*, 1488, ὦ φίλτατ' εἰποῦσ', εἰ λέγεις ἐτήτυμα.

1308.   κοὐκ ἔσθ' ὅπου
ὀργὴν ἔχοις ἄν.

The change from ὅπου to ὅτου is certainly slight, but I prefer to retain the MS. reading, which Jebb admits to be 'defensible.'

1314. ἤσθην πατέρα τε τὸν ἐμὸν εὐλογοῦντά σε
αὐτόν τέ μ'.

τε in the Aldine edition doubtless came—with many other readings—from *Ven.* 467 (V³) which has τὲ (*sic*) in the text. Tribrachs are more than usually frequent in the senarii of this play. The emphasis in αὐτόν τέ μ' is more natural, if πατέρα τε τὸν ἐμὸν precedes. Electra and Orestes in ll. c. by Jebb are speaking of the father of *both*.

1329. μήποτ' *ἂν τυχεῖν.

The change proposed by Porson, following Auratus, though not quite necessary, is simple and probable. So *CA*.

1330. *ἕως ἂν *αὐτὸς ἥλιος
ταύτῃ μὲν αἴρῃ.

Scaliger's ἕως for ὡς is also probably to be received.

1337. ἀνὴρ γὰρ ἡμῖν ἐστιν ἐκ Τροίας ἁλούς.

Jebb accents ἔστιν. Perhaps rightly.

1348. ὦ στυγνὸς αἰών.

αἰών here seems to mean simply='life,' as in Aesch. *Prom.* 862, Eur. *Bacch.* 95, Eur. *fr.* 801.

1354. ὦ τὰ πάντ' ἰδόντες ἀμφ' ἐμοῦ κύκλοι.

I seem not to have observed that L. has ἀμφ' ἐμοί, which Jebb reads. No doubt rightly.

1361. τἄλλα παιδεύει κακά.

*κακούς (Jebb) may be right, but in defence of κακά, cp. also Eur. *fr.* 939 ἀεί τι καινὸν ἡμέρα παιδεύεται.

1379. παύσοντας ἄλγους κἀποσῴζοντας νόσου.

κἀποσώσοντας, Jebb (Heath) is probably right.

1383. πῶς γάρ τις αἰσχύνοιτ' ἂν ὠφελούμενος;

ὠφελῶν φίλους (Jebb), from Buttmann, is certainly a good emendation.

1384. λέγεις δ' Ἀτρείδαις ὄφελος, ἢ 'π' ἐμοὶ τόδε;

τάδε, the reading of L. (omitted in my collation), is perhaps the true reading.

1385. σοί που φίλος γ' ὤν.

φίλος γ' ὤν is in any case *nom. pendens*, and the comma after που is needless. 'Methinks that, being thy friend, my meaning is friendly.'

1386. πῶς, ὅς γε τοῖς ἐχθροῖσιν ἐκδοῦναι θέλεις;

The slight change from ἐχθροῖσιν to ἐχθροῖσι μ', Jebb (Brunck) should, perhaps, be accepted.

1387. ὦ τᾶν, διδάσκου μὴ θρασύνεσθαι κακοῖς.

κακοῖς modal dative (Jebb). Perhaps. In ὦ τᾶν there seems to be an affectionate assumption of intimacy—'dear friend': Eur. *Heracl.* 688, *Bacch.* 802.

1401. ἅλις γάρ μοι τεθρήνηται γόοις.

'τεθρήνηται, impersonal' (Jebb). But is not the transition rather too abrupt?

1403. ἀντέρειδε νῦν βάσιν σήν.

Jebb here prefers the meaning to which I gave the second place (2) 'press thy foot against the ground.' He is probably right.

1431. ἃ δ' ἂν λάβῃς σὺ σκῦλα τοῦδε τοῦ στρατοῦ.

Jebb takes τοῦδε τοῦ στρατοῦ of the Achaean host (στρατεύματος, supra 1429). But does not the phrase here refer, not to the ἀριστεῖα, but to the *spolia opima* which he takes from those Trojans, Paris included, whom he slays with his bow? This avoids the supposed ellipse of τούτων, which, though of course possible, is rather awkward. This is Hermann's view.

1433. καὶ σοὶ ταῦτ'.

L. has καὶ σὺ ταῦτ', an impossible reading. See *Facsimile*.

1437. In Soph. *fr.* of *Philoctetes at Troy*, the wound was healed by Machaon; *Procl. Crestom.* p. 481, quoted by Nauck, p. 283.

1440. τοῦτο δ' ἐννοεῖσθ'.

Jebb admits that 'the middle was not less Attic than the active.' And the *Philoctetes*, a late drama, sometimes approximates to the language of prose.

PHILOCTETES

1443. †ἡ γὰρ εὐσέβεια συνθνῄσκει βροτοῖς.

It seems hopeless to defend ἡ γὰρ εὐσέβεια. One is almost driven to read οὐ γὰρ ηὐσέβεια with editors from Brunck downwards, although Tyrwhitt, a sound scholar, interpreted the traditional text, '*simul ad Orcum descendit, morientes comitatur.*' See Eur. *fr.* 734, ἀρετὴ δὲ κἂν θάνῃ τις οὐκ ἀπόλλυται, ζῇ δ' οὐκέτ' ὄντος σώματος· κακοῖσι δὲ ἅπαντα φροῦδα συνθανόνθ' ὑπὸ χθονός.

1448. κἀγὼ γνώμῃ ταύτῃ τίθεμαι.

It seems almost necessary to read γνώμην.

1460. For a metaphorical use of χειμάζεσθαι, see Eur. *Hipp.* 315, ἄλλῃ δ' ἐν τύχῃ χειμάζομαι.

1467.   χὠ πανδαμάτωρ
    δαίμων.

'The πανδαμάτωρ δαίμων is clearly Zeus' (Jebb). This was Buttmann's view. Hermann objects, '*πανδαμάτωρ ineptum foret Jovis epitheton; inepte etiam ille* δαίμων *appellaretur.*' The Scholiast hesitates between Heracles and Fortuna. I still prefer the former.

OEDIPUS COLONEUS

THE *Oedipus Coloneus* is said to have been produced for the first time by the poet's grandson in 402 B.C., some years after the author's death. The drama recalls a legendary time before the union of the townships, when Theseus was king of Athens and lord of the neighbouring communes. This description may be contrasted with the statement of Euripides in the *Hercules Furens*, that under Theseus the Athenians were a commonwealth of freemen. There are other indications of Oligarchic sympathies in the course of the play. It is also a remarkable feature of the drama that in celebrating the glories of Athens, the sanctities of the Colonus Hippius are made more prominent than the corresponding holy places on the Acropolis. The Athena worshipped is the Athena of the Knights, the Poseidon is he whose altar crowns the knoll, the olives are the olives of the Academy. Now it was within the precinct of Colonus, sacred to Poseidon, that the people were enclosed in order to vote for the constitution of the four hundred; and the name of Sophocles (of course uncertain whether the poet or not) occurs as that of one of the Probuli.

On these facts I base the following conjecture: (1) That the Colonus Hippius and the neighbouring region (like St. Germains) formed the aristocratic quarter, much as the Piraeus (a sort of Faubourg St. Antoine) was the resort of extreme democracy. (2) That the *Oedipus Coloneus* was composed under the influence of the aristocratic reaction. And (3) that for some reason connected with the political distractions of the time the drama was withheld from production until after the poet's death, when the amnesty had calmed political excitement, and a work of art which had the sanction of his name could be represented without danger to the state. (See *Classical Review* for February 1906.) The above is of course a mere conjecture, and another which I put forth is even more shadowy. It is in connection with the 'brazen threshold.' It seems to me possible that Oedipus, led by an inward intimation, finds his way at first to the place from which he ultimately disappears:—that when Antigone perceives the approach of the Chorus, and retires with Oedipus into the grove, the scene changes to another side of the precinct, where the Chorus enter, after having, as they themselves say, made the whole circuit of the sacred ground.

In a paper communicated to the *Journal of Hellenic Studies* for 1901, Sir George Young has discussed the question of the alternative routes indicated in the text as possible for the captors of the maidens, whom Theseus overtakes. He differs from Jebb, and agrees in so far with my note on l. 1060 (in the edition of 1879) in holding that the region to the westward of the snowy rock is the approach to Phyle through the ground to westward of the precipitous south-west end of Parnes. I agree with him also in thinking that the roads are imagined as converging towards Athens, or rather towards Colonus, for it is natural to suppose that travellers, or 'packmen,' would visit a richly inhabited quarter before making their way to the city. Also the phrase δίστομοι . . . ὁδοί (900) surely implied two roads and not more, debouching at a spot not far from Colonus. The traces of such convergence must long since have disappeared, when Colonus was no longer frequented, as in former years.

Sir George has also communicated to me his views as to ll. 57 and 1590, where the Scholiast, supposing the χαλκοῦς ὁδός to be meant in both places, seems to have noted a discrepancy:—ὃν ἐν ἀρχῇ εἶπεν χαλκόπουν ὁδόν (ὁδόν, MS.), τοῦτον νῦν ὑποτίθεται ἐκτὸς τῆς σκηνῆς, καὶ οὐκ ἔτι ἐν ὄψει τοῦ θεάτρου. To meet this I suggested the possibility of a change of scene after l. 116, where Antigone, having observed the approach of the Chorus, still invisible to the spectators, disappears with her father into the grove. The Coloniate elders, having made the circuit of the sacred precinct (135), then take their stand at a different point from that represented in the prologos; Oedipus being imagined as having been divinely led to the spot, where he was destined to part from all he loved on earth.

Professor Jebb adopted Hermann's solution:—*Sic potius existimandum videtur, latius patuisse illam loci liminis appellationem, ut partem comprehenderet loci, qui in scena conspiciebatur, pars autem extra scenam esset, et quidem ea, in qua hiatus esset ille qui designatur verius* ὁ καταρράκτης ὁδός . . . *ubi descensus patere ad inferos credebatur.*

It is commonly assumed (*L. and S.* s. v. βάθρον 4) that βάθροισι in this passage is to be understood of a stairway, and Jebb suggests that 'the myth was visibly symbolized by some artificial steps made at the top of the steep rift.' But does not the phrase rather signify the deep *foundations* of the brazen threshold, ῥίζησι διηνεκέεσσιν ἀρηρώς, as in the description of Hesiod (*Theog.* 812).

Sir George Young would read ὁδός with the MSS. in l. 57, and understands the Brass-paved Way to be 'the proper name given to some old foundations of a defensive work.' He adds 'That the Brass-paved Causeway is also an ἔρεισμ' Ἀθηνῶν may remind us of the Boulevards at Paris, of the Forburg at Reading, and similar names, given to sites of disused fortifications before a town.'

In the list of persons in L. the ξένος is given thus ξένος α λ η
(*i.e.* ἀλητής).

6. For φέροντα, cp. Eur. *Bacch.* 399, βραχὺς αἰών· ἐπὶ τούτῳ δέ τις ἂν μεγάλα διώκων τὰ παρόντ' οὐχὶ φέροι.

11. στῆσόν με κἀξίδρυσον, ὡς πυθοίμεθα.

I am not convinced that the opt. πυθοίμεθα, after the imperatives, which are conditioned by εἴ τινα βλέπεις, is 'impossible.'

14. πύργοι μὲν οἳ πόλιν στέγουσιν.

The question may be raised whether the walls of Themistocles are meant, or whether the πόλις is conceived as coextensive with the acropolis (Thuc. ii. 15).

16. χῶρος δ' ὅδ' ἱρός, ὡς ἀπεικάσαι.

The balance of evidence is rather in favour of ὡς σάφ' εἰκάσαι.

27. For ἐξοικήσιμος, cp. also Ar. *Ath. Pol.* 391, ἐξοικεῖν . . . Ἐλευσῖνα.

35. σκοπὸς προσήκεις †τῶν ἀδηλοῦμεν φράσαι.

'τούτων (the antecedent) is objective genitive after σκοπός' (Jebb). I agree. But, if so, must not σκοπός be taken in the more general sense of 'an informant'?

47. ἀλλ' οὐδὲ μέντοι τοὐξανιστάναι πόλεως δίχ' ἐστὶ θάρσος.

'οὐδὲ μέντοι would be weak' (Jebb). I think that it points the implied antithesis: '(I am afraid to let you stay where you are): *yet* I have not courage on the other hand to raise you up without authority.'

56, 57. ὃν δ' ἐπιστείβεις τόπον
χθονὸς καλεῖται τῆσδε χαλκόπους ὁδός.

In my Introduction, I suggested that Oedipus had been brought by Divine guidance to the immediate neighbourhood of the spot from which he was to take his final departure (1590 *f.*); that after the πρόλογος (at 116) there was a change of scene; and that the Chorus, whom Antigone had seen approaching, make their entrance on another side of the sacred grove. If this hypothesis, which I must own to be slenderly supported, is rejected, either τόπον—the place, distinguished from the whole region—includes both sides of the grove; or as Sir G. Young suggests, it may indicate some remains of an ancient structure, which could be traced from one side to the other. But neither suggestion is entirely satisfactory.

67. ἐκ τοῦ κατ' ἄστυ βασιλέως τάδ' ἄρχεται.

The words of Theseus himself in Eur. *Suppl.* 403-408, may be contrasted with this, especially 404, 405:

οὐ γὰρ ἄρχεται
ἑνὸς πρὸς ἀνδρός, ἀλλ' ἐλευθέρα πόλις.

71. ὡς πρὸς τί λέξων ἢ καταρτύσων μολεῖν;

So, Jebb. Rightly. μόλοι has crept in from the preceding line. It is observable that L has no punctuation at the end of this line.

79. οἵδε γὰρ κρινοῦσί σοι.

So Jebb. Rightly.

80. ἢ χρή σε μίμνειν.

εἰ χρή Jebb, with Brunck, etc. Perhaps rightly. But the imitation of Epic idioms is not infrequent.

OEDIPUS COLONEUS 237

92.   κέρδη μὲν οἰκήσαντα τοῖς δεδεγμένοις.

For the construction, cp. Eur. *Phoen.* 1043 *f.* ἔβα . . . | Οἰδίπους ὁ τλάμων | Θηβαίαν τάνδε γᾶν | τοτ᾽ ἀσμένοις, πάλιν δ᾽ ἄχη.

94.   σημεῖα δ᾽ ἥξειν τῶνδέ μοι παρηγγύα.

παρηγγύα : Jebb decides in favour of the interpretation to which I gave the second place (2), 'like παρεγγυᾶν σύνθημα . . . Cp. *supra* 46.' I agree.

104.   εἰ μὴ δοκῶ τι μειόνως ἔχειν.

I still prefer the explanation of the Scholiast to that of Hermann ; and I do not see why μειόνως ἔχειν may not mean 'to be deficient,' nor why the participle may not be added in explanation, to show the respect in which one falls short. Might not ἀρκούντως ἔχω ταλαιπωρῶν mean 'the misery which I suffer is enough,' as in *Ant.* 547, ἀρκέσω θνῄσκουσ᾽ ἐγώ, 'my death will be enough.' It would be a *personal* constr. = ἀρκούντως ἔχει μοι ἡ ταλαιπωρία.

107.   Cp. Eur. *Ion,* 30, οἶσθα γὰρ θεᾶς πόλιν.

112.   χρόνῳ παλαιοί.

I still think that the periphrasis expresses the feeling of awe with which the young girl regards the appearance of old age.

113.   σιγήσομαί τε καὶ σύ μ᾽ ἐξ ὁδοῦ πόδα κρύψον.

I believe that πόδα is right and expresses the dependence of Oedipus on his guide. The substitution of κρύψον for ἐξάγαγε or the like is due to condensation. 'Assist my going and hide me.'

115, 116. ἐν γὰρ τῷ μαθεῖν
ἔνεστιν ηὐλάβεια τῶν ποιουμένων.

I take this to be a general reflection. Cp. *e.g. El.* 990, 991.

121, 122. *προσπεύθου, λεῦσσε νιν,
προσδέρκου πανταχῇ.*

I follow Hermann. Jebb objects that λεύσσειν cannot mean 'to look for.' But is that certain? If it can, the same construction occurs in 135.

131, 132. ἀλόγως τὸ τᾶς
εὐφήμου στόμα φροντίδος
ἱέντες.

'Uttering without sound of words the voice of reverent thought.' I do not think that 'moving our lips' is implied.

133. τὰ δὲ νῦν τιν' ἥκειν
λόγος οὐδὲν ἄζονθ'.

I take ἄζονθ' absolutely—though of course with implied reference to the circumstances.

148. κἀπὶ σμικρᾶς μέγας ὥρμουν.

I retract the explanation given in my note, and would now prefer to read σμικρᾶς, with Blaydes,—understanding ἀγκύρας. Cp. Demosthenes *de Corona*, p. 319, οὐκ ἐπὶ τῆς αὐτῆς ὁρμεῖ τοῖς πολλοῖς. This parallel shows that the ellipse is idiomatic; and the figurative expression is more poetic. Cp. *fr.* 623, ἀλλ' εἰσὶ μητρὶ παῖδες ἄγκυραι βίου.

149, 150. ἀλαῶν ὀμμάτων.
ἆρα καὶ ἦσθα φυτάλμιος;

While explaining φυτάλμιος nearly as Jebb has done, I understand the whole phrase to mean simply, 'And art thou also blind?' ἦσθα, idiomatic, like ἦν in 117. Cp. *Aj.* 1077, κἂν σῶμα γεννήσῃ μέγα (Ajax was not *born* with a mighty frame); *fr.* 824, χῶρος ... ἀνθρώπου φρενῶν, | ὅπου τὸ τερπνὸν καὶ τὸ πημαῖνον φύει.

150. μακραίων *τις, ἐπεικάσαι.

The text here is uncertain. But my reading does not prevent the linking in thought of δυσαίων and μακραίων. Of the other emendations, I agree in preferring μακραίων θ' ὅσ' ἐπεικάσαι.

154. προσθήσεις τάσδ' ἀράς.

Jebb reads προσθήσει with Postgate and Blaydes. The question turns on our conception of the temper of the Coloniates. They are not devoid of pity, but their main anxiety is for the welfare of Colonus. 'Thou shalt not bring down (προσθήσεις) these curses,' viz. the wrath of the Eumenides, which would fall on Colonus if their sanctuary were violated. See below, note on 203, ὅτε νῦν χαλᾷς.

158-161. κάθυδρος οὗ
κρατὴρ μειλιχίων ποτῶν
ῥεύματι συντρέχει,
τῶν, ξένε πάμμορ', εὖ φύλαξαι.

Jebb decides in favour of the view to which I gave the second place (2), 'The bowl of pure water mingles with the flowing hydromel.' I accept his decision.

If τῶν is impossible, τό may be right. But the genitive, referring to the sanctities described in 157-159, may have

240   PARALIPOMENA SOPHOCLEA

been used, πρὸς τὸ σημαινόμενον, as if φύλαξαι were ἀπόσχου or the like. This reading agrees better with ἵνα . . . preceding.

172.   εἴκοντας ἃ δεῖ κοὐκ ἄκοντας.

'κοὐκ ἄκοντας would mean " and that, too, not unwillingly "—surely a weak sense' (Jebb). But I understand it to mean 'and not under compulsion' (as we shall have to do if we do not yield with a good grace). Cp. *infr.* 934, 935. Plato, *Legg.* 832 c, ἀκόντων ἑκοῦσα ἄρχει σὺν ἀεί τινι βίᾳ.

178.   ἐπίβαινε *πόρσω.

The change to ἔτι βαῖνε seems harmless, but unnecessary.

180.   προβίβαζε, κούρα,
προσω· σὺ γὰρ ἀΐεις.

The question whether some lines here are lost or not, may be left open, I think.

189. Cp. ἐπιβατεύειν in Herodotus. Also [Lys.] 6, § 15.

192.   τοῦδ' ἀντιπέτρου
βήματος.

αὐτοπέτρου, though conjectural (Musgrave), certainly yields a clearer sense than ἀντιπέτρου, which, however, as Jebb admits, may mean 'a ledge-like rock,' *i.e.* 'a stone seat having the appearance of native rock.'

195.   λέχριός γ' ἐπ' ἄκρου
λᾶος βραχὺς ὀκλάσας.

I am not confident as to the meaning I attribute to λέχριος, but it seems to accord better with the context here and in *Ant.* 1345. Cp. also Eur. *Hec.* 1026, λέχριος ἐκπεσεῖ: *Med.* 1168, λεχρία πάλιν | χωρεῖ, where the notion of 'sideways' does not seem to be in point. If I am right, λέχριος = leaning backwards, as προπετής = falling forwards.

199.   βάσει βάσιν ἁρμόσαι.

My view of βάσει, that it is a resting-place for the foot, attached to the seat, is supported by the Scholiast's words, ἐμόν ἐστι τοῦ (*l.* τὸ) ἁρμόσαι σου ἐφ' ἡσυχίας τὴν βάσιν τῇ καθέδρᾳ—although he is wrong in reading ἁρμόσαι (the infinitive). 'To fit step to step' = 'to walk carefully' is hardly a natural expression.

202.   ὤμοι δύσφρονος ἄτας.

'The doom of a dark soul' (Jebb).   Rather, more simply, 'cruel misfortune'.

203.   ὅτε νῦν χαλᾷς.

'Since now thou hast ease' (Jebb). I still prefer the interpretation of the Scholiast, ὅτε νῦν εἴκεις καὶ οὐκ ἀντιτείνεις ... Cp. Eur. *fr.* 340.

Κύπρις γὰρ οὐδὲν νουθετουμένη χαλᾷ

Ib. 362, *l.* 18.

φίλους δὲ τοὺς μέν μὴ χαλῶντας ἐν λόγοις κέκτησο.

The Chorus are strongly bent on enforcing obedience.

210.   μὴ μὴ μή μ' ἀνέρῃ τίς εἰμι.

'A threefold iteration would rather weaken than strengthen' (Jebb). I doubt this.

212. XO.† τί τόδε; OI. δεινὰ φύσις.

τί τόδε;—αἰνὰ φύσις (Jebb, with Hermann). I make no objection, though τί δέ;—δεινὰ (Elmsley) seems not less good.

220. OI. Λαΐου ἴστε τιν'; XO. 1.* ὤ. 2.* ἰοὺ ἰού.

I prefer (with Hermann in 1839) to give the interjections ὤ and ἰοὺ ἰού to different choreutae. The few words given to Oedipus are then more solemn.

229. οὐδενὶ μοιριδία τίσις ἔρχεται
ὧν προπάθῃ τὸ τίνειν·

Jebb's explanation of this line agrees with Hermann's: '*ob injuriam prius acceptam, si eam rependit.*' But the construction of τίνειν and the meaning given to it with τίσις preceding 'punishment for retaliation' are both rather harsh, especially as τίνειν in regard to injuries generally means to suffer for them rather than to repay. The citation of 1203, and Eur. *Or.* 109, is therefore not in point. I still incline to take τὸ τίνειν as epexegetic: 'No man is punished by the Fates in a case where he has been first injured that he should suffer on account of that.'

234. ἄφορμος ἐμᾶς χθονὸς ἔκθορε.

'ἄφορμος belongs to ἀφορμᾶν (there is no ἀφορμεῖν)' (Jebb). But in any case, the adj. is not derived from a verb: ἀπότιμος is not from an ἀποτιμάω, but from ἀπὸ and τιμή. And may not ἀφορμήσειν in [Eur.] *Rhes.* 98 be from ἀφορμεῖν?

243. πατρὸς ὑπὲρ τοὐμοῦ μόνου ἄντομαι.

μόνος in some connexions had little force beyond singling the noun to which it is attached for special emphasis, 'for my father and none else, I pray you', *i.e.* It is for my *father* I entreat. See *El.* 531, μοῦνος Ἑλλήνων, 'Of all these Greeks 'twas *he*'; *Trach.* 261, μόνον βροτῶν, 'He of all men'. *Infr.* 321, μόνης . . . Ἰσμήνης κάρα, 'Ismene and no other',—'It *is* Ismene'.

247.   ἐν ὑμῖν ὡς θεῷ.

The MS. reading ἐν ὑμῖν γὰρ ὡς θεῷ breaks the dactylic run, and gives a doubtful rhythm $- - \underline{\ } \cup \cup \dashv \underline{\ } \cup - \cup -$, which however may be compared with 242 and 249 $\underline{\ } \cup \cup \dashv \underline{\ } \cup -$. But the simple omission of γάρ, or (if the asyndeton offends) reading ἐν ὑμῖν δ', seems better than the introduction of the Aeolic ὕμμι.

252-4. I am now inclined to prefer the dactylo-iambic close—

οὐ γὰρ ἴδοις ἂν ἀθρῶν βρότον ὅστις ἂν, εἰ θεὸς
ἄγοι, 'κφυγεῖν δύναιτο.

Cp. Eur. *Hec.* 167-8—

πήματ', ἀπώλεσατ', ὠλέσατ'· οὐκέτι μοι βίος
ἀγαστὸς ἐν φάει.

258, 259.   κληδόνος καλῆς
μάτην ῥεούσης.

A flowing stream is the familiar symbol of that which has no fixity or permanence, but 'passes away'. That is the chief significance of ῥεούσης here, which, however, in the present context also suggests the image of a full, proud river.

244   PARALIPOMENA SOPHOCLEA

261. Cp. Eur. *Suppl.* 188, πόλις δὲ δὴ | μόνη δύναιτ' ἂν τόνδ' ὑποστῆναι πόνον.

263. For ποῦ cp. Bacchyl. iii. 38, ποῦ θεῶν ἐστὶν χάρις; and, for οἵτινες, Her. vii. 8 β, τὰς 'Αθήνας, οἵ γε . . .

264. Cp. Her. v. 71, τούτους ἀνιστᾶσι . . . ὑπεγγύους πλὴν θανάτου.

277, 278. καὶ μὴ θεοὺς τιμῶντες εἶτα τοὺς θεοὺς
μοίραις ποιεῖσθε μηδαμῶς.

It is admitted that the second negative here has an independent force. For this cp. also Plato, *Legg.* iii. 687 E, οὐ τοῦτο εὐκτέον . . . ἕπεσθαι πάντα τῇ ἑαυτοῦ βουλήσει, τὴν δὲ βούλησιν μηδὲν μᾶλλον τῇ ἑαυτοῦ φρονήσει, Lys. 24 § 26, μὴ τοίνυν . . . μηδὲν ἡμαρτηκὼς ὁμοίως ὑμῶν τύχοιμι τοῖς πολλὰ ἠδικηκόσιν: Andoc. i. 22, καὶ μὴ τοὺς μὲν παραδιδόντας μὴ ἐθέλειν ἐλέγχειν, τοὺς δὲ μὴ θέλοντας ἀναγκάζειν.

But the difficulty of μοίραις remains. It may be partly obviated, as Jebb remarks, by reading μοίρας with F, R². It has often occurred to me—considering the admissibility of Ionic forms in Tragedy,—that μοίραις ποιεῖσθ' ἐν μηδαμαῖς is not impossible, notwithstanding the *quasi-caesura*.

291. For μεταξύ, cp. Eur. *Hec.* 476.

303.   πολλὰ δ' ἐμπόρων ἔπη.

'And many rumours from wayfarers' (Jebb). I take δὲ adversatively. Although the distance is considerable, the rumour will soon reach his ears. The 'wayfarer' is probably Oedipus himself. Cp. Bacchyl. xvii. 36, στείχειν, ἔμπορον οἷ' ἀλάταν.

308. For εὐτυχὴς ... ἐμοί τε, cp. Pind. *Pyth.* v. 62, ὄφρα μὴ ταμίᾳ Κυράνας ἀτελὴς γένοιτο μαντεύμασιν.

313.   κρατὶ δ' ἡλιοστερὴς
κυνῇ.

Against ἡλιοσκεπής it may be urged that σκεπή is only shelter from wind and rain. See Plato, *Tim.* 76 D, where σκιά and σκεπή are distinguished.

321.   μόνης τόδ' ἐστὶ δῆλον Ἰσμήνης κάρα.

δῆλον, 'unmistakable', in contradistinction to the previous doubt, does not seem to me open to objection.

331. †ΟΙ. ἦ τῆσδε κἀμοῦ; ΙΣ. δυσμόρου δ' ἐμοῦ τρίτης†.

My reasons for leaving this line where it stands in the MSS., though marking it as doubtful, are given in my commentary (1879) and in *CA.*

333.   καὶ λόγοις γ' αὐτάγγελος.

The authority for λόγων is nearly equal to that for λόγοις, which however has the advantage of the 'harder reading'.

335.   οἱ δ' αὐθόμαιμοι ποῖ νεανίαι πονεῖν;

ποῖ = 'what has become of them', though harder, seems more expressive than ποῦ.

336.   δεινὰ δ' ἐν κείνοις τὰ νῦν.

Once more, I prefer the harder reading.

367, 368. πρὶν μὲν γὰρ αὐτοῖς ἦν ἔρις Κρέοντί τε
θρόνους ἐᾶσθαι μηδὲ χραίνεσθαι πόλιν.

'ἔρως, desire (436), is a necessary and a certain correction'
(Jebb). Without caring to dogmatize, I demur to this judgment. (1) Jebb does not object to joining αὐτοῖς Κρέοντί τε
on the score of Greek, and he decides in favour of taking
ἐᾶσθαι as passive: (2) it is therefore *allowable* to construe
'they strove with Creon (urging) that the throne should be
unoccupied': (3) this would be so far in accordance with
the advice of Teiresias in Eur. *Phoen.* 888 *f.* (quoted by
Meineke):

ἐκεῖνο μὲν γὰρ πρῶτον ἦν, τῶν Οἰδίπου
μηδένα πολίτην μηδ' ἄνακτ' εἶναι χθονός,
ὡς δαιμονῶντας κἀναστρέψοντας πόλιν.

(Creon would then of course be *regent* but not sovereign.)
The *Phoenissae* was produced, according to Dindorf, about
B.C. 415. (4) Without supposing any reference to an ἔρις
ἀγαθή, the antithesis between a former and a later ἔρις (the
latter of a fatal kind) is far more natural than that between
ἔρως and ἔρις κακή. (5) ἔρως does not suit well with ἐᾶσθαι
as infin. *passive*.

Meineke's objection to χραίνεσθαι is not well grounded.
For ἦν ἔρις with dative, cp. Eur. *Phoen.* 1462, ἦν δ' ἔρις στρατηλάταις. 'There was disputing between general and general.'

369. λόγῳ σκοποῦσι τὴν πάλαι γένους φθοράν.

'λόγῳ, in the light of reason' (Jebb). Rather, 'in their
argument', when they disputed with Creon. Cp. *Her.* v. 94,
§ 3, ἀποδεικνύντες τε λόγῳ οὐδὲν ... μετεὸν τῆς χώρης.

371. νῦν δ' ἐκ θεῶν του κἀξ* ἀλειτηροῦ φρενός.

κἀλιτηρίου (Jebb). Perhaps rightly.

OEDIPUS COLONEUS

383. ὅποι θεοὶ
πόνους κατοικτιοῦσιν.

ὅπου (Jebb). I still prefer ὅποι as a 'pregnant' use.

392. ἐν σοὶ τὰ κείνων φασὶ γίγνεσθαι κράτη.

φασί. 'We cannot supply "the θεωροί"' (Jebb). Why not, with τεθέσπισται preceding (388)?

401. ἡ δ' ὠφέλησις τίς θύραισι κειμένου;

Elmsley's θύρασι is not convincing here. θύρασι = 'out of doors', θύραισι = 'at their doors', like a beggar on the threshold.

402. κείνοις ὁ τύμβος δυστυχῶν ὁ σὸς βαρύς.

I think that Oedipus at least joins κείνοις with δυστυχῶν as well as with βαρύς.

405. μηδ' ἵν' ἂν σαυτοῦ κρατῇς.

I should not object to κρατοῖς if it had MS. authority. But I see no reason against κρατῇς.

420. φέρω δ' ὅμως.

'But still, such is the import of my tidings.' I still think this more natural than 'but I must bear it'.

422. Cp. [Eur.] *fr.* 1110, καὶ τέλος αὐτὸς ἔχει.

424. ἧς νῦν ἔχονται κἀπαναιροῦνται δόρυ.

The reading is not certain; but my defence of κἀπαναιροῦνται perhaps may stand. The Scholiast's explanation favours κἀπαναίρονται.

425. ὡς οὔτ' ἂν ὃς νῦν σκῆπτρα καὶ θρόνους ἔχει
μείνειεν.

Jebb's explanation of ὡς is that to which I gave the second place. The difference is slight.

426. The reading of AV^3, etc., πόλιν, construed with ἔλθοι, is perhaps to be preferred. See *infr.* 637, 1372.

432. πόλις τὸ δῶρον εἰκότως κατήνυσεν.

I do not press the objection to κατῄνεσεν.

436. οὐδεὶς ἔρωτος τοῦδ' ἐφαίνετ' ὠφελῶν·

While granting that the genitive is 'bold', and that M. Pappageorg's ἔρωτ' ἐς τόνδ' is extremely plausible (notwithstanding the *quasi-caesura*), I would, if possible, retain the MS. reading as more condensed and concentrated.

443. ἔπους σμικροῦ χάριν.

Cp. Eur. *Iph. A.* 1367, τοῦδ' οὕνεκ' οὐ σφαγήσεται.

454. παλαίφαθ' ἀμοὶ Φοῖβος ἤνυσέν ποτε.

ἤνυσέν ποτε, 'hath fulfilled at last' (Jebb). Is it not rather that as the main oracle had been so strikingly fulfilled, this particular prophecy also (93) was certain of fulfilment?

458. πρὸς *ταῖσδε *ταῖς σεμναῖσι δημούχοις θεαῖς
ἀλκὴν ποιεῖσθαι.

The reading is uncertain. But I doubt the necessity, asserted by Jebb, that an objective genitive with ἀλκὴν *must* mean 'the danger, *not* the interest defended'.

470. δι' ὁσίων χειρῶν θιγών.

I have never supposed a special allusion to blood-guiltiness here. But I still think that more is meant than *merely* washing the hands. I repeat 'the precept to wash the hands (Schndw.) is probably included, but with a ceremonial significance' (L. C., ed. 1879).

474, 475. θαλλοῖσιν ἢ κρόκαισιν ἢ ποίῳ τρόπῳ;
οἷός *γε νεαρᾶς νεοπόκῳ μαλλῷ λαβών.

'The objection to γε is that it supposes κρόκαισιν to be the genus of which μαλλῷ is a species' (Jebb). But γε sometimes adds as well as limits. I suppose ·κρόκαισιν to be properly soft woollen yarn suitable to form the woof in weaving, here used of a woollen fillet. To this suggestion γε may introduce a modified assent—'Yes, a woollen fillet, but composed of wool freshly plucked from a ewe-lamb.' σὺ seems otiose, and τε introduces an unmeaning complexity. I have nothing to object to νεοπόκῳ (newly plucked). Βαλών was probably the conjecture of some one to whom the idiomatic λαβών appeared superfluous.

479. Cp. πλημοχόη: Eur. *fr.* 592, *ib.* 148.

480. τοῦ τόνδε πλήσας θῶ;

Jebb takes θῶ, literally, of *placing* the bowl. I had understood the word more generally, of arranging or preparing the rite. Cp. 466. But Jebb's interpretation is quite unobjectionable.

487. δέχεσθαι τὸν ἱκέτην σωτήριον.

It is possible, as Jebb suggests, that σωτήριον includes both obtaining and conferring safety. But I still incline to think that the word forms part of the ritual of Colonus, without immediate reference to the case of Oedipus. Jebb's 'with a view to safety' may stand as an equivalent.

488. αἰτοῦ σύ τ' αὐτὸς κεἴ τις ἄλλος.

I accept σύ τ' αὐτὸς. See my note on *Ant.* 687.

489. μηδὲ μηκύνων βοήν.

μηκύνων, 'making loud' (Jebb). Yes. But in Plat. *Prot.* 329 A, μακρὸν ἠχεῖ surely refers to a *prolonged* sound.

498, 499. Cp. Eur. *fr.* 584, εἶς τοι δίκαιος μυρίων οὐκ ἐνδίκων | κρατεῖ τὸ θεῖον τὴν δίκην τε συλλαβών.

503. ἔρημον ἕρπειν οὐδ' ὑφηγητοῦ *γ' ἄνευ.

Without admitting that γε is 'intolerable', I have no objection to make to Hermann's δίχα.

511. ὅμως δ' ἔραμαι πυθέσθαι.

The *Oed. Coloneus* is a late play, like the *Philoctetes*, and polyschematism may be here and there admissible in both. See on *Phil.* 1151.

521, 522. ὦ ξένοι, ἤνεγκον †ἄκων μέν θεὸς ἴστω,
τούτων δ' αὐθαίρετον οὐδέν.

The difficulty of this passage has not been removed. E. L. Lushington, writing to me in 1886, defended *ἑκών, and proposed ἀλιτηρὸν for αὐθαίρετον. This removes the metrical irregularity and gives a real thought in place of a sophistic quibble. 'I acted willingly, indeed, but not wickedly.' Lushington censured οὖν as 'quite out of place, and very weak'. The position of μέν is also difficult in Jebb's reading. There is no antithesis between ἀέκων and αὐθαίρετον οὐδέν.

533.   ματρὸς κοινᾶς ἀπέβλαστον ὠδῖνος.

'Poetical Greek idiom would join κοινᾶς with ὠδῖνος rather than with ματρός' (Jebb). Perhaps rightly.

534.   *αἴδ' εἴσ' ἄρ' ἀπόγονοί τε καί.

In reading αἴδ' I followed E. L. Lushington. The double τε in Jebb's reading is difficult.

536.   ἰὼ δῆτα μυρίων γ' ἐπιστροφαὶ κακῶν.

'ἐπιστροφαί refers to the revival of the pangs in his soul by this questioning' (Jebb). Surely this is inadequate. The successive discoveries in *O. T.*, his self-blinding, the unnatural conduct of his sons, his exile—these are the ἐπιστροφαὶ κακῶν. Cp. Eur. *Androm*. 349, κακῶν τοσούτων οὐχ ὁρᾷς ἐπιρροάς;

540.   ὃ μήποτ' ἐγὼ ταλακάρδιος
            ἐπωφέλησα.

I am aware that my supposition, that μή with the aorist indic. here expresses an impossible wish with reference to past time, following the analogy of εἰ, ἵνα, ὡς, ὅπως with past tenses of the indicative, is bold, and perhaps violent; but I am not yet convinced that it is untrue. I acknowledge, however, the great ingenuity of Jebb's emendation.

545.   ἔχει δέ μοι.

ἔχει, sc. τὸ πρᾶγμα. Cp. Eur. *Phoen.* 995, τοὐμὸν δ' οὐχὶ συγγνώμην ἔχει. *Hel.* 505, δισσὰς δέ μοι | ἔχει φυλάξεις.

547.   καὶ γὰρ *ἀλοὺς ἐφόνευσα καὶ ὤλεσα.

Jebb throws contempt on Hermann's reading and the explanation of Döderlein, which was accepted by Hermann and Linwood, who remarks, '*Nexus est :* ἑάλων μὲν φονεύσας, καὶ ὀλέσας, *quod paullo insolentius effert* ἁλοὺς ἐφόνευσα.' The aorist participle sometimes denotes an action which is subsequent to that of the verb, while both are in past time. See Goodwin's *Moods and Tenses*, § 152. Here the inversion assists emphasis and concentration. 'I slew him—convicted of the deed.' As in 545, Oedipus admits the fact, but denies the blame. This correspondence of antitheses is destroyed by Mekler's reading. The apparently weak tautology, ἐφόνευσα καὶ ὤλεσα, may perhaps be accounted for by some reference to the formal language of Athenian Courts. In Jebb's reading, a dactylic line is ended with a cretic—ἀπώλεσᾶν | νόμῳ.

550.   Θησεὺς κατ' ὀμφὴν σὴν *ἀποσταλείς πάρα.

ἀποσταλείς. I see no reason for preferring Dindorf's reading to that of Turnebus. Hermann's ὃς ἐστάλη may be right. ἐφ' ἀστάλη assumes too much.

553.   τανῦν θ' ὁδοῖς
ἐν ταῖσδ' ἀκούων.

Jebb understands ὁδοῖς of Theseus coming from Athens to Colonus. Cp. 303, 304. But Theseus' knowledge in 555 does not go beyond what he has learnt from the σκοπός. The arrival of the traveller is more in point.

OEDIPUS COLONEUS

562. ὡς οἶδά γ' αὐτὸς ὡς ἐπαιδεύθην ξένος.

See Bacchylides xvii. (Θησεύς).

563. χὥς τις πλεῖστ' ἀνήρ.

ὥς τις πλεῖστα (sc. ἀθλήσας). See my note in *O. T.* 1219. I see no reason for accepting Dobree's reading, ὡς εἷς πλεῖστ'. It rather weakens the natural emphasis on πλεῖστα.

574. χὠ λόγος διέρχεται.

διοίχεται is of course an attractive variant. Jebb failed to see that the words I quoted from Plato, *Rep.* vi. 484 A, were διὰ μακροῦ τινὸς διεξελθόντος λόγου. If he preferred to read διεξελθόντες there, he should have said so. And I understand Demosthenes, 541, 22, to say 'when everything belonging to the laws, including ὑπωμοσίαι καὶ παραγραφαί (nominatives) had had its course (διεξεληλύθει).'

586. ἀλλ' ἐν βραχεῖ δὴ τήνδε μ' ἐξαιτεῖ χάριν.

'The favour which you ask of me lies in a small compass' (Jebb). Rightly.

588. πότερα τὰ τῶν σῶν ἐκγόνων, ἢ 'μοῦ λέγεις;

ἢ 'μοῦ. On re-reading my note of 1879, I see no reason for altering it. 'Do you mean the contest between your sons, or some conflict in which I am concerned?' (*CA*).

589. κεῖνοι κομίζειν κεῖσ' ἀναγκάζουσί με.

Kayser's ἄναξ, χρῄζουσι is extremely ingenious and attractive, but I am not convinced that the MS. reading

254 PARALIPOMENA SOPHOCLEA

is corrupt. An object for ἀναγκάζουσι (τινὰ or σέ) is easily supplied, and, after speaking distinctly of an ἀγών, it is not necessary that Oedipus should 'lead very gently up to the disclosure' etc.

590.   ἀλλ' εἰ θέλοντά γ'.

I am ready to accept θέλοντα.

596.   ἢ τὴν παλαιὰν ξυμφορὰν γένους ἐρεῖς;

'γένους="race" not "birth"' (Jebb). Rightly.

605. For χθῶν=πόλις, cp. Eur. *Heracl.* 968, τῇδ' ἀπιστῆσαι χθονί.

616, 617.   καὶ ταῖσι Θήβαις εἰ τανῦν εὐημερεῖ
καλῶς *τὸ πρὸς σέ.

I took εὐημερεῖ as impersonal. But τὰ is unobjectionable. V³, according to Castellani's collation, has τὸ. For the sentiment cp. Eur. *fr.* 594.

> ἀκάμας τε χρόνος περί γ' ἀενάῳ
> ῥεύματι πλήρης φοιτᾷ τίκτων
> αὐτὸς ἑαυτόν.

Theodectes *fr.* 9 (*N.* p. 804).

> ὁ μυρίος χρόνος
> τὰ πάντ' ἀμαυροῖ χὐπὸ χεῖρα λαμβάνει.

621.   ἵν' οὑμὸς εὕδων καὶ κεκρυμμένος νέκυς.

'ἵν'' could mean, "at a place where", at the grave (see on 411), but is better taken as="in which case", "when", since the moment of rupture (διασκεδῶσιν) would not be the battle at Colonus, but the preceding declaration of war'

(Jebb). It may be rejoined that δόρει implies actual conflict, and that 622 speaks of blood shed over the grave.

632, 633.   ὅτῳ πρῶτον μὲν ἡ δορύξενος
κοινὴ παρ' ἡμῖν αἰέν ἐστιν ἑστία;

Jebb decides for the reading and interpretation which I placed second, but which I rather preferred. I should therefore now read ὅτῳ.

637.   χώρᾳ δ' *ἔμπολιν κατοικιῶ.

I should now read ἔμπολιν with Jebb, accepting Musgrave's conjecture.

668, 669.   εὐίππου, ξένε, τᾶσδε χώρας
ἵκου τὰ κράτιστα γᾶς ἔπαυλα.

Jebb takes these lines as I do, except that εὐίππου χώρας seems to me to refer especially to the Colonus Hippius.

674.   τὸν οἰνῶπ' ἀνέχουσα κισσόν.

I admit that τὸν οἰνωπὸν ἔχουσα κισσόν is possibly right. But I am not convinced that ἀνέχουσα = 'maintaining' (as a favourite haunt) is certainly wrong.   See Pind. *Pyth.* ii. 89 (θεὸν).

ὃς ἀνέχει ποτὲ μὲν τὰ κείνων, τοτ' αὖθ'
ἑτέροις ἔδωκεν μέγα κῦδος.

685. Cp. Eur. *Ion*, 889, κρόκεα πέταλα . . . ἀνθίζειν χρυσανταυγῆ.

687.   Κηφισοῦ νομάδες ῥεέθρων.

I still prefer to take νομάδες actively ('the springs that feed the runnels'). Jebb says 'There is no example of an adjective of this form (as σποράς, στροφάς, φορβάς) having an active sense.' But surely φορβάς is active in *Phil.* 700 and *fr.* 279? ('the bounteous earth,' Jebb).

688.　ἐπ' ἤματι.

Jebb does not quote Heraclitus (*fr.* 32, ed. Bywater) νέος ἐφ' ἡμέρῃ ἥλιος.

692, 693.　οὐδ' ἁ
χρυσάνιος Ἀφροδίτα.

I should now read thus with Jebb, with θεαῖς for θείαις in the strophe (680).

702.　τὸ μέν τις οὐ νεαρὸς οὐδὲ γήρᾳ
σημαίνων.

I should now read οὐδὲ in deference to Jebb's decision. But I am not convinced that γήρᾳ='in old age' is beyond the limit of usage in Tragedy. συνναίων 'has palaeographic probability', but is feeble here.

710, 711.　εἰπεῖν ... αὔχημα μέγιστον,
εὔιππον, εὔπωλον, εὐθάλασσον.

αὔχημα εὔπωλον, etc., seems 'forced', especially since αὔχημα is in apposition, and is hardly supported by Bacchyl. iii. 12, πλείσταρχον Ἑλλάνων γέρας, which Jebb (*l. c.*) compares with it. I still think that the two lost syllables ‿‿ contained a pronoun governed by εἰπεῖν (γέ νιν).

716.　ἁ δ' εὐήρετμος ἔκπαγλ' ἁλία χερσὶ †παραπτομένα πλάτα.

Jebb's conjecture, προσαρμοζομένα, is attractive; but it seems more poetical to take πλάτα, by the familiar synecdoche, of the ship, than literally of the oar. I have suggested παραϊσσομένα, assuming the Epic quantity (ᾱ in *arsi*) to be retained, as in Eur. *Tro.* 1086, ἐμὲ δὲ πόντιον σκάφος | ἄισσον πτεροῖσι πορεύσει, where ἄισσον is answered by Αἰγαίου in the antistrophe, and in Pind. *N.* v. 43, ἤτοι μετᾰΐξαντα, corresponding to γαμβρὸν Ποσειδάωνα, etc.

721.   νῦν σοὶ τὰ λαμπρὰ ταῦτα δὴ φαίνειν ἔπη.

σοί here and in *Phil.* 1165 (sc. πάρεστιν), though without other parallels, appears to me idiomatic.

729, 730.   ὁρῶ τιν' ὑμᾶς ὀμμάτων εἰληφότας
φόβον νεώρη.

Cp. Eur. *fr.* 457, αἰδὼς ἐν ὀφθαλμοῖσι γίγνεται, τέκνον.

735.   ἀλλ' ἄνδρα τόνδε τηλικόνδ' ἀπεστάλην
πείσων.

The MS. reading τηλικόνδ' seems much more pointed than the conj. τηλικόσδ'. As Mr. Palmer well observes, the age and feebleness of Oedipus was a plausible reason for persuading him 'to put himself under the care and protection of his friends'.

737.   ἀλλ' ἀνδρῶν ὕπο.

ἀστῶν is certainly the stronger reading, and may be right, though ἀνδρῶν has much better authority.

755.   ἀλλ' οὐ γὰρ ἔστι τἀμφανῆ κρύπτειν, σύ νιν.

I see no sufficient reason for placing a colon at κρύπτειν. It makes rather an abrupt asyndeton.

761, 762.   κἀπὸ παντὸς ἂν φέρων
λόγου δικαίου μηχάνημα ποικίλον.

I distinctly prefer the alternative which Jebb rejects,

'taking λόγον δ. as defining gen. with μηχάνημα: "thou who from anything wouldst borrow a crafty device consisting in a fair plea."' See the parallels adduced by Jebb.

764.   ἐν οἷς μάλιστ' ἂν ἀλγοίην ἁλούς.

'Because his dearest wish now is that his grave should bless his friends and harm his foes' (Jebb). Rightly. For ἑλεῖν, of crossing or foiling a design, cp. Eur. *Med.* 372, τἄμ' ἑλεῖν βουλεύματα.

786.   κακῶν ἄνατος τῶνδ' ἀπαλλαχθῇ χθονός.

τῆσδ' is harmless, but τῶνδ' (masc.), though awkward, may be right. Jebb strangely joins κακῶν τῆσδε χθονός—and so L. and S. But I should have thought that 'to get off scot free from this land (or from the land of these men'),—*i.e.* from conflict with her—was quite a natural expression. Cp. Plat. *Soph.* 254 D, ἀθῴοις ἀπαλλάττειν (absolute use): *Legg.* xii. 953 A, ὅπως ἂν . . · ἀβλαβεῖς τοῦ δρᾶσαί τε καὶ παθεῖν ἀπαλλάττωνται: *Theaet.* 183 C, τοῦ τε σοῦ ἑταίρου ἀπηλλάγμεθα: *Rep.* 329 D, δεσποτῶν . . . ἀπηλλάχθαι: *Alc.* i. 1050, ἐμοῦ οὐκ ἀπαλλάττει: *Gorg.* 514 C, ἐπειδὴ τῶν διδασκάλων ἀπηλλάγημεν: *Rep.* 366 A, *Legg.* ii. 721 D, Lys. xxviii. 8, τοιούτῳ τρόπῳ τῆς πόλεως ἀπαλλαγῆναι. Creon knows of the oracle, and the Chorus have heard the prophecy of Oedipus.

787, 788.   ἐκεῖ
χώρας ἀλάστωρ οὑμὸς ἐνναίων ἀεί.

It seems at first sight more rhythmical and more consistent with the use of χώρα to join χώρας ἀλάστωρ, with Jebb. But ἀλάστωρ οὑμός is stronger if taken separately. For an extended or generalised use of χώρα, cp. Plato, *Legg.* 747 E, μέγιστον διαφέροιεν ἂν τόποι χώρας: *Rep,* 423 B, ὅσην χώραν ἀφορισαμένους τὴν ἄλλην χαίρειν ἐᾶν.

792.   ὅσῳπερ καὶ σαφεστέρων κλύω.

I should read either ἐκ with L or καὶ with A, but not the conflation of both (κἀκ) with Jebb.

808.   χωρὶς τό τ' εἰπεῖν πολλὰ καὶ τὰ καίρια.

τὰ καίρια seems more pointed than τὸ καίρια.

816.   ἦ μὴν σὺ κἄνευ τῶνδε λυπηθεὶς ἔσει.

Musgrave's τοῦδε for τῶνδε makes the meaning clearer, but is hardly certain, although τῶνδε may be an error due to the same word occurring in the previous line.

832.   τοὺς ἐμοὺς ἄγω.

Cp. Eur. *Heracl.* 139.

        Ἀργεῖος ὢν γὰρ αὐτὸς Ἀργείους ἄγω
ib. 267.
        ἄξω γε μέντοι τοὺς ἐμοὺς ἐγὼ λαβών.

848, 849.   οὔκουν ποτ' ἐκ τούτοιν γε μὴ σκήπτροιν ἔτι
             ὁδοιπορήσεις·

Jebb reads ὁδοιπορήσῃς, perhaps rightly, but the point is uncertain. The future makes a stronger end of the clause.

861.   ΧΟ. δεινὸν λέγεις. ΚΡ. ὡς τοῦτο νῦν πεπράξεται.

The Triclinian reading is for once the best. There is no special point in λέγοις ἄν, and the reservation on the part of Creon—ἢν μὴ etc.—shows that he is not so rash at this moment as he becomes (874) after the curse of Oedipus.

260   PARALIPOMENA SOPHOCLEA

866. ψιλὸν ὄμμ' ἀποσπάσας.

I do not think that ὄμμα can at once mean 'darling' and 'means of sight'. That the latter is meant appears from the context. Nor can ψιλόν be simply 'defenceless'. Cp. the use of μόνην in 895. There is an *oxymoron* intended, 'the eye of one who has no eyes'. Cp. Job xxix. 15, 'I was eyes to the blind, and feet was I to the lame'. But the helplessness of the young maiden adds to the pathos of the expression.

868.   τοιγὰρ σὲ καὐτὸν καὶ γένος τὸ σόν.

It is needless to change καὐτὸν to τ' αὐτὸν against the MSS. *ib.* θεῶν. Such genitives are often unemphatic if not pleonastic. See note on 1085.

885.   ἐπεὶ πέραν
περῶσίν *γε δή.

Jebb and Hermann are possibly right in saying that πέραν cannot be metaphorical = 'they are passing all bounds'. On the other hand, it may be noted that the Chorus in imagining the subsequent encounter (1047, 1059 *f.*) speak of places within the Athenian boundary. If πέραν is taken literally, the expression is hyperbolical. There is a mark (¨) over πέραν in L, indicating a gloss which does not appear. See 155 *supra*, περᾷς.

900.   ἔνθα δίστομοι
μάλιστα συμβάλλουσιν ἐμπόρων ὁδοί.

The question of the 'two roads' will be treated on 1054. Roads from Phyle and Eleusis, long since obliterated, would naturally converge towards a place so frequented as Colonus.

917.   πόλιν κένανδρον.

κένανδρον: 'destitute of inhabitants' (Jebb). Rather 'void of men or manhood': cp. Aesch. *Pers.* 118 *f.*, μὴ πόλις πύθηται κένανδρον μέγ' ἄστυ Σουσίδος . . . γυναικοπληθὴς ὅμιλος.

934.   εἰ μὴ μέτοικος τῆσδε τῆς χώρας θέλεις.

Jebb rightly comments on the *ironical* use of μέτοικος.

939.   ἐγὼ οὔτ' ἄνανδρον τήνδε τὴν πόλιν λέγων.

'Schneidewin's νέμων . . . is clearly right' (Jebb). I doubt. The repetition of the same word with different meaning is no cause for suspicion: and for λέγων='account', 'esteem', cp. Aesch. *Prom.* 994, καὶ σὲ δ' ἐν τούτοις λέγω: *Eum.* 48, οὔτοι γυναῖκας, ἀλλὰ Γοργόνας λέγω, and note on *Ant.* 32.

945, 946.   ὅτῳ γάμοι
ξυνόντες εὑρέθησαν ἀνόσιοι τέκνων.

I still think that τέκνων is a descriptive genitive—'the unholy marriage of a son' (*sc.* with his mother). As Jebb observes, there is 'a certain designed obscurity.' But it is not necessary that the genitive should be one of relation ='marriage with a son'.

965.   τάχ' ἄν τι μηνίουσιν εἰς γένος πάλαι.

Cp. Eur. *Hipp.* 831 *f.*

πρόσωθεν δέ ποθεν ἀνακομίζομαι
τύχαν δαιμόνων
ἀμπλακίαισι τῶν
πάροιθέν τινος.

977.   πῶς γ' ἂν τό γ' ἆκον πρᾶγμ' ἂν εἰκότως ψέγοις;

I have no objection to reading πῶς ἄν with Jebb.

262　PARALIPOMENA SOPHOCLEA

1007.　　　　　　　　　　ἥδε τοῦθ' ὑπερφέρει.

The MS. evidence certainly favours τοῦθ' rather than τῷδ', and I should have thought that either might stand.

1016.　　　　　　　　　οἱ μὲν *ἐξειργασμένοι.

The reasoning in favour of ἐξειργασμένοι (F. W. Schmidt's conjecture) is irresistible.

1020, 1021.　　　　　εἰ μὲν ἐν τόποισι τοῖσδ' ἔχεις
　　　　　　　　　τὰς παῖδας ἡμῖν.

I now agree with Jebb that Elmsley's ἡμῖν (for ἡμῶν of the MSS.) is probably right.

1023, 1024.　　　　　　　　οὓς οὐ μή ποτε
χώρας φυγόντες τῆσδ' ἐπεύξωνται θεοῖς.

The difference between 'glorying before the gods' after a victory, and 'making grateful vows to the gods' (Jebb) is a rather shadowy one. In other respects, Jebb's interpretation agrees with mine.

1034.　　　　　　　　ἦ μάτην τὰ νῦν τέ σοι
δοκεῖ λελέχθαι.

Whether τανῦν or τὰ νῦν should be read here is uncertain.

1038.　　　　　　　　　χωρῶν ἀπείλει νυν.

I think that νυν here is simpler and not feebler than νῦν.

1040.　　　　　ἢν μὴ θάνω 'γὼ πρόσθεν, οὐχὶ παύσομαι.

Cp. Eur. *H. F.* 534, 535.

ξύγγνωθί μοι,
εἰ πρόσθεν ἥρπασ' ἃ σὲ λέγειν πρὸς τόνδε χρή.

1046.   τὸν χαλκοβόαν Ἄρη.

The clatter of shields and swords in battle is poetically imagined as the brazen voice of Ares.

1051, 1052.   θνατοῖσιν, ὧν καὶ χρυσέα
κλῂς ἐπὶ γλώσσᾳ βέβακε.

Jebb decides in favour of the interpretation (Hermann's) to which I gave the second place in 1879, referring ὧν to θνατοῖσιν. I believe he is right.

1055-1057.   τὰς διστόλους
ἀδμῆτας ἀδελφὰς
αὐτάρκει τάχ' ἐμμίξειν βοᾷ.

While agreeing generally in Jebb's view, I still think that the dative may be governed by ἐμμίξειν (or ἐμμείξειν), not in the sense of conflict, but of being present in the *mêlée*. See my note of 1879.

1061.   Οἰάτιδος ἐκ νομοῦ.

Jebb thinks Hartung's εἰς νομόν, 'certain', because 'the ellipse of χῶρον is surely impossible'. This is hardly convincing, with χώρους immediately preceding.

'The place meant is not certain' (Jebb). I am still inclined to think that the 'snowy rock' must be the western end of Parnes and that the pass of Phyle is meant. The pasturage of Oea may have extended farther to the N. than is indicated on Jebb's chart. In any case ῥιμφαρμάτοις ἁμίλλαις involves an hyperbole. The question of the two roads is discussed by Sir George Young in *J. H. S.* for 1901.

1065. ἁλώσεται.

Jebb's interpretation nearly agrees with mine, only I take 'the enemy' vaguely thought of, rather than Creon, to be the subject.

1068, 1069.   ὁρμᾶται †κατ' ἀμ—
πυκτήρια φάλαρα πώλων†.

Jebb 'cannot believe κατὰ ἀμπυκτήρια to be Greek', when so understood. I am not convinced of this. For ἀμπυκτήρια πώλων, cp. Eur. *Alc.* 428, τέθριππά θ' οἳ ζεύγυνσθε καὶ μονάμπυκας | πώλους. The difficulty is increased by the doubtfulness of the reading in the corresponding line of the strophe, 1054. In 1879 I proposed to read (1054) ἔνθ' οἴομαι ἐγρεκύδοιμον (epithet of Pallas in Hes. *Theog.* 925), and (1068, 1069), κατὰ | λάμπρ' ἀμπυκτήρια πώλων.

For Hermann's χαλῶσ', however, cp. Hes. *Scut.* 308, ῥυτὰ χαλαίνοντες.

1076, 1077.   γνώμα τάχ' †ἀνδώσειν
τὰν δεινὰ τλᾶσαν, δεινὰ δ'εὑροῦσαν πρὸς *αὐθαίμων πάθη.

Jebb's and Bücheler's conjecture τάχ' ἀντάσειν τᾶν ... τλασᾶν ... εὑρουσᾶν is extremely ingenious. But the meeting of the chorus with the maidens is hardly in point. Elmsley suggested to read ἐνδώσειν with πάθη as subject and τᾶν ... εὑρουσᾶν gen. pl., 'that the sufferings of the maidens who have so much endured and have been treated so hardly by their kindred shall soon subside, *i.e.* be relieved' Cp. *Iph. A.* 942—

ἡ δεινὰ τλᾶσα κοὐκ ἀνεκτὰ παρθένος.

Another expedient is to read *ἐκδώσειν, 'that they will surrender' (with accusatives following). Cp. *Her.* i. 3, οὐ δόντες αὐτοὶ δίκας οὐδὲ ἐκδόντες.

1082, 1083.   κύρσαιμι *τῶνδ' ἀγώνων
           θεωρήσασα τοὐμὸν ὄμμα.

κύρσαιμι *τῶνδ' ἀγώνων is close to the MSS. and seems harmless, whatever is made of 1083. With regard to this, I admit that the grounds for αἰωρήσασα are strong. Cp. *e.g.* Eur. *Suppl.* 1047—

   Ευάδνη.   ἥδ' ἐγὼ πέτρας ἔπι . . .
              δύστηνον αἰώρημα κουφίζω, πάτερ.

On the other hand, before finally condemning θεωρήσασα, other cases, especially in Euripides, of the transitive use of intransitive verbs (βαίνειν, χορεύειν, *H. F.* 686, 871) should be considered. Professor E. L. Lushington said, 'I still support the old reading. θεωρ. ὄμμα, 'let my eye be spectator,' is a boldness of expression which in Sophocles shocks me not'.

1085.   ἰὼ Ζεῦ, πάνταρχε θεῶν.

I observe that θεῶν, in Jebb's emended order of words (ἰὼ θεῶν πάνταρχε), confirms the MS. reading of 868.

1087.   γᾶς τᾶσδε δαμούχοις

I still think that δαμούχοις (pl. for sing.) refers to Theseus, not to the Coloniates.

1113, 1114.   κἀναπαύσετον
           τοῦ πρόσθ' ἐρήμου τοῦδε δυστήνου πλάνου.

I do not think that *l.* 1114, with Jebb's reading κἀναπνεύσατον, can refer to the brief and hurried experience of the maidens after the capture. I take the words as they stand to mean that the presence of both his daughters comforts him, now that he has found a resting-place after the long wandering; in which he had indeed been led and tended by Antigone, but such alleviation of misery could not be compared with his present joy (ἔχω τὰ φίλτατ', etc.).

1118. καὶ σοί τε τοὔργον τοῦτ' *ἐμοί τ' ἔσται βραχύ.

I do not feel that Wex's emendation of this line

οὗ *κᾶστι τοὔργον· τοὐμὸν ὧδ' ἔσται βραχύ

is convincing, and I prefer to leave it as Hermann corrected it, though under the ban of Jebb.
For ἔργον of an easy task, cp. *Phil.* 26, τοὔργον οὐ μακρὸν λέγεις.

1199. πρὸς τὸ λιπαρές.

Cp. Eur. *Hec.* 745.

ἆρ' ἐκλογίζομαί γε πρὸς τὸ δυσμενὲς
μᾶλλον φρένας τοῦδ' . . .

and, for the general meaning, *Her. Fur.* 534-5, ξύγγνωθί μοι, εἰ πρόσθεν ἥρπασ' ἃ σέ λέγειν πρὸς τόνδε χρή.

1176. τί σοι τοῦτ' ἐστὶ λυπηρόν, κλύειν;

The emphasis is on κλύειν' (Jebb). Yes. I therefore prefer τοῦτ' to *τοῦδ' which would claim the emphasis for itself.

1187. τά τοι καλῶς
εὑρημέν' ἔργα τῷ λόγῳ μηνύεται.

There is surely some force in Mr. Palmer's argument against Hermann's *κακῶς here: 'Antigone intimates that Polynices might have some honourable purpose in seeking a conference, something by which Oedipus might be benefited rather than injured. This proved to be the case, for when admitted to an interview, he most solemnly affirms that he was come for the support of his father, and that if the events of the war against his brother turned out prosperously, he purposed bringing back his father to his home and country. ... If it is borne in mind that Antigone addresses her father with a view to propitiate his goodwill towards his son, nothing can be conceived more ill-adapted to that end, than to insinuate the evil surmise, that most basely as his son had acted towards him hitherto, he might possibly be meditating some further cruelty against his father; and by admitting him to a familiar converse it was possible he might betray the secret purposes of his heart.'

1190.   τὰ τῷν *κάκιστα δυσσεβεστάτων, πάτερ.

τὰ τῶν κακίστων δυσσεβέστατ', ὦ πάτερ (Jebb) certainly involves less change than any other emendation. But Toup's τὰ τῶν κακίστων κἀσεβεστάτων, 'the deeds of most vile and impious men,' has something to recommend it.

1191.   θέμις σέ γ' εἶναι.

I agree with Jebb in thinking that the evidence for θέμις indeclinable is 'neither large nor altogether satisfactory'. But I also approve his judgment in retaining provisionally the traditional text.

1192.   ἀλλ' αὐτόν—εἰσὶ χἀτέροις.

Here also I think that some of Mr. Palmer's reasoning is worth quotation. 'If ἀλλ' αὐτόν were uttered in a tone of earnest entreaty, and the speaker abruptly added what follows, I can conceive that it would be very intelligible, and if so, the touching effect of the entreaty would be heightened by the very fact that the sentence was unfinished.' The *aposiopesis* is qualified by the resumption in 1201 ἀλλ' ἡμὶν εἶκε. A somewhat similar breaking off is found in 1648:

τὸν ἄνδρα—τὸν μὲν οὐδαμοῦ παρόντ' ἔτι—
ἄνακτα δ' αὐτὸν . . .

1204.   βαρεῖαν ἡδονὴν νικᾶτέ με.

ἡδονή, singular, in the sense of that which gives pleasure— such as the obtaining of a boon, is rare; and I am therefore still inclined to think that βαρεῖαν ἡδονὴν is an oxymoron— 'your words win me over with a charm which is sorely against my will'—although the cognate accusative in this case is slightly more 'bold'.

1209.   σὺ δ' ὤν
        σῶς ἴσθ'.

This correction of the MS. reading seems probable, but not certain.

1211.   ὅστις τοῦ πλέονας μέρους χρῄζει τοῦ μετρίου παρεὶς
        ζώειν.

Jebb decides in favour of the interpretation which I placed second (2)—supposing an ellipse of χρῄζειν before τοῦ μετρίου. And so *CA*. But it still deserves to be considered whether a genitive with παρίημι (as with ἀμελεῖν, ὀλιγωρεῖν, etc.) is 'impossible'. For παρείς cp. Eur. *Iph. A.* 387, τὸ λελογισμένον παρεὶς | καὶ τὸ καλόν.

OEDIPUS COLONEUS 269

1215. πολλὰ μὲν αἱ μακραὶ ἁμέραι κατέθεντο.

κατέθεντο: 'lay up' (Jebb). I prefer 'lay down from their store', 'contribute'—a 'subjective' use of the middle. So in *Theaet.* 209 C, πρὶν ἂν ἡ σιμότης αὕτη τῶν ἄλλων σιμοτήτων ... διάφορον μνημεῖον παρ' ἐμοὶ ἐνσημηναμένη καταθῆται, καταθέσθαι is 'to deposit from itself'.

1219, 1220. ὅταν τις ἐς πλέον πέσῃ
τοῦ θέλοντος.

'Assuredly τοῦ θέλοντος in this context is not Greek' (Jebb). It may be so. Perhaps the nearest parallel is Eur. *Iph. A.* 1270:

οὐ Μενέλεώς με καταδεδούλωται, τέκνον,
οὐδ' ἐπὶ τὸ κείνου βουλόμενον ἐλήλυθα.

But is τοῦ δέοντος not rather prosaic? I admit that it is rendered plausible by the Scholiast's paraphrase—ἐς πλέον τοῦ προσήκοντος. I did not take τοῦ θέλοντος as = 'wish for prolonged life', but 'the state of willing', *i.e.* 'the life that is accompanied by the will to live'.

1225. μὴ φῦναι τὸν ἅπαντα νικᾷ λόγον.

Add to the familiar parallels—Bacchyl. v. 160—the words of Heracles on meeting the shade of Meleager:

θνατοῖσι μὴ φῦναι φέριστον,
μήτ' ἀελίου προσιδεῖν
φέγγος.

τὸν ἅπαντα νικᾷ λόγον, 'exceeds every possible estimate' (Jebb). I prefer as more natural 'stands first on the whole reckoning', not 'when the balance is struck between the good and evil of being born', but 'when all so-called goods have been appraised'.

1230.   ὡς εὖτ' ἂν τὸ νέον παρῇ, κούφας ἀφροσύνας φέρον.

Is τὸ νέον infancy or youth? This depends upon the way in which παρῇ is taken. Jebb with Schneidewin derives it from παρίημι: 'once a man has passed the time of infancy with its light unconsciousness'. For παρῇ, Jebb compares Bacchyl. iii. 88, πολιὸν π[αρ]έντα γῆρας, where προέντα, 'casting off old age', is equally possible. Cp. *Il.* ix. 446, γῆρας ἀποξύσας θήσειν νέον ἡβώοντα, H. Ven. 229, H. Cer. 276, γῆρας ἀπωσαμένη. But it is questionable whether in this case the plural ἀφροσύνας or the use of φέρον can be accepted. This was felt by Nauck when he conjectured (not very happily) for *l.* 1230, κοῦφος, ἀφροσύνης γέμων. The pl. ἀφροσύνας recalls the Homeric καταπαυέμεν ἀφροσυνάων (*Od.* xxiv. 457, cp. xvi. 278) said with reference to the suitors' insolences: cp. Bacchyl. xiv. 57 *f.*, ἀφροσύναις | ἐξαισίοις θάλλουσ' ἀθαμβής | Ὕβρις. And for τὸ νέον in such a connexion, cp. Eur. *Androm.* 184, 185:

κακόν γε θνητοῖς τὸ νέον, ἐν δὲ τῷ νέῳ
τὸ μὴ δίκαιον ὅστις ἀνθρώπων ἔχει.

Fr. adespot, 538 :

τὸ νέον ἅπαν ὑψηλόν ἐστι καὶ θρασύ.

Hesiod's silver race die off on reaching puberty, ἀλγε' ἔχοντες | ἀφραδίης (*Op. et D.* 133, 134).

1231.   τίς πλάγχθη πολύμοχθος ἔξω;

Jebb reads with Herwerden, τὶς *πλαγὰ πολύμοχθος ἔξω, an ingenious emendation. But if it were true, would not the line be remarkable for the absence of a verb? If τίς καμάτων may mean 'what trouble?' may not κάματος be supplied by anticipation in the earlier part of the line? For trouble personified as 'wandering', cp. Aesch. *Prom.* 275, 276:

ταυτά τοι πλανωμένη
πρὸς ἄλλοτ' ἄλλον πημονὴ προσιζάνει.

1248. αἱ δ' *ἐννυχιᾶν ἀπὸ ῥιπᾶν.

'Sophocles here named the Rhipaean mountains, "beyond utmost Scythia", as representing the *North*' (Jebb). His note on this passage, with the reference to Arist. *Meteor.* i. 13, is thoroughly satisfactory.

1250. ἀνδρῶν γε μοῦνος.

'With no escort at least' (Jebb), who censures my interpretation 'he and no man else' as 'somewhat weak'. I hold, on the contrary, that it is natural and dramatic that Antigone should interpose these words *sotto voce*, and that Oedipus in his blindness and extreme anxiety should not at once apprehend their import. Cp. 321, μόνης τόδ' ἐστι δῆλον Ἰσμήνης κάρα.

This view was defended in my Essay on *Tragic Drama*, p. 122. See also Jebb's note on *Trach.* 184.

1266. *τἀμὰ μὴ 'ξ ἄλλων πύθῃ.

For τἀμὰ, cp. Eur. *fr.* 797:

ἐξ ἐμοῦ γὰρ τἀμὰ †μαθήσῃ κλύων.

(*πάντ' εἴσῃ, ci. Meineke.)

1270. ἄκη μὲν ἔστι.

Jebb so accents, perhaps rightly.

1279. οὕτως *ἀφῇ γε.

Jebb reads με with Dindorf, and objects to γε. But the addition of the participle serves to emphasise οὕτως, 'Not *thus* at all events' (without speaking).

1282. ἢ δυσχεράναντ᾽, ἢ κατοικτίσαντά πως.

'Neither δυσχεραίνειν nor κατοικτίζειν is ever causative in classical Greek.' I yield the point as to κατοικτίζειν, for κατοικτίσαντα may mean—not 'having moved to pity' but—'having moved through the expression of pity'. But I still think that δυσχεραίνειν here is causative, and that such a use is not more singular than that of ὀργαίνω in *O. T.* 335, καὶ γὰρ ἂν πέτρου | φύσιν σύ γ᾽ ὀργάνειας—where as here the 1st aorist is in question. Cp. the 1st aorists of πτήσσω and ἐκπτήσσω. (Eur. *Hec.* 179).

1298, 1299.   ὃν ἐγὼ μάλιστα μὲν
τὴν σὴν Ἐρινὺν αἰτίαν εἶναι λέγω.

I still think that μέν opposes τὴν σὴν Ἐρινὺν to other efficient causes, which are not adduced. Jebb takes τ. σ. 'Ε. to mean 'the Fury who pursues thee'. This seems 'forced'. It is occasioned by Jebb's assumption that the notorious Curse of Oedipus is ignored in the present drama. On this, see below, note on 1375 f. Even if it were so, the 'Erinys' here spoken of might be merely the wrath resulting from the unnatural treatment which Polynices has confessed in 1265 *f.* and for which a father's Erinys might be expected to pursue a son. But I do not think that the poet has departed so far from the universal tradition. Cp. 1433, 1434.

1337.   τὸν αὐτὸν δαίμον᾽ ἐξειληφότες.

ἐξειληχότες is certainly a probable variant.

1348.   τῆσδε δημοῦχος χθονός.

The arguments for δημοῦχοι (L pr.) and δημοῦχος (L^c cett) are nearly balanced. But Jebb's note here (I quote from the 2nd edition 1889) is inconsistent with that on 458: 'But below, 1087 γᾶς ... δαμούχοις = the Athenians, 1348 δημοῦχος χθονός = the King.'

1358, 1359. ὅτ' ἐν πόνῳ
ταὐτῷ βεβηκὼς τυγχάνεις κακῶν ἐμοί.

Cp. Eur. *fr.* 196, ἐν ὄλβῳ μὴ σαφεῖ βεβηκότες.

1361. ὥσπερ ἂν ζῶ.

I still think that ὥσπερ ἂν ζῶ = 'In whatever way I live' ('utcunque vivam' Herm.) is sufficiently supported by the analogy of ὅσπερ ἂν in *Od.* xvii. 586, οὐκ ἄφρων ὁ ξεῖνος, ὀίεται, ὅσπερ ἂν εἴη, or, as Monro now reads, οὐκ ἄφρων ὁ ξεῖνος ὀίεται, ὥς περ ἂν εἴη. The allusion to Polynices' remarks in 1256 ff. is quite in keeping with the context here.

1372, 1373. οὐ γὰρ ἔσθ' ὅπως πόλιν
κείνην ἐρεῖ τις.

My explanation of these words—'there is one who never shall call her by the dear and honoured name of City'—is essentially the same with Hermann's: 'Quemadmodum si de patriâ sermo esset, nemo offenderetur, si scriptum videret οὐ γὰρ ἔσθ' ὅπως πάτραν | κείνην ἐρεῖ τις, ita, quum de civitate agitur, recte dictum est πόλιν, quae est civitas, cujus quis civis est.' So Creon uses the word in lines 837, 858 of this play, and in 1417 πόλιν = τὴν σὴν πόλιν, and a similar brachylogy occurs in Eur. *Heracl.* 202, πόλιν μὲν ἀρκεῖ. Polynices has spoken of defeating his brother, but not of overthrowing Thebes, as would be implied by πόλιν ... ἐρείψεις. And although Antigone in pleading with him uses the phrase πάτραν κατασκάψαντι, she does so in order to remind him that the result of such a conflict must be disastrous either way.

1375.   τοιάσδ' ἀρὰς σφῷν πρόσθε τ' ἐξανῆκ' ἐγώ.

With reference to Jebb's view of this passage, I will only here repeat what I said in 1879: 'The curse thus solemnly recalled is the original curse of the old story, and not a mere incidental utterance like that in 421 f.' This does not seem to me at all undramatic.

1378, 1379.   καὶ μὴ 'ξατιμάζητον, εἰ τυφλοῦ πατρὸς
τοιώδ' ἔφυτον· αἵδε γὰρ τάδ' οὐκ ἔδρων.

'καὶ μὴ 'ξατιμάζητον, sc. τοὺς φυτεύσαντας' (Jebb). This is the received interpretation, but, to my thinking it leaves the connexion of the following clause, εἰ ... ἔφυτον, rather obscure. Jebb takes εἰ as = ὅτι and makes the father's blindness the ground of the sons' contempt. But in this case the addition of τοιώδε confuses the sense. The emphatic order of the words rather suggests 'seeing that ye, his offspring, behaved *so cruelly* to a father who was *blind*'. I take the clause thus understood to be the object of ἐξατιμάζητον, where the compound has the force of ἐξουθενεῖν, ἐκφλαυρίζειν in later Greek. When duly punished, they would no longer think lightly of their offences. ἀτιμάζειν is followed by an infinitive (*i.e.* an object clause) in Eur. *H. F.* 608, 609:

οὐκ ἀτιμάσω
θεοὺς προσειπεῖν πρῶτα τοὺς κατὰ στέγας.

γὰρ in 1379 means that the heinousness of the sons' misbehaviour is accentuated by the dutifulness of the daughters.

1382.   Δίκη ξύνεδρος Ζηνὸς ἀρχαίοις νόμοις.

Jebb construes Ζηνὸς with ξύνεδρος and explains ἀρχαίοις νόμοις as a 'causal dative'. I prefer to understand with Hermann: 'Pro Jove dixit Ζηνὸς ἀρχαίοις νόμοις, quia sensus, qui verbis subest, eo redit ut dicat, *si quidem Justitia incolumes servat Jovis antiquas leges.* Viderat hoc Brunckius.'

1389, 1390. καὶ καλῶ τὸ Ταρτάρου
στυγνὸν πατρῷον ἔρεβος, ὥς σ' ἀποικίσῃ.

The darkness of Erebus obscures interpretation here. As often elsewhere, Hermann's note is especially helpful. He wrote as follows (ed. 1839): 'Puto hic dici: *invoco invisam Tartari caliginem, quae patrem meum Laium tegit, ut te hinc abstrahat.*' But the solemn words cannot simply mean that Polynices should be taken to the place of the dead: and, as Jebb rightly observes, any allusion to the manner of Laius' death would be out of place: 'It seems hardly the fit moment for Oed. to recall his own parricidal act.' I speak with diffidence, but I believe the imprecation to signify that Polynices shall not be 'gathered to his fathers'. The body of Laius had been brought home and laid in the royal burial-ground. But 'a horror lived about' his tomb, not merely because he was slain by his son, but because by his unnatural crimes and by disobedience to Apollo, he had brought the anger of the Erinyes upon his race. Consequently, the darkness there beneath was not simply the darkness of death —the *Erebus* apostrophised by Ajax as his only light:— the vault opened directly upon *Tartarus*, the hopeless prison-house (Eur. *Hipp.* 1290; cf. also *Or.* 1225, ὦ δῶμα ναίων νυκτὸς ὀρφναίας πάτερ). But even from thence, from his natural resting-place, Polynices is to be exiled. I therefore take ἀποικίζειν here to mean—not to *take*, but to *send* abroad, 'unto another home' (Eur. *Hipp.* 629), viz. (perhaps) the mound raised by Creon's followers over his mangled remains upon the open plain (*Ant.* 1203, 1204). Even the sepulchre of his sires, guilt-haunted as it is, rejects him. For ἀποικίσῃ, cp. Eur. *Hipp.* 629, ὃ σπείρας ... πατὴρ ... ἀπῴκισ'.

1397, 1398. οὔτε ταῖς παρελθούσαις ὁδοῖς
ξυνήδομαί σοι.

Jebb, with Wecklein, reads σου, but the combination of

datives is not more awkward than similar occurrences elsewhere, and the pause at the end of the line would lessen the harshness in delivery. Though an impersonal dative elsewhere follows συνήδομαι, σοι is here more pointed.

1406. τὰ σκληρὰ πατρὸς κλύετε †τοῦδ' ἀρωμένου.

Jebb reads ταῦτ' for τοῦδ',—a probable correction, as I admitted in 1879, but not 'certain'.

1418. πῶς γὰρ αὖθις αὖ πάλιν.

Jebb admits the possibility of the MS. reading, and I prefer to retain it.

1424. ὁρᾷς τὰ τοῦδ' οὖν ὡς ἐς ὀρθὸν ἐκφέρει
μαντεύμαθ'.

Jebb is perhaps right in treating ἐκφέρει as second person middle. Tyrwhitt's ἐκφέρεις amounts to the same thing. But I still think that the reasoning in my note has some force, and the order of the words rather favours making τὰ . . . μαντεύματα the subject; cp. *Trach.* 824, ὁπότε τελεόμηνος ἐκφέροι | δωδέκατος ἄροτος for an equally rare use of ἐκφέρειν, and, for the construction, *Her.* v. 92 β, τὸ . . . χρηστήριον . . . φέρον τε ἐς τὠυτό . . .

1435. σφῷν δ' εὐοδοίη Ζεύς, τάδ' εἰ τελεῖτέ μοι
θανόντ'.

Jebb reads σφὼ with Hermann (1839). The point is unimportant, and can hardly be determined by late usage. In any case εὐοδοίη is from εὐοδοῦν. τάδ' εἰ τελεῖτέ μοι | θανόντ'. Jebb reads with Lobeck, τάδ' εἰ θανόντι μοι | τελεῖτ.' As I have said elsewhere, I am not convinced that ι of the dative is *never* elided in Tragedy: in the present

passage the order of the words in the MS. reading, with
θανόντ' at the beginning of the line, and in epexegesis, is
by far more natural and expressive. And a change from
dative to accusative is not impossible (Aesch. *Cho.* 410).

1440.   εἰς προὖπτον Ἅιδην.

Eur. *Hipp.* 1366, προὖπτον ἐς Ἅιδην στείχω: Bacchyl. iii.
51, ὁ γὰρ προφανὴς θνα- | τοῖσιν ἔχθιστος φόνων.

1454.   ὁρᾷ ὁρᾷ ταῦτ' ἀεὶ χρόνος, †ἐπεὶ μὲν ἕτερα.

In dealing with this corrupt passage Jebb accepts στρέφων
for ἐπεὶ from Schneidewin, altering δέδια to δέδοικα in the
antistrophe. I prefer to read *ἀφεὶς μὲν ἕτερα = 'letting some
things go', *i.e.* no longer upholding them. This has the
advantage of continuing the cretic or paeonic rhythm, instead
of interrupting it with a diiambus.

1463, 1464.   ἴδε μάλα, μέγας ἐρείπεται
κτύπος ἄφατος ὅδε διόβολος.

Jebb, transposing ὅδε and otherwise changing the order
reads:

μέγας, ἴδε, μάλ' ὅδ' ἐρείπεται
κτύπος ἄφατος διόβολος.

I prefer Hermann's method, of introducing a second νέα
in the strophe. For (1) ἴδε μάλα = 'lo again!' seems
idiomatic—see my note, comparing also *Her.* i. 134, vii. 186:
and (2) the dochmiac metre is thus sustained throughout.

1466.   †οὐρανία γὰρ ἀστραπὴ φλέγει πάλιν.

Jebb defends the MS. οὐρανῖα (with synizesis). Bothe's
οὐρανοῦ (from heaven) or Jebb's conj. οὐρανῷ seems preferable.

1472. ἥκει τῷδ' ἐπ' ἀνδρί.

'The doom . . . advances to take him' (Jebb). Perhaps rightly. Cp. Aesch. *Prom. s. f.* τοιάδ' ἐπ' ἐμοὶ ῥιπὴ Διόθεν . . . στείχει.

1478 f. The reading here depends on the antistrophe. Jebb's reading of 1491, 1492,

ἰὼ ἰώ, παῖ, βᾶθι, βᾶθ', εἴτ' ἄκρα
*περὶ γύαλ' ἐναλίῳ

is hardly defensible in making βᾶθ', εἴτ' ἄκρᾰ = ἀμφίστᾰτᾱι in a continuous series of dochmiac and paeonic rhythms. My revered teacher, Professor E. L. Lushington, in writing to me after the appearance of Jebb's edition, was still confident of his own emendation:—

1479, 1480.   διαπρύσιος ὄτοβος· ἵ-
              λεως, δαῖμον, ἵλεως, εἴ τι γᾷ
1492, 1493.   ἐπιγύαλον ἐναλίῳ
              Ποσειδανίῳ θεῷ τυγχάνεις.

The only changes are the Attic form ἵλεως, and the vocative with the omission of ὦ. Hermann had anticipated ἐπιγύαλον.

I have the same authority for retaining ἐναισίου (or ἐναισίῳ) δὲ συντύχοιμι in 1482. I do not think that the general aspiration is 'intolerably weak'.

1488. τί δ' ἂν θέλοις τὸ πιστὸν ἐμφῦναι φρενί;

τὸ πιστὸν, 'the pledge' (Jebb). I do not think that 'pledge' answers fully to πιστόν here. Rather (1) 'What is the matter requiring mutual trust?' Oedipus is anxious that Theseus may find him able to speak connectedly and convincingly. Or possibly (2) 'Why wouldst thou have fixed in thy mind the condition which inspires confidence?'

1493. Ποσειδανίῳ θεῷ.

For the MS. reading Ποσειδαωνίῳ, cp. Bacchylides v. 70, Πορθαονίδα, on which Kenyon observes: 'Scanned as a quadrisyllable, āo coalescing by synizesis into one long syllable.'

1501. σαφὴς μὲν αὐτῶν.

I do not think ἀστῶν for αὐτῶν a 'certain correction'. The Coloniates are not ἀστοί,—only δημόται.

1510. ἐν τῷ δὲ κεῖσαι τοῦ μόρου τεκμηρίῳ;

Jebb is perhaps right in rejecting 'On what sign of thine end dost thou rely?' But his own reading, 'What sign *holds thee in suspense?*' also introduces an alien thought. The verb elsewhere simply indicates the situation in which a person finds himself. 'What present circumstance affecting thee is a signal of impending doom?'

1521. οὗ με χρὴ θανεῖν.

The place described in 1590 is not (as Jebb says) that where Oedipus died, but only where he was last seen, except by Theseus (1648 f.).

1524, 1525. πρὸ πολλῶν ἀσπίδων ἀλκὴν ὅδε
δορός τ' ἐπακτοῦ γειτονῶν ἀεὶ τιθῇ.

γειτονῶν. It is the neighbourhood of the tomb which gives security to Athens. The Thebans are not γείτονες to the Athenians: and if the genitives are joined, γειτόνων (*sic*) is an unnecessary addition to ἐπακτοῦ.

1536. θεοὶ γὰρ εὖ μὲν, ὀψὲ δ' εἰσορῶσ'.

Jebb's remark, that the order of words lays the stress on

ὀψέ, is probably right, and justifies his view of the relation of this verse to the preceding. The wicked are emboldened by the apparent long-suffering of the Gods.

1541. μηδ' ἔτ' ἐντρεπώμεθα.

I believe that Jebb is right in his defence of ἐντρεπώμεθα, and that the idea of the verb is that of persons who, instead of 'facing the music', turn to look at one another.

1555. μέμνησθέ μου θανόντος.

I still rather prefer Elmsley's μεμνῆσθε.

1561. ἐπιπόνῳ μήτε βαρυαχεῖ.

I should now read as above to correspond with 1572, ἀδάματον φύλακα παρ' Ἅιδᾳ ⌒⌣ ⌒ ⌒ ⌒⌣ ⌒ –

1562. ξένον *ἄρ' εὖ *κατανύσαι.

I still read as above—but doubtfully, and in 1573, λόγος *ἐσαιὲν ἀνέχει.

1565, 1566. πολλῶν γὰρ ἂν καὶ μάταν
πημάτων ἱκνουμένων.

I believe that the MS. text here is sound: καὶ not= 'and' but='even'. The participle takes the place of an hypothetical clause,—εἰ καὶ πολλὰ πήματα ἱκνεῖτο μάταν, 'Although many miseries came with no relief'. In ordinary lives suffering is followed by joy (*Trach.* 129), but it has not been so in the life of Oedipus. Hence μάταν='without consequent happiness'. The other meaning, 'without cause', is also possible, *i.e.* 'undeservedly'. But I prefer the former. The imperfect participle is sufficiently supported by the instances given in Goodwin's *Moods and Tenses*, § 140.

1567.   πάλιν σε δαίμων δίκαιος αὔξοι.

I see no reason for objecting to σε as explained by the Scholiast: ἀποστρέφει τὸν λόγον πρὸς τὸν Οἰδίπουν.

1570.   φασὶ πολυξέστοις.

Jebb's reading *ταῖσι πολυξένοις is extremely plausible: but (1) φασὶ, expanded in what follows—λόγος αἰὲν ἀνέχει, is not alien from the manner of Sophocles (*Phil.* 706-711; *El.* 1384-1397); and (2) long syllables in the place of short ones are so frequent in this antistrophe, indicating a retarded rhythm (ἀνικάτου, ἄντρων, βῆναι) that πολυξέστοις need not be condemned as unmetrical, while, as regards the meaning, a graphic or pictorial epithet suits better with the image of Cerberus than the more commonplace notion of the innumerable dead. The 'iron gates' (*Il.* viii. 15), are kept in good repair.

1574.   ὄν, ὦ Γᾶς παῖ καὶ Ταρτάρου,

τὸν is certainly euphonic; but there is a distinct pause after ἀνέχει· (or ἔχει·) which may excuse ὄν.

The 'son of Earth and Tartarus' is surely Death, as in Jebb's note (2nd edition), and not Cerberus, as implied in his note on Bacchyl. v. 62.

1575.   κατεύχομαι ἐν καθαρῷ βῆναι.

I believe ἐν καθαρῷ βῆναι = 'to leave a clear path' to be an oxymoron not beyond the Sophoclean limit. It is equivalent to μὴ ἐμποδὼν βῆναι.

1584.   ὡς λελοιπότα
κεῖνον τὸν ἀεὶ βίοτον ἐξεπίστασο.

I still hold to the 'heretical' view that τὸν ἀεί here and *infr.* 1701 is an elliptical expression, rendered tolerable by vernacular use, for εἰς τὸν ἀεὶ χρόνον. See note on *El.* 1075.

1591. χαλκοῖς βάθροισι γῆθεν ἐρριζωμένον.

I take βάθροισι not of 'steps' real or imaginary, but of the deep *foundations* of the steep-down threshold. See Introd. to this play, *supra* p. 234.

Cp. Eur. *Phoen.* 1131, 1132.

ὅλην πόλιν
φέρων μοχλοῖσιν ἐξανασπάσας βάθρων.

Rhes. 287, 288.

οἳ κατ' Ἰδαῖον λέπας
οἰκοῦμεν αὐτόρριζον ἑστίαν χθονός.

1593. κοίλου πέλας κρατῆρος.

The same double occurs here as *supr.* 158 *f.*, whether the κρατήρ was a real bowl, or a natural hollow in the rock.

1595. τοῦ τε Θορικίου πέτρου.

The significance of the Thorician stone is, of course, open to conjecture.

1604. ἐπεὶ δὲ παντὸς εἶχε δρῶντος ἡδονὴν.

Jebb suggests ἔρωτος, but wisely retains δρῶντος in his text. The absence of the article may be accounted for, if we render 'he was pleased with all (his requirements) being *in act*'. Just as in ἀργόν (1605) an attribute of the doer is transferred to the deed (cp. τό γ' ἆκον πρᾶμα, 977), so the active participle takes the place of the passive. This is bold, but not too bold, I think.

1608. οὐδ' ἀνίεσαν
στέρνων ἀραγμοὺς.

Cp. also Eur. *I. T.* 318, οὐκ ἀνίεμεν πέτροις | βάλλοντες.

1632.   δός μοι χερὸς σῆς πίστιν ἀρχαίαν τέκνοις.

πίστιν ἀρχαίαν : Jebb reads ὁρκίαν with Pappageorg, and while agreeing with Bellermann that my version of ἀρχαίαν, 'that time-honoured pledge', is the only sound one, adds, 'But in such a context we surely want something more than so general an epithet.' I hold, on the contrary, that any more particularising epithet would weaken the natural force of χερὸς σῆς πίστιν. Theseus is to pledge his word to the maidens to satisfy Oedipus. It would be superfluous for him to tender an oath to them. Cp. *Phil.* 813, Eur. *Med.* 21, 22.

1649, 1650.   τὸν ἄνδρα, τὸν μὲν οὐδαμοῦ παρόντ᾽ ἔτι
ἄνακτα δ᾽ . . .

Cp. also Eur. *Alc.* 300-2 (ed. Murray).

αἰτήσομαι γάρ σ᾽—ἀξίαν μὲν οὔποτε·
δίκαια δ᾽.

1662.   εὔνουν διαστὰν γῆς ἀλύπητον βάθρον.

ἀλύπητον certainly *implies* that Oedipus had a painless end. But the order of the words suggests that grammatically it is not a secondary predicate, but a general epithet.

1673, 1674.   ᾧτινι τὸν πολὺν
ἄλλοτε μὲν πόνον ἔμπεδον εἴχομεν.

For the dative cp. also Eur. *Iph. A.* 1339, ᾧ σὺ δεῦρ᾽ ἐλήλυθας, and, for the form ᾧτινι, Bacchyl. v. 50 :

ὄλβιος ᾧτινι θεὸς
μοῖράν τε καλῶν ἔπορεν . . .

Andoc. 2. § 10, γνοὺς τὰς ἐμαυτοῦ συμφοράς, ᾧτινι . . .

284 PARALIPOMENA SOPHOCLEA

1677. *ἔξεστιν μὲν εἰκάσαι, φίλοι.

I maintain this reading, and greatly prefer to interpret, 'you can guess'. She naturally shrinks from a direct reply, and leaves it to the Chorus to infer the fact from seeing the maidens return alone.

1678. ὡς μάλιστ' ἂν εἰ πόθῳ λάβοις.

If the MS. reading is 'intolerable', εἰ is easily changed to ἐν, as Jebb does, according to Canter's conj. approved by Hermann. I will only make two remarks on Jebb's note:—
(1) No one, so far as I am aware, ever construed 'ὡς μάλιστ' ἂν πόθῳ λάβοις, εἰ (λάβοις)'. Hermann's rendering is 'ὡς μάλιστ' ἂν (βαίης scilicet vel λάβοις), εἰ πόθῳ λάβοις. *obiit, quo modo maxime mortem accipias, si exoptatam accipias*' :— mine was, 'As you would above all choose the mode of your departure, if you could choose by longing' (ὡς μάλιστ' ἂν λάβοις τὸ βῆναι, εἰ πόθῳ λάβοις). (2) My second remark is this: Jebb's interpretation of Canter's conjecture ἐν πόθῳ λάβοις assumes the use of λαμβάνω for a mental conception, which he condemns in *Ant.* 439.

1682. ἐν ἀφανεῖ τινι μόρῳ *φερόμεναι.

Hermann's φερόμεναι seems to me more imaginative, as well as nearer to the MSS., than φερόμενον. For the use of the middle, cp. *Aj.* 647 (χρόνος) φύει τ' ἄδηλα καὶ φανέντα κρύπτεται.

1694. τὸ φέρον ἐκ θεοῦ καλῶς
*μηδὲν ἄγαν *φλέγεσθον.

Emendation, here and *infra* 1715 ⨀, is rendered more doubtful by a haunting uncertainty, like that which troubled us in the parodos, 182 *f.*—whether the κομμός was intended

OEDIPUS COLONEUS

to be antistrophic throughout. I do not think that Wecklein's method, adopted by Jebb, is any better than that of Hermann, and Dindorf—τὸ φέρον ἐκ θεοῦ καλῶς, etc., which harmonises better with the sequel (οὔ τοι κατάμεμπτ' ἔβησαν).

1697. πόθος <τοι> καὶ κακῶν ἄρ' ἦν τις.

Hartung's insertion of τοι after πόθος is probable.

1698. καὶ γὰρ ὃ μηδαμὰ δὴ φίλον <ἦν> φίλον.

Jebb is also right in adopting Brunck's substitution of φίλον ἦν for τὸ φίλον. Cp. Bacchyl. iii. 47, τὰ πρόσθε δ' ἐχθρὰ φίλα· θανεῖν γλύκιστον.

1702. οὐδὲ γέρων ἀφίλητος ἐμοί ποτε.

Good reasons are given for suspecting γέρων, but the correction seems extremely uncertain. Nor does γέρων seem after all impossible, if we compare the γῆρας ἄφιλον of the Chorus in 1237.

1704. XO. ἔπραξεν; AN. *ἐξέπραξεν οἷον ἤθελεν.

'The first ἔπραξεν is itself an argument for the second' (Jebb). Hardly, when it is considered how often a phrase is thus varied in repetition.

1712. ὤμοι, γᾶς ἐπὶ ξένας θανεῖν ἔχρῃζες, ἀλλ'
ἔρημος ἔθανες ὧδέ μοι.

This emendation, which Jebb accepts from Wecklein, is probably right, although Hermann's view of the passage was attractive.

1715.   ὦ τάλαινα, τίς ἄρα με πότμος . . .

As the interpolation comes from the misplacing of a line (1735) I do not see why αὖθις ὧδ' should be retained.

1718, 1719.   *ἐπαμμένει σέ τ', ὦ φίλα, *τὰς πατρὸς ὧδ' ἐρήμας;

Hermann's ἐπαμμένει for ἐπιμένει, and the addition of τὰς before πατρός, should probably be adopted with Jebb.

1734, 1736.   ποῖ δῆτ' . . .
αἰῶνα τλάμον' ἕξω;

Again I see no reason for altering the *pregnant* ποῖ; to ποῦ;

1734-1750. Jebb's suggestion that the lines here given to Antigone were given by the poet to Ismene, but transferred because of the difficulty of the fourth actor, is extremely ingenious and worth considering.

1741.   τί δῆθ' ὑπερνοεῖς;

Graser's correction, ὅπερ νοεῖς for ὑπερνοεῖς, though approved by Hermann, is surely rather flat. Of other emendations, if ὑπερνοεῖς must be rejected, ὑπερπονεῖς appears the best.

1751.   παύετε θρῆνον.

So Jebb, rightly, from L² etc.

1751, 1752.   ἐν οἷς γὰρ
χάρις ἡ χθονία ξύν' ἀπόκειται
πενθεῖν οὐ χρή.

Reading ξύν' ἀπόκειται with Jebb and Reisig, I still

prefer to take οἷς as masculine;—ἐν οἷς=ἐν τούτοις ἐν οἷς:—
'It is wrong to mourn amongst those with whom the
kindness of the dead is treasured as a public benefit.'
Cp. 1518, 1519:

ἅ σοι
γήρως ἄλυπα τῇδε κείσεται πόλει.

Oedipus is now a blessed shade, and his favour is identified
with that of the powers below. Cp. Aesch. *Cho.* 476, μάκαρες
χθόνιοι, Pind. *Pyth.* v. 136, χθονίᾳ φρενί. This is said as
Theseus and his train are seen approaching.

1758.   ἀλλ' οὐ θεμιτὸν κεῖσ' <ἐστὶ> μολεῖν.

While agreeing that such a paroemiac as ἀλλ' οὐ θεμιτὸν
κεῖσε μολεῖν (MS.) is unlikely, I prefer to complete the
dimeter by the simple insertion of ἐστί.

1773.   δράσω καὶ τάδε, καὶ πάνθ' * ὁπόσ' ἄν.

I now agree in preferring ὁπόσ' ἄν to ὅσα γ' ἄν.